These Kids

These Kids

*Identity, Agency, and Social Justice
at a Last Chance High School*

KYSA NYGREEN

THE UNIVERSITY OF CHICAGO PRESS   CHICAGO AND LONDON

KH

KYSA NYGREEN is assistant professor in the School of Education at the University of Massachusetts, Amherst.

The University of Chicago Press, Chicago 60637
The University of Chicago Press, Ltd., London
© 2013 by The University of Chicago
All rights reserved. Published 2013.
Printed in the United States of America
22 21 20 19 18 17 16 15 14 13   1 2 3 4 5

ISBN-13: 978-0-226-03142-2 (cloth)
ISBN-13: 978-0-226-03156-9 (paper)
ISBN-13: 978-0-226-03173-6 (e-book)

Library of Congress Cataloging-in-Publication Data

Nygreen, Kysa.
   These kids : identity, agency, and social justice at a last chance high school /
Kysa Nygreen.
      pages ; cm.
   Includes bibliographical references and index.
   ISBN 978-0-226-03142-2 (alk. paper) — ISBN 978-0-226-03156-9 (pbk. : alk.
paper) — ISBN 978-0-226-03173-6 (e-book)   1. Evening and continuation school
students—California—Psychology.   2. High school dropouts—California—Psychology.
3. Evening and continuation schools—California.   4. Failure (Psychology) in
adolescence.   I. Title.
   LC5552.C3N94 2013
   374′.809794—dc23

                                                           2012043143

10/20/14

Contents

Acknowledgments

Many individuals have helped me develop, sharpen, and strengthen the ideas in this book. I first want to recognize the youth participants in the Participatory Action Research Team for Youth (PARTY) group, all of whom are now full-grown adults. Without them, this book could not exist. These youth graciously let me into their lives; gave their time, hearts, and minds to pursuing social justice; and helped me learn alongside them. I am thankful for their blunt honesty with me even when I struggled to listen, and their endless reserves of compassion and forgiveness. I also wish to thank all the students, teachers, and staff at "Jackson High" for allowing me to conduct this research and for sharing so much of their time and knowledge with me. I owe special thanks to "Ms. Barry," for giving us her classroom once a week for a youth-led social justice class. Confidentiality agreements prevent me from naming them personally, but they know who they are.

At the University of California–Berkeley, where I was a doctoral student when this research began, I benefited from a tight student cohort in the Social and Cultural Studies Program: Andrea Dyrness, Soo Ah Kwon, Patricia Sanchez, Shabnam Koirala, Emma Fuentes, and Amanda Lashaw. All are colleagues in the very best sense of the word, and each of them contributed to the PARTY project and this book. Patricia showed me how to create my own small participatory action research project with youth. Soo Ah read every chapter of my dissertation, providing helpful advice and emotional support. Years after we graduated, Amanda took time to offer a careful, critical reading of my first book proposal. Her feedback was extremely valuable not only for improving the proposal but also for strengthening the quality of my analysis. Andrea has been an ongoing source of support for more than thirteen years. As a study partner, research partner, writing partner, ally, and friend, she has provided valuable feedback and thoughtful advice that have greatly shaped and improved this book. The members of my dissertation committee at Berkeley made it possible for me to pursue this work and offered much valuable support: Ingrid Seyer-Ochi, Carol Stack, John Hurst, and Ruthie Gilmore. While at Berkeley, I also benefited from the intellectual mentorship of Stuart Tannock, Daniel Perstein, and Glynda Hull. I especially want to recognize John Hurst for giving me courage to take many intellectual, political, and pedagogical risks. As well, Stuart Tannock continually pushed me to ask deeper, more critical questions about education and schooling; his enduring influence on my thinking was evident to me as I wrote and reworked this book many years later.

The University of California President's Postdoctoral Fellowship provided me the time and space to begin conceptualizing this book, and an institutional home at the University of California–Santa Cruz (UCSC), where I was privileged to receive mentorship from two extraordinary scholars, Greta Gibson and Ron Glass. I can trace many of the larger arguments of this book back to discussions I had with each of them during my postdoctoral fellowship years. Greta helped me see that focusing on the unique aspects of the continuation high school as an ethnographic context could be an intellectually fruitful approach. She was the person to suggest the book's title, *These Kids*, and she helped with practical aspects of writing a book proposal and contacting publishers. Ron helped me develop and refine many of the arguments about "college for all" that appear in chapters 5 and 6. He suggested literature that deepened my understanding of how my "small" participatory research project was connected to "big" issues of inequality and the social construction of failure. He patiently listened to my anxieties and gave me confidence that helped me move forward when I was on the verge of giving up. And he has provided valuable feedback on multiple drafts of this work at several points in the last seven years.

Numerous other colleagues also provided feedback on the manuscript in whole or in part: Peter Demerath, Christine Sleeter, Deirdre Kelly, Denise Ives, Flavio Azavedo, Laura Valdiviezo, Cathy Luna, Pamela Perry, Jennifer Cannon, Liz Boner, and three anonymous reviewers. I especially want to acknowledge Deirdre Kelly, as well as the anonymous reviewers, for reading the full manuscript and offering supportive yet constructive comments that helped me improve it. Peter Demerath offered consistent intellectual support and valuable comments on my writing. I also owe a big thanks to Liz Boner for providing early feedback on chapters 1 and 2 during my preliminary stages of conceptualizing this book; her suggestions decisively shaped its direction. Still others contributed ideas that influenced and enriched this book in various ways: Anna Rios Rojas, David Barillas-Chon, K. Wayne Yang, Judy Pace, Beth Rubin, Ruth Kim, Sally Galman, and Barbara Madeloni. I want to acknowledge Ruth Kim for being the first to suggest I read Holland, Lachicotte, Skinner, and Cain's (2001) book on figured worlds, and Liz Boner, who pointed me in the direction of discourse theory, especially works by James Gee (2001), Jan Blommaert (2005), and Norman Fairclough (2003). A conversation with Beth Rubin at a conference in 2008 strengthened my thinking about figured worlds theory and how it could apply to my analysis of last chance high schools. Sally Galman was a consistent, reassuring sounding board and role model for juggling writing with new motherhood. Barbara Madeloni helped me connect my arguments to the neoliberal assault on education and gave me courage to advance a bolder critique.

At UCSC, four excellent research assistants helped me review the literature on last chance high schools and their students: Yazmin Duarte, Mariella Saba, Yolanda Diaz-Houston, and Linnea Beckett. The doctoral students in my graduate seminar on participatory action research inspired me to be more transparent and self-reflexive in my writing; among them, I especially recognize Yunnie Snyder, Melissa-Ann Nievera-Lozano, Alisun Thompson, and Derrick Jones. At the University of Massachusetts–Amherst, three research assistants helped me stay organized: Holly Graham, Jennifer Cannon, and Brenda Muzeta. For two years, the doctoral students in my urban education seminar pushed my thinking and humbled me with their experience, passion, and commitments to social justice. I am deeply thankful for the consistent, caring support of Elizabeth Branch Dyson at the University of Chicago Press. Elizabeth immediately understood what I wanted to accomplish in the book and worked tirelessly with me to bring that vision to fruition. Much of my endurance over these many years is due to Elizabeth's persistent and supportive presence. Two additional mentors, Timiza Wagner and Lahairoi Carlisle, have been a constant source of inner strength, wisdom, and insight. Their unwavering faith in me helped tremendously in the long haul of writing this book.

The PARTY project was funded by an Applied Social Issues Grant from the Society for the Psychological Study of Social Issues (SPSSI) and a Spencer Research Training Grant from the UC Berkeley Graduate School of Education. Additional funding to help me analyze the data and write up the dissertation was received through the UC Berkeley Mentored Research Award, Flanders Fellowship, and Regent's Fellowship (Dean's Normative Time Grant). The University of California President's Postdoctoral Fellowship Program provided crucial funding and academic support for my writing. Funding from UC Santa Cruz Faculty Research Grants and the University of Massachusetts–Amherst School of Education allowed me to hire research assistants to support research for the book. The University of Massachusetts–Amherst Book Publication Subvention Program provided additional funding to support publication.

I want to thank Arin Dube for believing in this work and for pushing, expanding, and strengthening my thinking in many directions. My parents, Nancy and Ted Nygreen, and parents-in-law, Syamalima and Dipak Dube, have also been valuable sources of inspiration and support. I owe a tremendous debt of gratitude to my mother-in-law, Syamalima, who gave countless hours of her time toward infant care, cooking, laundry, and housecleaning so that I could sleep through the night and work on this book by day in the weeks and months immediately after the birth of my son. Kiran Nygreen Dube was born in the midst of writing this book, and has brought greater joy to my life than I ever thought possible. His loving spirit and deep belly laugh have helped me through the sometimes lonely and difficult stretches of writing that were a necessary part of this process. Finally, I want to acknowledge my grandparents, Glen and Beverly Nygreen, who taught me my earliest and most enduring lessons about social justice. Educators both, they embodied a powerful combination of scholarship, pedagogy, and activism that I have spent my life striving to emulate. Although they are not alive to read this book, their example deeply influenced it.

Introduction: The Paradox of Getting Ahead

In a small conference room at a local city college, three young graduates of Jackson High School and I sat around a gray hexagon-shaped table for our third weekly meeting of the Participatory Action Research Team for Youth (PARTY). I passed out copies of a funding proposal I had written, explaining to the youth that it was a draft and I wanted their feedback. I began reading aloud, starting with the title: "The Youth Research Team: A Participatory Action Research Project." I continued:

> The Youth Research Team is a small group of urban youth (aged 16–20) working collaboratively with me to research and design and implement a "transformative educational project." The youth researchers attend or recently graduated from a continuation high school where I worked previously as a classroom teacher. Since the students at our school are involuntarily transferred from a regular high school, they typically arrive with low GPAs and histories of truancy, contributing to low engagement and high rates of absenteeism/attrition at the school—

"Wait, wait, wait. Hold up," D interjected. A nineteen-year-old African American young man, D had been out of school for just over a year. "Why do you say we're from a continuation high school?" Initially surprised, I responded, "Well, it contextualizes the project, gives them a sense of who we are and why we want to make a difference in our school." "I don't like it," D responded resolutely. "It makes us look like fuckups." Slightly defensive, I explained it was just the opposite: "Oh no, actually your background is a *strength*. It shows the things you've overcome. It's like the point of our whole project." D studied the document and continued, "I don't like this part either," pointing to the page, "about the GPAs, low engagement, all that." We sat in silence for a moment before I uttered a soft "Uh-huh. What do you guys think?" looking at Louis and Lolo, who had been listening in silence. D answered instead, "I said it makes us look like fuckups."

D's alma mater, Jackson High, was an alternative high school to which students were involuntarily transferred if they fell significantly behind in credits toward graduating. Located in a racially and socioeconomically diverse California city, Jackson was a small high school serving approximately 120 students, most of whom, like D, were African American and low income. Official documents asserted that the school was designed to meet the needs of its at-risk students by offering greater flexibility, individualized attention, and a small school environment. While Jackson did indeed offer these advantages, the act of removing some students (disproportionately poor and of color) from the regular high school and placing them in a special one for remediation served to mark these young people and their school with an indelible stigma. Far from being a "strength"—as I claimed in my defense to D—attending Jackson High identified a student as a failure, delinquent, or problem. This, in turn, had powerful implications for students' emerging identities.

In this book, I explore the impact of school failure on the identity formation of youth who, like D, found themselves at the bottom of a vastly differentiated educational hierarchy. "These kids," as I call them here, are variously labeled with terms like *troubled, at-risk*, and *low achieving*. They are usually found at the margins of the education system—in alterative and continuation programs, in remedial and special education classes, or outside of school altogether. Here they learn, both implicitly and explicitly, that *they* are the problem professional educators and reformers are trying so hard to fix. They are made aware that school failure, much more than other types of failure, is significant for determining the kinds of people they can become and the kinds of lives they can expect to live. Their status as school "failures" activates deep-seated narratives and assumptions about them, rooted in racialized notions of deficiency and cultural deprivation. This is the "hidden curriculum" (Apple 1979) of educational failure, and like all hidden curricula, it powerfully shapes students' sense of themselves as learners, civic actors, and people. In this book, I interrogate this hidden curriculum of failure and, in so doing, seek to expose and raise questions about one of the central dilemmas of American schooling: the paradox of getting ahead.

What Is the Paradox of Getting Ahead?

Education in the United States is inextricably tied up with the idea of getting ahead. Few would deny that getting ahead is an important, legitimate, and desirable goal of getting an education, and the metaphor of getting ahead plays prominently in the public discourse on education—as the legislative names "No Child Left Behind" and "Race to the Top" clearly suggest. Yet, absent from this collective narrative of getting ahead is the ever-present reality of hierarchy. To get ahead in school requires getting ahead of others, and the most successful students are those who get ahead of the greatest number of others. In the era of No Child Left Behind, our nation has rhetorically embraced the belief that all children can and should get ahead in school. Dominant educational discourses lead us to view "getting ahead" as an unqualified good and "falling behind" as a problem to be fixed. They also portray getting ahead as an option that is theoretically open to everyone who simply works hard for it.

The paradox of getting ahead refers to the persistent American belief and repeated public statements that all children can "get ahead" and "succeed" in school. It is a paradox because, in the context of American schooling, "getting ahead" and "getting left behind" are two sides of the same coin (Varenne and McDermott 1999; Labaree 2010). Every year, hundreds (if not thousands) of educational researchers produce studies that help us understand how more children could "get ahead" and "succeed" in school. This research may contribute to making schools marginally more equitable and humane, but the role of schooling in *producing* a hierarchy of achievement too often remains obscured. Proclamations that sound benign—like "every child can succeed" and "all students can get ahead"—mask the existence of hierarchy and paint a deceptive picture of the possibilities for true equality in and through schooling. This is because they obscure the fact that, in addition to providing opportunities for getting ahead, American schools are also saddled with the task of sorting students into unequal labor market roles (Varenne and McDermott 1999; Labaree 1997, 2010; Carnoy and Levin 1985; Kantor and Tyack 1982). This is the paradox of getting ahead, and it means that no matter how hard we try, "school failure," in some form or another, will always be with us.

For decades, scholars have pondered this fundamental paradox of schooling, and many have concluded that the emphasis on getting ahead in school undermines possibilities for meaningful learning and democratic education (e.g., Demerath 2009; Pope 2003; Labaree 1999; Carnoy and Levin 1985; Varenne and McDermott 1999). In this book, I examine the paradox of getting ahead from the perspective of a teacher/researcher at a "last chance high school"—the term Deirdre Kelly (1993a) applies to high schools that, like Jackson High, are designed for students who have been academically unsuccessful and labeled at risk for dropping out. Last chance high schools sit at the crossroads of two contradictory purposes of American education: to provide multiple opportunities for upward mobility and to sort students into unequal labor market roles. They are at once a second chance for students who have failed, and a bottom track in the highly stratified structure of secondary education. For most students who attend them, transfer to a last chance high school is the final stop in a long line of failed interventions, disciplinary actions, or attempts at academic remediation. At the end of this line, the transfer process serves as a quasi-official acknowledgment that a student has failed in the race to get ahead in school. These schools are stigmatized as "dumping grounds" for "throwaway kids," and students are labeled as failures the moment they walk through the door (Kelly 1993a).

Because last chance high schools exclusively serve students who have already been designated as failures, these schools throw the paradox of getting ahead into sharp relief and force us to contend with the dilemma of educational hierarchy in ways that may be easier to ignore at other kinds of schools. In the six years I spent at Jackson High as a teacher and researcher, I worked hard to help every student I encountered "move up" in the world and "get ahead" in his or her life. It was important to me, as it is for most educators, to believe in every student and help all students reach their goals. But even as I strove to help all my students get ahead, I sometimes found myself wondering if this aim was theoretically achievable at all. I never questioned the inherent abilities of my students; I knew that, with a different set of life circumstances and opportunities, almost all of them would have been able to achieve mainstream definitions of "success" in school and the workplace. My question, instead, was about whether success for all of them was a *social* possibility: was there, in fact, enough "success" to go around (Varenne and McDermott

1999; McDermott 1987)? As a teacher at a last chance high school, the best message I had to offer my students was to "try hard" so they might "beat the odds" and get ahead in life. With my colleagues, we tried to create "exceptions" so that more of our students might do exactly that. But we did not, collectively, question the necessity of the achievement hierarchy itself, or the justice of a system that creates and then relegates its "losers" to poverty-wage work and silenced political voices. This hierarchical system, and its very real consequences for our students' lives, simply appeared inevitable. It saturated our consciousness as a taken-for-granted and entirely "natural" way of organizing learning.

In this book, I aim to disrupt these assumptions by following in the tradition of educational anthropology to "make the familiar strange" (Spindler 1982). I hope to expose the limitations on social justice that I felt intuitively but could not articulate during my six years at Jackson High. In the past, my attempts to name these limitations were stifled by fear that doing so could imply I was giving up on Jackson students or trying to justify low expectations of them. Despite all its injustices, I knew that schooling offered Jackson students their best hope for achieving some degree of upward mobility. And I could not conceive of a better way forward than that of trying to make the existing hierarchical system more fair and meritocratic, so that more Jackson students might become exceptions to the rule of social reproduction. I did not have access to the language or systems of meaning that might enable me to imagine any alternatives; in short, I lacked a discourse of educational justice capable of transcending the paradox of getting ahead. This book attempts to take some small steps toward forging that alternative discourse. Rather than accept the achievement hierarchy as a necessary product of schooling, I ask: What is and should be the purpose of education in a system that must also produce hierarchies of ranked achievement with consequences for economic distribution? What does it mean to pursue social justice for "all" students inside a system like this? Is it possible to reconceptualize schooling to eliminate such hierarchies altogether? What would we construct in its place?

I am not the first person to raise these questions about the American educational system, and surely will not be the last. The dilemma of hierarchy has long vexed educators and scholars with commitments to social justice and other critical and democratic pedagogies. My purpose in this book is to breathe new life into these questions at a historical moment in which the *hierarchization* of education is accelerating at an astounding rate (chapter 1). As this book goes to press, the dominant discourse of education reform is actively advancing a vision of education as a private good—a commodity that individuals compete to accumulate in greater amounts as they strive to get ahead of one another in an educational marketplace—while the discourse of education for democracy has been severely marginalized or at times abandoned altogether (Lipman 2011; Labaree 2010). Meanwhile, the application of market-based competition to all aspects of education is being promoted as a solution to deepening educational and economic inequalities—contributing even further to the trends of educational commodification and hierarchization (Lipman 2011; Ravitch 2011; Watkins 2011). At this historical moment, then, it is particularly urgent for educators to keep critical questions about the democratic purposes of education at the front and center of our scholarship. In this book, I aim to contribute to this long-standing conversation among education scholars while also advancing a vision of educational justice that is grounded in a concern for the well-being and dignity of all students, but especially for those at the bottom of the educational achievement hierarchy. Second, I aim to humanize these issues by examining them through the lenses of ethnography and participatory action research with youth.

About This Book

This book is about the work of the Participatory Action Research Team for Youth (PARTY) at Jackson High and the five young adults who participated in it along with me. It tells the story of PARTY as one modest attempt to enact social and educational change through participatory action research (PAR) and social justice education in the context of a last chance high school. I initiated the PARTY project as a doctoral student, building from four years of experience as a classroom teacher, substitute, and volunteer at Jackson High. As I explained to the youth participants, PAR is a process that brings people together to: (1) identify common social problems affecting their lives and communities; (2) design questions and research to critically investigate those problems; and (3) engage in collective action that builds from the research process and advances social change (Cammarota and Fine 2008; McIntyre 2000; Berg and Schensul 2004). I was a doctoral student at the time, and looking for a way to bridge theory with practice while staying connected to the youth at Jackson. As a budding researcher, I hoped to study the dynamics of educational inequality at Jackson High, but I also wanted to do more than simply document what I found. Instead, I hoped to pursue a research program that could potentially empower Jackson youth to demand better and more equitable educational opportunities. PAR offered a compelling model for engaged scholarship of this sort.

I was still in close contact with three young graduates of Jackson High—Lolo, Louis, and D, who had once been my students. After they graduated and I had moved on to graduate school, I continued to meet with each of them on a regular basis. Sometimes we just met to talk and catch up over a meal or a cup of coffee; other times I helped them with a résumé, job search, or assignment for a community college class. D's grandmother and uncle lived across the street from me, and we often chatted with each other from our respective front porches. I also attended church occasionally with Louis and Lolo, and had been present at some of Lolo's major family celebrations. So when I decided to explore the possibility of a PAR project at Jackson High, Lolo, Louis, and D were the first people I turned to. They agreed to help me start a project, and I booked a room at the local city college for weekly two-hour meetings. Over the next two school years, we recruited additional members and continued to hold weekly meetings in which we discussed issues in our lives, current events in the news, and ideas about education and social change. In the first year, we also developed research questions about Jackson High, learned about different research methods, conducted a survey of Jackson students, conducted interviews and participant observation at various schools, attended conferences and lectures and political events together, and invited guest speakers to share about their own research for social change. In the second year, we developed and taught a class in "social justice" at Jackson High. The decision to teach a social justice class was the action, chosen collectively by PARTY members, that emerged from the process of PAR. We gained permission from the US government teacher at Jackson to lead an eighty-minute class period once a week for one semester. Three PARTY members stayed on to teach the class, and we continued to hold weekly meetings to reflect and plan.

This book is about the PARTY project and its members as we conducted research and planned for, taught, and reflected on a social justice class at Jackson High. It explores how we wrestled with questions about inequality and social justice, and attempted to take individual and collective action in light of our emerging understandings. As a "theoretically informed case study" (Gonzalez, Moll, and Amanti 2005) grounded in critical and sociocultural theories of identity and agency, it examines how each of us, as individuals and as a group, constructed and enacted identities as learners, teachers, and civic actors in and through the work of PARTY. It interrogates the connections between our emerging identities and our acts of agency and resistance. And it presents fine-grained ethnographic analyses of key moments in the PARTY project to illuminate how broader macro relations of power played out at the micro level of human action and interaction. At the same time, this book explores some of the macro relations of power and historical trends that defined the terrain PARTY had to negotiate. These include enduring philosophical dilemmas about the purposes of education in an unequal society; the historic role of schooling in social sorting and preparing youth for labor market roles; and the contradictions of pursuing social justice "for all" inside a system that is organized to produce hierarchies of achievement with consequences for economic distribution.

The micro and macro levels of analysis in this book are deeply interconnected and inform each other. If we begin, as Varenne and McDermott (1999) suggest we do, with the assumption that school failure is *produced* rather than *revealed* in schools, it follows that the purpose of social analysis is not to discover the characteristics of students who "fail" or "succeed," but to examine the processes through which the categories themselves are produced, recognized, legitimized, challenged, and transformed. Along these lines, my goal in this book is to uncover some of the micro- and macro-level processes that contribute to sustaining "school failure" as a meaningful social category with significant implications for the lives of children and the broader culture. I examine how the social category of failure is constructed through discourse, and illuminate how this discourse is reproduced, challenged, and contested by a group of youth who have been so labeled. I examine the perspectives and identity practices of these youth, not as a way to help "us" understand "them" but as a lens to help us conceptualize failure as a socially constructed category.

Theoretical Foundations and Arguments

This book advances two central claims, each of which builds from and dialogues with a distinct body of literature. First, I draw from a long tra-

dition of critical educational ethnographies that have examined schooling as a site of identity formation (e.g., Bettie 2003; Davidson 1996; Demerath 2009; Eckert 1989; Foley 1990; Ferguson 2001; Fine 1991; Weis
1990). This body of literature shows that school is not just a place where
students learn (or don't learn) academic curricula and skills; it is also a
place where they develop a sense of what kind of people they are, where
they belong in the world, what they are capable of and entitled to, and
what they can expect in the future. This body of work has exposed how
student identities are connected to the hidden curriculum (Apple 1979)
of schooling, especially the implicit messages conveyed through practices of tracking, sorting, and labeling of students.

A centerpiece of this literature is its engagement with the structure-
agency debate, a long-standing staple of sociological research. Put simply, this debate focuses on the degree to which our individual biogra-
phies are shaped by social forces beyond our control (i.e., "structure")
or by our own individual choices and actions (i.e., "agency"). In the field
of education, this debate has centered on explaining why and how low-
income kids disproportionately wind up in low-status educational tracks
and, by extension, in low-wage occupations that lock them into subordinate class locations (e.g., Bowles and Gintis 1976; MacLeod 2008; Willis 1981). This is a process called *social reproduction*—a term that refers to the role of schools in reproducing class inequality. Educational
scholars have long sought to understand the degree to which students
"choose" these different educational tracks, or are forced into them by
social structures beyond their control.[1] Critical research in this tradition has tended to document the powerful weight of structure while also
seeking to understand the potential (and limits) of student agency and
resistance in challenging, subverting, or transforming that structure (Giroux [1983] 2003; Willis 1981; Solorzano and Delgado Bernal 2001). A
related body of research in education has examined the potential (and
limits) of *teacher agency* in challenging or interrupting patterns of social
reproduction by transforming the structures and practices of schooling
from within (Giroux [1983] 2003; Lipman 1997, 2003; Pease-Alvarez and
Thompson 2011).

This book draws lessons from and talks back to both bodies of research—on student and teacher agency, respectively—by exploring how
the youth PARTY members sought to challenge and change the social
conditions of their lives through their work as participatory researchers
and as social justice educators. This book does not attempt to resolve

the structure-agency debate, but it does provide insight into what I call the *discursive dimension of structure*—that is, the power of discourse, or shared meaning systems, to shape identity and thereby constrain the exercise of agency. In analyzing the PARTY project, I show how acts of agency and resistance were always possible, *and* how they were limited at every turn by constraints that were largely *discursive-ideological* rather than purely structural (Kim 2000; see also chapter 2). To develop these arguments, I apply the theory of "figured worlds" (Holland et al. 2001) to unpack how identity and agency are embedded within shared meaning systems as well as social relations of power. (Chapter 2 contains a more detailed discussion of figured worlds theory.) Throughout the book, I employ a sociocultural understanding of identity as a fluid and active concept—a practice of identification—rather than a fixed characteristic of individuals (Gee 2000). I argue, and illustrate ethnographically, that the discourses available in the figured worlds we inhabit make some identities more readily available than others, thereby placing constraints on action such that socially reproductive results remain the most likely outcome most of the time—even when we attempt to engage in resistive practice.

The second body of literature I engage with examines historic and contemporary debates about the role of education in society, particularly in relation to social inequality and labor market institutions (e.g., Tyack and Cuban 1997; Grubb and Lazerson 2004; Kliebard 1999; Kantor and Tyack 1982). From this literature, David Labaree's (1997) seminal essay on the contradictory purposes of American education provides a foundational framework that I employ throughout the book. In this essay, Labaree identifies three overarching goals that have historically been assigned American education. The first, what he calls "democratic equality," aims to prepare students as *citizens* who are capable of participating in and upholding the institutions of democracy. Emphasizing the civic purposes of education, the democratic equality paradigm supports policies and pedagogies that advance egalitarianism, a common curriculum, and skills for civic engagement. The second goal, what he calls "social efficiency," aims to prepare students as *workers* who meet the needs of employers and the economy. Emphasizing the economic purposes of education, the social efficiency paradigm supports policies and pedagogies that advance a differentiated curriculum (corresponding to the differentiated labor market) and skills for the workplace. The third goal, what he calls "social mobility," aims to provide students with opportunities for upward mobility. Emphasizing the instrumental purposes of education in the competition for individual advancement, the social mobility paradigm supports policies and pedagogies that advance opportunities for mobility as well as the stratification of educational credentials. Labaree argues that American schools have historically pursued all three goals simultaneously, even though they often work at cross-purposes.

The second part of Labaree's argument is that the "social mobility" goal has become increasingly dominant in American education in the last generation, overshadowing the goals of democratic equality and social efficiency. This, he claims, has consequences for the quality of teaching and learning in schools, and for society as a whole. Unique among the three goals, social mobility is the only one that frames education primarily as a *private* good for individual gain. Educational credentials are treated as commodities, increasingly pursued for their "exchange value" instead of their "use value." One result, he argues, is the accelerated trend toward credentialism, or the pursuit of educational credentials for their own sake rather than the knowledge they symbolize. A second result is credential inflation, or increasing credential requirements for jobs whose actual skill requirements have not changed. Both of these trends undermine deep learning and possibilities for democratic education in schools, he argues, because they provide incentives for students to learn only the minimum amount needed to achieve requisite credentials and to advance above others in the competition to get ahead. Elsewhere, Labaree has argued persuasively that our society's collective obsession with "getting ahead" in school often undermines the goal of getting an education (see Labaree 1999 for elaboration of this point), and other scholars have advanced similar arguments (e.g., Pope 2003; Demerath 2009; Callahan 2004; Vojak 2006). Significantly, Labaree notes that despite the increasing dominance of the social mobility goal in shaping educational practice, policy, and discourse, overall levels of mobility have not substantially changed (1997, 69–70).

In this book, I draw from Labaree's work (1997, 1999, 2010) to argue that the dominance of the social mobility goal weakens possibilities for social justice education in schools. By social justice education, I refer to educational approaches sharing two core pedagogical and political principles.[2] First, social justice education is education for critical consciousness and praxis (Freire 2000). This means it empowers students to think critically about the social world, to question taken-for-granted assumptions and ideologies, to become producers and not merely consumers of knowledge, and to take action for collective social change. Social justice education calls on teachers to provoke critical inquiry and dialogue, foster deep learning instead of rote memorization, affirm students' civic experiences and identities, and promote a vision of the collective or public good. It also recognizes the inherently political, nonneutral nature of all knowledge and the institutions of schooling, with a particular eye toward identifying and dismantling patterns of institutionalized oppression within the educational system and outside it. The second core principle of social justice is equity: social justice education explicitly aims to improve the life chances and quality of life for marginalized and last chance students *as a group*. In my understanding, this notion of equity differs from the more familiar educational goal of promoting *individual* upward mobility. Instead, it suggests a vision of social justice for *all* students—those who are getting ahead in school and those "others" against whom getting ahead is made possible.

Many critical educators and scholars have advanced compelling visions of social justice education and offered practical ideas for implementing it more authentically in schools.[3] However, we have not systematically and directly confronted the paradox of getting ahead as a serious obstacle to social justice "for all." In fact, we have too often done the opposite, buying into the glorification of social mobility by celebrating how education can help (individual) marginalized students achieve "success" through staying in school, going on to college, and obtaining professional middle-income jobs. I hope this book will challenge us to reconsider the costs of reproducing this discourse. With the last chance high school as my vantage point for engaging these issues, I argue that the social mobility paradigm undermines, rather than supports, our efforts to practice meaningful social justice education in schools and to bring about social justice for marginalized and last chance students as a group. This book calls on educators with commitments to social justice and other critical and democratic pedagogies to engage seriously with—rather than continue to deny, minimize, and dodge—the enduring dilemma of hierarchy and the paradox of getting ahead.

Methodological Approach

This book is based on two years of participant observation with the PARTY group and a total of six years working at Jackson High. While facilitating the PARTY project, I took ethnographic field notes and audio-recorded every group meeting. The transcripts of weekly PARTY meetings were an especially important data source, and this book contains several long stretches of dialogue from them. I conducted audio-recorded semistructured interviews with all PARTY members and eight students in the social justice class, but an even richer source of data was the additional time I spent informally with key youth participants— giving rides, visiting their homes, providing tutoring, helping with scholarship essays, talking on the phone, or grabbing a bite to eat. In these unstructured interactions, conversations tended to be more authentic and impromptu. I always took field notes during or immediately after these informal conversations with the youth. The period of formal data collection lasted two school years, but this book draws insights from my six years of experience working at Jackson High and the relationships I maintained with the youth participants before the PARTY project and since.

In addition to my ethnographic data, this book draws extensively from secondary sources to contextualize and historicize PARTY's work and draw connections between the micro and macro levels of analysis. Deirdre Kelly's (1993a) seminal historical analysis of continuation (last chance) high schools is the foundation for chapter 1, which recounts much of that history and employs Kelly's key analytical frames for interpretation. In preparing chapter 1, I also consulted a range of additional secondary sources and historical policy documents, and I conducted content analysis of contemporary policy, practitioner, and research texts about last chance high schools and their students. Chapters 5 and 6 also make extensive use of secondary sources about the academic-vocational divide, the labor market for non-college-educated workers, and the arguments for and against policies of "college for all" and vocational education.

Finally, this book incorporates methods of participatory action research (PAR) and autoethnography, as its central findings derive from my analysis of a PAR project in which I was a key participant. As I report on the work of PARTY, I periodically acknowledge my own role and reflect on the choices I made as facilitator. A theme that weaves throughout each chapter is an ongoing dialogue between the "me of then" and the "me of now," as I reflect on the choices I made and the words I uttered then with the clearer perspective of hindsight.[4] This dialogue between the "me of then" and the "me of now" incorporates analytic and narrative elements of autoethnography (Ellis and Bochner 2000), and often generates analyses that are relevant to the larger arguments of the book. But although I incorporate autoethnography throughout, my goal is to retain a primary analytic focus on the youth participants and the social contexts of their lives. In this way, I attempt to heed the call for honest self-reflexive writing without drowning out the important voices and perspectives of the youth, who remain the protagonists of this story.

It is important to point out how this book differs from most other academic writing about PAR. There are few scholarly books in print that contain extended case studies of a single PAR project (for example, McIntyre 2000; Maguire 1987; Dyrness 2011). With the important exception of Dyrness 2011, the existing book-length case studies of PAR projects have tended to focus on explaining the rationale for the PAR method, defending its research validity, showing how to practice it, and examining its limits and possibilities as a mode of inquiry or an approach to working with youth. These works are aimed primarily at university-based researchers who are, or wish to be, practitioners of PAR. Taking these works as a point of departure, this book assumes the validity of PAR and operationalizes it as a research method. Unlike many academic books and articles based on PAR projects, this book is not primarily *about* using PAR. Rather, it is a book that *uses* PAR, together with critical ethnographic methods, to explore broader questions of identity, agency, and social reproduction that have long been central to sociocultural research in education.

Representational Dilemmas

Nearly two decades ago, feminist and PAR scholar Patricia Maguire expressed her concern that the academic literature on PAR was filled with self-congratulatory, glossy accounts of PAR projects achieving success (Maguire 1993). These accounts, she argued, made PAR appear to be a simple, straightforward process that nearly always produced positive results. Maguire confessed that reading this literature filled her with feelings of inadequacy and self-doubt about her own PAR project. Rather than helping her understand the complex dynamics of doing PAR, she wrote, the literature left her feeling "immobilized and intimidated by ideal standards" (ibid., 158). She called for more PAR scholars to produce honest, nuanced, self-reflexive accounts of our work in order to encourage ourselves and others to "learn by doing" (ibid., 158).

Many scholars have heeded Maguire's call by publishing such accounts of PAR projects (e.g., Kelly 1993b; Langhout 2006; Kirshner 2010; LeCompte 1995), and this book attempts to do the same. It focuses on a PAR project that was largely (though not wholly) *un*successful at creating social change. My purpose in telling this story is not to critique the project, the methodology of PAR, or the individual participants. Instead, I draw from sociocultural theory to analyze the participants' practices as we *attempted* to enact social and educational change in and through the PAR process. The PARTY project is the ethnographic context (along with the last chance high school) from which I examine questions of identity, agency, and practices of social and educational change. It is a fitting context for engaging these questions because it was a space in which young people and I were actively trying to understand and challenge patterns of social inequality that we witnessed and experienced. In my view, the fact that we largely failed to effect change does not make the project less worthy as an object of study. In fact, it helps illuminate some of the sociocultural practices and discourses that may lead other educators and youth to achieve *reproductive* ends even while pursuing *resistive* goals.

Many scholars and practitioners of PAR have worked hard to gain legitimacy for this method within the academy, and some might reasonably worry that an account such as mine could provide ammunition to critics who would like to discredit PAR as a research method. I am sympathetic to these concerns about methodological representation, but I believe the literature on PAR stands to benefit from more honest, nuanced, self-reflexive accounts of real PAR projects—including those that fall short of our expectations along with those that far exceed them. For scholars who are serious about legitimizing PAR in academic research, I believe it is important to *use* PAR as a methodology to answer research questions on a range of topics relevant to educational scholars and not simply on the topic of PAR itself, no matter how important that topic may be to PAR practitioners. This book aims to take us in this direction and, as such, should strengthen rather than weaken the place of PAR in the academic social sciences. Just as the methodology of ethnography has benefited from the "reflexive turn" prompted by critiques of feminists and scholars of color, so too will the methodology of PAR be strengthened by our willingness to write honestly and self-reflexively about the ethical, political, and intellectual dilemmas of this method.

Power, Positionality, and the "Me of Then"

The youth PARTY members ranged in age from sixteen to twenty-one and included African American, Filipino, mixed-race (black/Latino), and white individuals. All were working-class or poor, and none had a college graduate among their close friends or family members. In contrast, I was twenty-six years old when the project started and came from a family with race, class, and educational privilege: I am of European American heritage and the third generation in my family to receive a PhD degree. As a former Jackson teacher, I spoke on behalf of the group to other teachers and the Jackson principal. As a doctoral student, I initiated, funded, and facilitated the project. And I had something immediate to gain from it—a dissertation and an advanced academic degree— while the benefits to the youth were less immediate and tangible.

During the project, I tried to reduce the impact of these power asymmetries in several ways. I emphasized that all group decisions would be made by consensus. I provided a small stipend (thirty dollars per week) to the youth as recognition that their time was valuable and that rewards should be accrued by all of us. I invited the youth to present with me at academic conferences. I sought their feedback on all written work I produced about the project, including funding proposals and dissertation drafts. I delegated to youth as much of the formal communication with Jackson staff members and the principal as possible. Despite these actions, I continued to hold disproportionate power. My combined privileges of race, class, and educational advantage allowed me to exercise voice within (and on behalf of) the group. I alone could veto any decision the group made, and I alone could call the project off at any time— for if I quit, the project would end. (The same was not true for the youth participants, some of whom did drop out only to be replaced by other youth.) Elsewhere, I have described my relationship to the PARTY group as a form of false egalitarianism: like color-blind racism, my repeated insistence that we were "all equal" in fact obscured and exacerbated real power differences (Nygreen 2009).

Only by analyzing the transcripts, field notes, and analytic memos in the years after the project ended was I able to recognize the extent of my privilege in the group and its harmful effects on our work. What I saw was that, in many ways, my own actions contributed to the reproduction of power inequalities, the silencing of youth voices, the perpetuation of my own agenda, and the confirmation of my own sense of entitlement. It was painful to recognize these truths about myself in the data. As I analyzed and wrote up the results of the project, I tried hard to avoid a fully honest discussion of my role. In fact, the doctoral dissertation I initially wrote about PARTY included only a cursory accounting of these issues. After completing the dissertation, I was tempted to put PARTY in my past and move on to other projects. However, I felt strongly that I still had a story to tell—one that had not yet been told, and that I was not ready to throw away altogether. That is the story I attempt to tell in this book. In preparing the book, I revisited all of the transcripts, field notes, and analytic memos from PARTY—three years after the project came to a close. With the benefit of distance, I was able to view my own words in these texts as "data," and subject them to the same type of critical analysis to which I subjected the words of the youth. While it was often difficult to read myself this way, I no longer reacted with the same defensiveness that I had during the first round of analysis. I was able to differentiate between the "me of then" and the "me of now," and to analyze the "me of then" as a character in the ethnographic story. The story I tell in this book reflects the perspective of the "me of now" with the benefits of additional insight that the intervening years of life have afforded me.

Still, as I wrote this book, I often hesitated to include scenes that might reveal my weaknesses as a facilitator. A candid description of my role would require a level of self-examination that promised to be difficult and painful. I dreaded having to admit the degree to which deficit thinking (Valencia 1997) and internalized dominance (Tatum 2003) had sometimes shaped my actions, and I feared that a truly honest account would have to reveal this. Moreover, I wondered about how to include myself honestly without making the story all about me, for I wanted to stay focused on the youth and the issues they faced at Jackson High. My intention was not to write a memoir of my own personal development; it was to tell a story of one group's modest attempt to wrestle with complex issues of educational inequality and to enact change through PAR and social justice education at a last chance high school. I was confident that this story could also shed light on the problems posed by the paradox of getting ahead and the limits of existing discursive frameworks for pursuing a vision of educational justice for all students. It is with these goals in mind that I tell the story of PARTY in the subsequent pages of this book.

Outline of the Book

Part 1: Social and Historical Contexts

The first two chapters lay the groundwork for the story of PARTY by discussing the historical, ethnographic, and discursive contexts of the project. Chapter 1 introduces readers to Jackson High and provides a historical perspective by tracing the evolution of California's continuation high school system—the state's largest "last chance" program—from its inception in 1919 to the present. Drawing heavily from Deirdre Kelly's (1993a) seminal historical analysis of the continuation high school system, I examine official policy narratives about these schools from each historical period, emphasizing how they have defined the purpose of continuation schools and the constituency of students who attend them. First, I show how continuation high schools have developed in the context of increasing *educational hierarchization* over the past century of education reform. Following Kelly (1993a), I argue that instead of providing an alternative for students, continuation high schools have increasingly reproduced the deep structures and practices of mainstream schooling. Second, I explore how the concept of a last chance high school was constructed, in tandem with the last chance *student*, as a particular kind of school serving a particular kind of kid—a defective and inferior adolescent for whom special schooling in a segregated context was (presumed to be) needed. This "kind of kid"—the troubled, maladjusted, or at-risk youth—remains a staple of contemporary policy, practitioner, and research discourse on educational failure, which I refer to as the "discourse of these kids."

In chapter 2, I examine how youth PARTY members and prospective PARTY members from Jackson High School interacted with the "discourse of these kids" by alternately mobilizing, reproducing, opposing, or contesting it. The social category of failure was imposed on Jackson youth such that they routinely had to contend with it, answer to it, explain or justify or deny it. In dominant educational discourse, the category of school failure encompasses more than a student's performance on school-based assessments: young people in this category are constructed not only as failed *students* but also as failed *persons*, and these failures are tied to notions of inherent intelligence and social class (Rose 2005b). In this discursive landscape, Jackson students and graduates worked hard to construct identities as deserving, capable, and intelligent young adults. In doing so, however, they often reproduced the very images and tropes they were trying to escape. In addition to developing these arguments, this chapter introduces the key youth participants in PARTY and the core theoretical concepts of the book: identity, discourse, agency, and figured worlds.

Part 2: Theorizing Identity and Agency

Chapters 3 and 4 tell the story of PARTY as we conducted collaborative research and took action by designing and teaching a social justice class at Jackson High. These chapters provide fine-grained ethnographic analyses of PARTY group practices with an eye toward refining theories of identity and agency. Chapter 3 focuses on weekly PARTY meetings as a space of deepening critical consciousness among the youth participants. This chapter describes our work in the first year and a half as we developed research questions, conducted a survey of Jackson students, analyzed our findings, conducted additional research, and made the choice to teach a social justice class at Jackson High. It also draws from theories of critical consciousness and civic identity formation to examine the youth's participation in weekly PARTY meetings through these lenses. It explores how the youth participants made sense of their lived civic experiences—especially their encounters with the educational and criminal justice systems—and how they imagined possibilities for exercising agency within the constraints of this sociopolitical context. It then examines the goals of the social justice class and the ways in which youth PARTY members discursively connected the work of teaching to a larger vision of collective action for social change. In this way, the social justice class was conceived as a political intervention with explicitly civic and collective goals—resonating with Labaree's (1997) "democratic equality" purpose of education.

Chapter 4 traces what happened as PARTY moved from theory to practice—from envisioning and planning a social justice class to actually teaching one at Jackson High School. Through ethnographic vignettes from the social justice class and weekly PARTY meetings in which we reflected on the class, this chapter demonstrates that, despite our attempt to implement an alternative and liberatory model of education for social change, we largely reproduced the practices and discourses of traditional classroom teaching. It theorizes these classroom dynamics and the reproductive outcomes of the class by drawing from sociocultural theories of teacher identity, agency, and figured worlds. It examines how the social context of Jackson High, and the more generalized figured world of schooling, shaped the emerging teacher identities of PARTY members, including myself, and our ability to exercise agency as individuals and as a collective. Building from the arguments advanced in chapter 2, this chapter shows how the figured world of schooling, and the discourses and identity categories that pervade that figured world, shaped and constrained our capacity for agency, thereby increasing the likelihood of reproductive outcomes.

Part 3: Dilemmas of Social Justice at the Last Chance High School

In chapters 5 and 6, I extend outward from the PARTY group to a broader focus on the last chance high school as a context that reveals and magnifies the paradox of getting ahead and the limits it places on social justice education. In chapter 5, I explore internal PARTY debates about the curricular goals of social justice education, particularly those focused on the meaning of academic standards and preparation for college and careers. Although PARTY members shared the goal of empowering Jackson students to become critical agents of social change, we brought different paradigms of educational justice to the table, which embodied different worldviews about the means and ends of social justice education at a last chance high school. Core debates within PARTY concerned the meaning and role of academic skill building and "standards" in the social justice class, and the relative value of academic versus vocational preparation for empowering Jackson students in their transition to adult roles. This chapter contextualizes PARTY's intragroup debates by connecting them to the realities of the postindustrial labor market and the historic struggle to define the purpose of high school at the bottom of the educational hierarchy.

In chapter 6, I reflect on the book's key arguments and consider their implications for educators who wish to advance social justice for all students. I explore the logic and limits of current educational justice discourses, such as "college for all," and ask what alternative visions of educational justice might enable us to transcend the paradox of getting ahead. This paradox is thrown into sharp relief at the last chance high school, but it encompasses all levels of schooling. I argue for a new discourse of educational justice that challenges the paradigm of individual mobility and articulates a vision of justice for all students, especially marginalized and last chance students as a group. To move toward this vision, I argue that educators should reframe our priorities from closing the achievement gap to closing the *consequence gap*. Only then might we begin to imagine a new pedagogy of social justice for "these kids."

PART I

Social and Historical Contexts

Situating Jackson High: Last Chance High Schools and the Discourse of These Kids

The Maytown City School District operated one comprehensive high school, the well-regarded Maytown High, a large and racially diverse school with over three thousand students. Most local residents knew this as the city's only public high school and did not know, or easily forgot, that a second high school operated just a few blocks away. Located on a busy intersection at the corner of Cesar Chavez Boulevard and Henry Street, Jackson High was a nondescript, modest complex of freshly painted portable classrooms enclosing a small interior courtyard of grass and cement. Although few Maytown residents were aware of its existence, Jackson High was a school where students fulfilled basic graduation requirements and earned high school diplomas, and where credentialed teachers and administrators worked under the same employment contract as those in the rest of the school district. But Jackson was a continuation high school, and even though every school district in California is required to maintain at least one such school, continuation high schools remain largely absent from the general public's consciousness (Kelly 1993a). Further, among Maytown residents who did know about Jackson—because they either worked in the school district, lived nearby, or had a child transferred there—the school's reputation was decidedly negative, seen as a dumping ground for the worst students in the city.

Maytown is a small city of approximately one hundred thousand residents in the middle of a large, urbanized metropolitan area. Its population in 2000 was 59.0 percent white, 16.0 percent Asian, 14.0 percent

African American, 5.0 percent from "other races," and 6.0 percent multi-racial. Ten percent of residents were classified as Latino/a (of any race), and less than 1.0 percent each as Native American and Pacific Islander.[1] Maytown is home to many well-educated professionals with high-status occupations, and median family income is substantially higher than state and national medians.[2] Despite these signs of privilege, Maytown contains substantial socioeconomic diversity, and it is a city in which race and class are largely conflated such that lower-income neighborhoods are predominantly African American (and increasingly Latino) while higher-income neighborhoods are predominantly white. When I arrived at Jackson as a classroom teacher, the school was 81.0 percent African American (compared with 36.0 percent at Maytown High), 4.0 percent white (compared with 41.0 percent at Maytown High), and 54.0 percent of its students qualified for free/reduced-price meals (compared with 5.7 percent at Maytown High).[3] Its students came disproportionately, if not entirely, from the poorest neighborhoods of the city. With a mix of apartments, small single-family homes, and public housing units, these neighborhoods were known around the city as centers of gun violence, street crime, and poverty. Underscoring this image, small corner liquor stores and street signs warning potential drug dealers to stay away were visible on almost every block.

Like most continuation programs in the state, Jackson provided only the bare basics of a high school education—just enough to fulfill minimum requirements for a diploma but too little to qualify a student for admission to a state university. In addition to being excluded from college preparatory courses, Jackson students were barred from participation in extracurricular activities at Maytown High, including sports, even though Jackson itself offered no extracurricular programs. Every year, fierce debates ensued about whether Jackson students should be allowed to attend Maytown High School's homecoming festivities, prom, and graduation ceremonies. Many Maytown parents, administrators, and teachers considered the Jackson students too dangerous and threatening to participate in these activities.

Approximately 10 percent of California's secondary students attend continuation high schools (Ruiz de Velasco et al. 2008), and yet relatively little educational research has focused on these schools. In this chapter, I attempt to make up some of this ground by providing a thorough history and discussion of continuation high schools, their development, and relative positioning vis-à-vis "regular" high schools. Deirdre Kelly's book *Last Chance High* (1993a) provides perhaps the most thorough history of continuation high schools available in print. In it, Kelly reconstructs the history of these schools from their inception in 1919 through the 1980s, focusing on their role and positioning within the overall system of secondary schooling. Drawing extensively from Kelly's work, this chapter highlights two key insights that are significant to the story I will tell about the PARTY project at Jackson High. First, instead of providing an alternative for students, Kelly argues, continuation high schools have largely reproduced the deep structures and practices of mainstream schooling. Second, her analysis shows how continuation students have persistently been defined in opposition to normative standards of the "successful" student and with the use of deficiency tropes that position continuation students as inferior.

Building from these points, this chapter shows how policy discourses associated with the establishment and maintenance of a last chance high school system contributed to the development of a new social category or "kind of kid": the at-risk, dropout-prone youth for whom special schooling in a segregated context is (presumed to be) needed. In using the term *kind of kid* throughout this and future chapters, I am drawing from James Gee's (2000) notion of "kinds of people" to refer to social categories that become sources of identity. At Jackson High, other teachers and I often used the phrase *these kids* as a shorthand way of talking about this particular kind of kid. This term appeared in comments such as "These kids need discipline" or "I don't know how to handle these kids!" As a classroom teacher myself, when I talked about "these kids," I meant to convey a bundle of unspoken assumptions and meanings: as opposed to "normal" or "mainstream" high school students, "these kids" were constructed as deficient, deviant, and difficult. In this chapter, I show that *these kids* was not simply a localized term used among Jackson teachers but representative of a broader public discourse about youth who are socially located at the bottom end of the educational hierarchy. I identify what I call the *discourse of these kids*—a dominant educational discourse defining who these kids are, what they need, why they are a problem, and what the purpose of high school is (or should be) for them. I examine the historical development of this discourse as well as its scope and reach in contemporary policy, practitioner, and research texts. This historical and discursive analysis of continuation high schools and their students provides essential context for understanding the dynamics of the PARTY project and Jackson High.

The (Attempted) Makeover of Jackson High

In my second year as a teacher at Jackson, the school's negative reputation was addressed in a faculty meeting. Eight Jackson teachers—four
black and four white, including me—sat around a rectangular conference table. At the head sat our principal, Mr. Jones, and the principal
of Maytown High, Ms. Dawson, both African American. After brief
introductions, the principals informed the teachers that Jackson High
was going to change. It looked bad, they told us, to be a predominantly
black school in a racially diverse city, especially when enrollment was involuntary rather than a choice. Two things needed to happen: Jackson
needed to become "diverse," and enrollment needed to become voluntary. It would be our responsibility to recruit and retain a more diverse
student body at Jackson. At this point, the middle-aged African American man who taught math asked the principals if by "diverse" students
they meant white students. Without the slightest hesitation, Ms. Dawson replied affirmatively. Then an older African American woman who
had taught at Jackson for more than a decade cleared her throat and proceeded slowly, as if contemplating her words with great care, and asked
Ms. Dawson if she could please explain what white students in the city
of Maytown would ever choose to enroll at Jackson. Ms. Dawson again
replied without any hesitation. There were plenty of students, she said,
who were alienated from the mainstream educational system—hippies,
punks, skaters, ravers—and these were the kids we should target for recruitment to Jackson High.

   Although not mentioned at this faculty meeting, this was not the first
time Jackson had sought to rehabilitate its image by attracting white students of the hippie-punk-raver variety. In the late 1960s, the school officially changed its name from South End Continuation High School to
Jackson High School. The move was intended to eliminate the stigma associated with South End, which by then had become known as a dumping ground for the district's worst students. Then as now, South End was
a predominantly African American and high-poverty school, in sharp
contrast to the racial and socioeconomic diversity of the city of Maytown
and its other public schools. Under a visionary new principal, the newly
named Jackson High implemented a program of nontraditional pedagogy and branded itself an "alternative" high school. At the time, the
school district was experimenting with several small alternative schools,

and an emergent alternative schools movement was spreading across the country. In this context, Jackson was able to present itself as one of several new alternative programs that students could choose to attend. Although Jackson High was still technically a continuation school—meaning students could be involuntarily transferred there for poor academic performance—it also started to attract voluntary students, among them a sizable number of white and middle-class students seeking a progressive alternative.

But the era of Jackson as an alternative school was short-lived. By the time I arrived in the late 1990s, it had long since regained the stigma previously associated with South End, and it had lost the racial and class diversity that had brought it some temporary status. So, in the years following the faculty meeting with Ms. Dawson, Jackson High underwent another name change and implemented a series of reforms in an attempt to become "diverse." The school was renamed Maytown Alternative Program (MAP).[4] It scrapped the block schedule—according to which classes met every other day for ninety minutes—and replaced it with a traditional schedule in which each class met every day for forty-five minutes.[5] It lengthened the school day by ninety minutes and added a ninth grade, demonstrating that it was now a "real" high school (as opposed to a continuation program, which typically had shorter school days and served grades ten through twelve only). A new (white) principal, Mr. Galo, was brought in from the central administration office to replace Mr. Jones. And, remarkably, the school district abandoned the policy of involuntary transfer. From then on, counselors at Maytown High could recommend struggling students for transfer to Jackson (now MAP) but could not, technically, compel them to transfer.

Despite these efforts, between 1998 and 2004 the school remained predominantly African American (fluctuating between 72 and 78 percent), followed by Latino/a (12 to 14 percent), with a small number of white and Asian / Pacific Islander students.[6] In the year that ninth graders were recruited as its first voluntary cohort, about five white freshmen enrolled (in a class of approximately twenty-five students).[7] By the end of their sophomore year, all of these voluntary white students had transferred out—either to Maytown High, the independent studies program, private schools, or other school districts. Although the involuntary transfer process had been technically abandoned, in practice the policy of recommending students for transfer operated in much the same way and resulted in the same population of students winding up at Jackson. In short, despite efforts to reinvent itself as an "alternative" program with higher status, Jackson High continued to look strikingly like a continuation high school by every measure.

The story of Jackson's failed attempt at transformation is emblematic when placed in its social and historical context as a continuation or "last chance" high school in California (Kelly 1993a). Deirdre Kelly's book *Last Chance High* (1993a) shows that continuation high schools have occupied the bottom rung in a vastly differentiated educational hierarchy for nearly a century and have always experienced the stigma associated with that role. As Kelly demonstrates, continuation high schools have repeatedly sought legitimacy by adopting new narratives to portray both their mission and their students in a more positive light, but these attempts have tended to be short-lived, routinely drowned out by more powerful images of continuation students as genetically and culturally deficient racial outsiders. Moreover, instead of creating true alternatives, repeated reforms have resulted in programs that look *more* like traditional high schools rather than less, and often focus on attracting higher-status students instead of seeking ways to serve the existing student body more effectively. Both of these points were evidenced in Jackson's transformation into MAP.

The remainder of this chapter reconstructs much of the history of continuation high schools that was first published in Kelly's book (1993a), and then extends this history to the present day. The first three sections recount the three major time periods that Kelly identified: expansion and growth (1918–30), decline and transformation (1930–65), and reborn as alternative schools (1965–83). I follow with a fourth section based on my own analysis of the current historical moment, the era of accountability (1983 to the present). For each of these four time periods, I examine policy, practitioner, and research texts about continuation high schools with attention to two themes: the definition of the continuation *student* and the purpose of the continuation *school*. To research this history, I consulted a range of secondary sources and historical documents, and conducted my own independent analysis of contemporary policy, practitioner, and research texts, but I am deeply indebted to Kelly's work for providing the essential analytical frames and questions that anchored my inquiry. In addition to helping us think about the social construction of failure and the social category of "these kids," the history of continuation high schools reveals the enduring challenge of defining a purpose for education at the bottom of the educational hierarchy. Further, it sheds light on a set of processes that I refer to as the *hierarchization* of education.

Expansion and Growth: 1918–30

The continuation high school emerged during the first three decades of the twentieth century, an era in which high school was becoming the new frontier of educational advancement. From 1900 to 1930, high school enrollment roughly doubled every decade (Martin 1961). As enrollments grew, so too did a public belief in the power of schooling as a solution to new social problems (Perkinson 1995; Tyack and Cuban 1997). Accordingly, the reformers of the day sought to keep more young people in school for longer periods of time, and their success in accomplishing this was largely seen as a measure of general social progress (Kliebard 1999; Tyack and Cuban 1997). In this new social context, leaving school before graduation came to be defined as a "problem" for the first time, and some reformers saw continuation schools as a solution. The idea for continuation schools (as well as the name) came from the German education system, where working youth attended a part-time school for four to eight hours per week. Inspired by the German model, a reform movement in the United States emerged in the early twentieth century to establish part-time continuation schools here (Imber 1985; Katznelson and Weir 1988; Kliebard 1999). By 1920, twenty states, including California, had passed legislation mandating the establishment of part-time continuation schools (Mayman 1933, 195). And by 1930, thirty-four states and US territories (including Puerto Rico and Hawaii) had established part-time continuation programs, and these programs were serving up to 340,000 young people a year (Kelly 1993a)—approximately 8 percent of all students enrolled in public secondary schools (Beales 1941).[8]

It is this system of part-time schooling for working minors that has grown into the continuation high school system of today. From its inception, the target continuation student was a high school–aged youth who had left school to enter the workforce. State laws, as well as the federal Smith-Hughes Act, all specified the young *worker* as the primary constituency of continuation schools. Serving the needs of "juvenile workers" or "working minors," as they were interchangeably called, was widely accepted as the purpose continuation schools were expected to fulfill (Wright 1929; Keller 1924; Mayman 1933; Williamson 2008). The plight

of young workers—many of them from poor and immigrant families—
was beginning to gain the attention of reformers and the public. Low
wages, dangerous working conditions, long hours, and the lack of upward mobility were all issues that young workers faced. Many proponents of continuation schools claimed they could address these issues by
offering vocational education and guidance that would help working and
work-bound students seek and secure better jobs within the manual labor occupations for which they were destined (Kantor and Tyack 1982;
Kliebard 1999; Imber 1985). Vocational education was also promoted
as a more "relevant" curriculum for working and work-bound students,
compared with the "irrelevant" academic curriculum, thus contributing to reformers' efforts to keep more students in school for longer periods of time (Kantor and Tyack 1982; Kliebard 1999). The general idea
that schooling should prepare students for labor market roles—what is
known as *vocationalism*—began to take root during this era (Kliebard
1999; Kantor and Tyack 1982). Accordingly, many continuation programs emphasized vocational training and vocational guidance with the
goal of helping young workers secure better jobs, decrease exploitation
and poverty, and achieve upward mobility (Mayman 1933; Imber 1985).
These schools also emphasized citizenship skills such as patriotism and
obedience, and "life skills" such as hygiene and the value of marriage
(Imber 1985; Mayman 1933).

Unfortunately, Imber (1985) found little evidence that vocational education ever helped continuation students command higher wages or
obtain better jobs. The problem, he argues, was that most continuation
students were working in jobs at the very bottom of the occupational hierarchy that offered few options for upward mobility, regardless of any
additional training they might receive in school. In the early part of
the twentieth century, he explains, "the majority of child workers were
employed in factories whose flat, bottom-heavy organization made advancement unlikely. Thus, continuation schools failed to recognize that
there would be no career ladder for most who started work as children
regardless of how well they could read, write, or operate their machine"
(ibid., 58). In short, the problems that continuation students faced—of
low wages, dangerous working conditions, exploitation, and few labor
rights—seemed to stem not from their lack of training but from the nature of the labor market itself. Imber (ibid.) concludes that continuation schools "proved powerless in their attempt to provide a solution
for the sorry plight of child workers, a problem which was not educa-

tional but rather the result of the socio-economic structure of the larger society" (58).

Although official descriptions of continuation students emphasized their status as workers, there is some evidence that the actual population of continuation schools has always included unemployed youth as well as those who were simply unsuccessful in regular high schools. As early as 1926, the California Board of Education published a bulletin stating, "To these [continuation] schools come the pupils who were the most serious educational, disciplinary, or social problems in the full-time school . . . merely because they belong to the age group for whom part-time schools were designed" (quoted in Williamson 2008, 8). Likewise, a continuation school principal in New York City bemoaned that far too many of his students were "doing nothing except continually seeking employment, or, what is more to be deplored, some are not anxious to seek or get a job" (Keller 1924, 86). He went on to describe his students as a mix of working youth along with "boys and girls unable to learn and therefore scholastic failures" (ibid., 95).

Whether describing the young workers or the "scholastic failures" attending continuation schools, deficiency-oriented tropes about these students pervaded the professional and academic discourse. In his aptly named book *The Education of the Ne'er-do-well*, a continuation school principal described his predominantly immigrant students as lacking the "mental equipment" for academic work (Henry 1916, 28). Another continuation school teacher described her students as incapable of rational thought; "the wage-earning adolescent is, in fact, peculiarly unused to reasoning" (Phillips [1922] 2009, 20), she wrote, and thus becomes "prey to superstition of the crudest kind" (ibid., 21). She described the continuation student as potentially dangerous, claiming that "his almost fierce desire for concrete social relationships finds expression through gangs and secret societies" (ibid., 17). When describing the challenges of vocational training with continuation students, one principal wrote, "Not only must the teacher supply the technical knowledge of occupations and diagnose aptitudes and abilities, but he must arouse or infuse the will-to-do. Thousands of years of heredity plus fifteen years of environment against four hours a week of an educational experiment present awful odds" (Keller 1924, 87). In this statement, the principal identifies both genetic ("thousands of years of heredity") and cultural ("fifteen years of environment") deficiencies as the cause of his students' laziness (or lack of "will-to-do"). In 1931, a study comparing working minors to full-time secondary students concluded, "Every investigation of mental differences between school and working children has shown a decided superiority on the part of school children" (Goldberger 1931, 1).

These early texts written by continuation teachers, administrators, and researchers reflect a discourse of deficiency in which continuation students were framed as both distinct from, and inferior to, "regular" high school students. In these writings, practitioners and scholars attempted to generalize about continuation students, to identify their specific needs and define what made them unique, under the guise of serving them better in the continuation school. Through this process, a new social category or "kind of kid" was being constructed. It was not just a "working minor" but also a deficient, defective, and problematic kind of student, associated with foreignness, low intelligence, laziness, lack of skill, poor upbringing, genetic inferiority, and possible danger (i.e., gang affiliation). In every comparison made—IQ, work ethic, morality, even aesthetics—the continuation student came out as inferior when compared to a presumed but usually untheorized "regular" or full-time student. This discourse of deficiency resonates with what we now call color-blind racism (Bonilla-Silva 2006) because it conveys racial and ethnic meanings without the necessity of naming race. What was ostensibly a straightforward institutional category, the "working minor," became value laden as other social meanings were attached to it, many of them with racial undertones.

Decline and Transformation: 1930–65

In the years between 1930 and 1950, the system of part-time continuation schools all but disappeared from the national map, with the notable exception of California. The demise of these schools was precipitated by a steep decline in enrollments that began in the early 1930s (Imber 1985; Kelly 1993a; Mayman 1933). Both the lack of available jobs during the Great Depression and the tightened enforcement of child labor laws reduced the number of youth in the labor force (Mayman 1933; Kelly 1993a). At the same time, there was increased pressure on regular high schools to keep students in school full-time, and reforms aimed at this goal were successfully implemented across the country (Imber 1985). By 1950, high school education had been so thoroughly differentiated by tracking that many saw no need for a separate continuation school (ibid.). Most comprehensive high schools now offered multiple tracks that included programs in vocational training and guidance—areas that had once been the domain of continuation education. As a result, most states eliminated their continuation programs in the 1940s and 1950s, but California managed to maintain its institutional infrastructure and reinvent the program with a new purpose serving a new clientele (Kelly 1993a; Williamson 2008). As such, the period of 1930 to 1965 can be seen as one of decline and transformation: nationwide, continuation schools quietly disappeared, but in California, they survived by transforming their purpose and expanding their definition of the particular kind of kid for whom these schools existed.

As discussed previously, there is evidence that nonworking students had attended continuation schools since their inception. These students included some who were temporarily unemployed as well as others who transferred to continuation schools simply because they were unsuccessful or unhappy in full-time school. Yet in the early years, these nonworking students were rarely if ever mentioned in official policy texts. This began to change when, in 1929, a California state law required unemployed youth who were enrolled in continuation programs to attend school for fifteen hours per week instead of the standard four hours per week required of working youth (Williamson 2008). This was the first "official" acknowledgment that nonworking students were even enrolled in continuation programs, and it created two groups of students at these schools: the four-hours-per-week (employed) group and the fifteen-hours-per-week (unemployed) group. Throughout the 1930s, the latter group grew more numerous as the youth labor market dried up, periods of unemployment lasted longer, and increasing numbers of students never sought work at all. The shortage of working students threatened to render the continuation school obsolete. If they were to survive, continuation schools had to present themselves as more than just a part-time program for employed youth (Kelly 1993a).

This shift in purpose occurred in the 1950s through the fusion of working and nonworking continuation students into a single social category. In 1955, an influential state-commissioned study opened with the bold assertion that all continuation students, whether employed or not, shared a basic characteristic that defined them as a group: a lack of "adjustment" to full-time schooling:

As periods of unemployment lengthened during the depression years it became evident that many minors subject to compulsory attendance upon continuation education classes shared a characteristic which was related to employment status *only in a secondary sense*. This characteristic was lack of
adjustment in the full-time school. Many who left full-time school for a job
on the pretext of economic need were in no greater financial difficulties than
others who relied upon after-school employment. Lack of adjustment to the
program or the environment of the regular full-time high school led these
youth to drop out. (Shaffer 1955, 1, emphasis added)

This passage reveals a conceptual shift in the glue holding the continuation student category together. Employment status was irrelevant
in this formulation; the fundamental trait shared by all continuation students was their lack of adjustment to full-time schooling and, hence, the
need to provide them with "adjustment education" in a part-time program. Chief among the report's recommendations was a call for continuation education to be redefined as "a program serving *all those students* who have limitations, unusual problems, or responsibilities which
make it inadvisable for them to attend the regular secondary school program" (ibid., 105, emphasis added). This recommendation was significant because it expressly called for a shift in focus from a school serving
working youth to one designed for all students who were not successful in regular school—in other words, a school serving *failing* youth. As
the recognized constituency of continuation schools shifted, so too did
narratives about the purpose of these schools. Increasingly, "life adjustment" was framed as the primary purpose of continuation education, su-
perseding vocational and civic training (Kelly 1993a).

In the 1950 edition of the *Handbook on Continuation Education in
California* (published by the California Department of Education), the
"working student" remained in the official description of the continuation school's clientele, but the image of the "unadjusted" student occupied a much more central place throughout the text. In lieu of a meaningful definition of the "unadjusted student," the handbook offered the
following passage:

These [unadjusted students] may be classified as students who are retarded
in school, students with little interest in the school program, students needing remedial work in certain fields, students with limited physical capacity,

students returning to school after long periods of absence, transfers, late en-
rollees, students needing special guidance such as habitual truants, juvenile
court problems, behavior cases, health problems, and students requiring re-
habilitation. (Jones 1950, 3)

Lists like this—what I call the grab-bag frame—were to become a
staple in texts about continuation schools and their students. As educators and policymakers tried to describe the nonworking students at these
schools, their descriptions often read as laundry lists of traits, characteristics, and circumstances that might be causes, aggravators, correlates,
or outcomes of poor school performance. These were simply added to
the former descriptor of "working student," thus leading to a grab-bag-
like description of continuation students in the form of a list. For example, the district superintendent in El Monte, California, explained, "In
our continuation classes we find the employed, the married, the delinquent, the average, the bright, the malcontent, the sullen, the emotion-
ally disturbed, and so on" (Hicks 1945, 76). A teacher in San Diego described her continuation class this way: "The moron and superior adult
are represented, the maladjusted and the delinquent, wealthy and poor,
married and divorced, native and foreign born" (Markey 1940, 162). And
a sociologist writing in the 1960s noted, "Among these students are habitual truants, behavior problems in the regular school, juvenile court
wards, retarded students and those requiring special instruction in particular fields, students with health problems, and those with little motivation in school" (Elder 1966, 326).

As in previous decades, deficiency tropes permeated the discourse
about these students, as when the 1950 *Handbook on Continuation Education in California* explained:

Sometimes their capacity for personal improvement, which is affected by
their heredity and their physical and social environment, is more restricted
than that of their more fortunate fellows; sometimes their human relationships are impaired by the broken and underprivileged homes from which they
come; often their economic proficiency is substandard because of their lack
of ability, inadequate training, poor health, and improper work habits and
attitudes; frequently their effectiveness as citizens is lessened by their igno-
rance, indifference, lack of good home training, dissatisfaction with school,
and many other factors which cause general maladjustment. (Jones 1950, 4)

In this passage, continuation students are defined principally in terms of their shortcomings or deficiencies: a "restricted" capacity for personal improvement, "impaired" human relationships, "substandard" economic proficiency, and ineffectiveness as citizens. The causes of their short-comings are located in both genetic ("heredity") and environmental fac-tors, including their home and family lives, revealing a perspective shaped by notions of genetic and cultural deficiency. Continuation students are described as lacking a proper work ethic and good home training, and being civically ignorant and apathetic. All of these diagnoses and tropes are presented under the guise of understanding continuation students better in order to meet their needs more successfully. But their impact also reinforces powerful images of genetic and cultural deficiency that may unwittingly serve to legitimize students' low social and educational status.

In short, the years between 1930 and 1965 were marked by new narra-tives about *who* continuation students were (from "working" to "malad-justed" youth) and the *purpose* of continuation education for them (from a part-time program offering schedule flexibility to an intervention pro-gram offering "psychological adjustment" for the maladjusted and de-linquent) (Markey 1940, 160). Two additional developments in this time period were important in shaping the continuation high school of to-day. First, around 1950, the term *continuation* high *school* started to re-place *continuation school* or *continuation program* in policy texts. This is likely related to the fact that real high school credits were now, for the first time, being awarded for coursework completed in continuation pro-grams, and continuation students could even pursue a high school di-ploma (Jones 1950). Continuation high schools were, in fact, starting to look more like regular high schools—accepting all students, lengthening their school day, and awarding credits and diplomas.

As continuation high schools started to look more like regular high schools, they also became more distinctly recognizable as *low-status* high schools serving low-status students. As such, concerns about the growing stigmatization of continuation programs emerged in policy, practitioner, and research texts (Kelly 1993a).[9] These concerns were com-pounded by the overrepresentation of African American and immigrant students in continuation schools. As one sociologist observed, "Consid-ering the characteristics of the [continuation] school and large number of Negro students enrolled, a civil rights group would have little diffi-culty in describing it as a 'dumping ground' for Negro students" (Elder

1966, 340). These concerns about stigma and racial segregation helped set the stage for their reinvention as "alternative schools" in the 1970s—foreshadowing Jackson High School's own attempted reinvention, recounted earlier in this chapter, in the early 2000s.

Reborn as Alternative Schools: 1965–83

The alternative and free schools movement that spread across the country in the late 1960s and early 1970s provided a context for continuation schools to challenge their growing stigmatization and, in some places such as Maytown, to blossom into marginally respected alternative programs. The movement for alternative schools was based on a rejection of traditional schooling as an outdated and dehumanizing institution (Swidler 1980). Central to the movement was a belief that every child learns differently and should therefore be able to choose an educational program that fits his or her unique learning styles and interests (Mottaz 2002). The alternative school philosophy also held that the cause of school failure was not located in students themselves but rather within the structures and practices of mainstream schooling with its rigid standards, authoritarian power relations, factory-style pedagogy, and decontextualized knowledge. A national alternative schools movement led to thousands of new alternative high schools being established nationwide by 1975 (ibid.). These alternative schools allowed teachers, parents, and other community members to experiment with nontraditional pedagogy that ran counter to the dominant forms of instruction found in mainstream high schools (Swidler 1980).

In this social and political context, continuation high schools found new justification for their existence and a competing set of narratives to describe their mission and students.[10] With many new alternative schools in the mix, continuation programs could portray themselves as one more "choice" in a vast array of options. And with the rising popularity of a critical discourse on mainstream schooling, an antideficit perspective on continuation students could begin to emerge. Although continuation schools continued to suffer from stigma (see Voss 1968, 17–18; Camp 1980, 47), there were now well-circulated competing narratives available to portray the schools and the students who attended them from a less deficit-oriented perspective: instead of locating the causes of school failure inside students, official narratives began to speak about a *mismatch* between traditional forms of schooling and the unique needs, problems, and circumstances of continuation students.

In official policy texts, the grab-bag frame persisted as the dominant way to describe who continuation students were and what made them unique. The obligatory reference to working students as a distinct group within this grab bag remained up through the 1968 edition of the *Handbook on Continuation Education in California*, which divided continuation students into two groups: "those who drop out of school for financial reasons and the *much larger group* of those who are unadjusted to full-time school" (Voss 1968, 4, emphasis added). The handbook went on to describe both groups of students using a grab-bag-like list of traits and characteristics:

> All may be classified as having unusual problems, situations, and responsibilities. For the most part, they may be characterized as those who do not or cannot attend regularly; those for whom a large school fails to provide a happy or constructive environment; those who do not benefit from group learning experiences and who may even limit benefits to others. Also included are students with little interest in the regular school program; students needing remedial work in certain fields; students with limited physical capacity; and students returning after long periods of absence. Still other students are those transferring or enrolling late; those needing special guidance, such as habitual truants; those involved in juvenile court actions; those with behavioral problems; those with health problems; and those needing rehabilitation or readjustment training for other reasons. (ibid., 4)

A noteworthy addition to the grab bag occurred in the 1968 edition of the handbook, the first to acknowledge pregnant girls as a distinct subgroup of the continuation program's target population (Kelly 1993a). References to pregnant and parenting students have remained in subsequent editions of the handbook.

The 1973 edition of the handbook was the first to omit the by now formulaic reference to working students. It read simply, "The largest single group of students requiring attention through the continuation education program is comprised of those who drop out of full-time school or who are potential dropouts whose problems require that they transfer from the regular school" (Eales 1973, 2). It then proceeded to offer a grab-bag list of reasons for which these students might have become potential dropouts, or why they might be in need of special help in a continuation school. Another significant discursive shift occurred in the 1960s when continuation high schools officially adopted the goal of providing access to a high school diploma. The 1968 edition of the handbook states, "As now defined, continuation education is a program that leads toward a high school diploma" (Voss 1968, 1). This centering of the diploma reflects the gradual trend of continuation high schools toward becoming smaller, watered-down versions of traditional high schools (Kelly 1993a)—ironically occurring at the very same moment when they were being touted as "alternatives."

The Era of Accountability: 1983 to the Present

Today, the California Department of Education's website states simply that "continuation education is a *high school diploma program* [emphasis added] designed to meet the needs of students sixteen through eighteen years of age who have not graduated from high school, are not exempt from compulsory school attendance, and are deemed at risk of not completing their education."[11] California is now the only state in the country to maintain a system of schools called "continuation" high schools, but similar last chance programs exist in other states—typically under the name of "alternative schools"—for students at the bottom of the educational hierarchy (Laudan 2006; Kleiner, Porch, and Farris 2002). Like the continuation high school system in California, these "alternative" high schools tend to emphasize dropout prevention while providing a second-chance (or last chance) route to the high school diploma. Reflecting the trend toward increased educational credentialism, it is the diploma itself, not the knowledge it represents, that is put forward as the central purpose of schooling for "these kids."

In the two decades that have passed since the publication of Deirdre Kelly's book in 1993, the idea of a standardized curriculum for all children (ensured through standardized testing and accountability measures) has become a centerpiece of education reform. As well, the increasing reliance on standardized tests has produced ever more elaborate mechanisms for differentiating between "higher-" and "lower-" performing students (Lipman 2003, 2011). In this time, the high school curriculum has steadily become narrowed around the core academic subject areas that are tested, and continuation high schools are no exception. Like the movement for vocational education in the early twentieth century, the movement for standardization around academic or college preparatory subject area coursework has often been justified on the grounds of expanding opportunity for upward mobility.[12] Yet rather than facilitating mobility, the impact of curricular standardization has arguably been to reify social and educational hierarchies while strengthening only the appearance of equal opportunity: the more curriculum is standardized—offering the "same" content to all students—the easier it becomes to determine "better" and "worse" performances and thus to produce a ranked hierarchy of achievement. In comprehensive high schools, terms such as *regular* and *honors* get tacked onto course names as a way of differentiating higher and lower levels in what is ostensibly the "same" curricular content. This dual process of simultaneous curricular standardization and stratification can be summarized as a process of *educational hierarchization*. As seen throughout this chapter, the trend of educational hierarchization is evident in the history of continuation high schools: as these schools increasingly mimicked regular high schools in their form and content, they also became increasingly identifiable as low-status schools for failing students rather than alternatives for working students. In this way, homogenization and stratification went hand in hand.

Most continuation high schools today feature a traditional academic curriculum that is oriented toward passing California's high school exit exam (EdSource 2008), and intended to offer students the possibility—or at least the illusion of the possibility—of returning to the regular high school once they have turned their academic performance around (Williamson 2008). This goal of returning to the regular high school reflects and reinforces the current dominant paradigm of social mobility. Rather than vocational, civic, or "life adjustment" training, today's last chance high schools seek to provide "these kids" with yet another opportunity to get ahead in school. In this framework, educational justice is defined as the opportunity for (individual) social mobility achieved through access to a uniform, standardized, academic curriculum. "These kids" might be on the bottom of the educational hierarchy now, we reason, but if they try very hard, they still have the possibility of getting ahead. As such, our answer to the dilemma of educational hierarchy is to produce the illusion that no student actually has to occupy its bottom rungs, except by choice.

I conducted a review of policy, practitioner, and research texts about continuation and other last chance high schools to see how these schools and their students are conceptualized in the body of "official knowledge" that exists about them today.[13] This review revealed three prevailing themes that, I contend, represent the contours of a professional discourse about last chance high schools and their students. First, as in the past, today's official texts about last chance high schools assume that there exists a particular kind of kid who does not succeed in regular high school and is therefore best served in a last chance program. As in the past, this "kind" is routinely defined in terms of a grab-bag list of traits and characteristics that include causes, correlates, and consequences of educational marginalization. As an example, note how the No Child Left Behind Act defines youth in this category:

> [A] school aged individual who is at-risk of academic failure, has a drug or alcohol problem, is pregnant or is a parent, has come into contact with the juvenile justice system in the past, is at least one year behind the expected grade level for the age of the individual, has limited English proficiency, is a gang member, has dropped out of school in the past, or has a high absenteeism rate at school. (title I, part D, "The Prevention and Intervention Programs for Children and Youth Who Are Neglected, Delinquent, or At-Risk)

In this text, being an English learner and being a gang member are listed together as comparable deviant-coded characteristics of students. Seemingly disjointed items are placed on the list without explanation of how they are linked. And there is no discussion of the fact that many students with these characteristics perform perfectly well in so-called regular schools. The repeated use of these grab-bag lists in policy, practitioner, and research texts contributes to the construction of continuation/ alternative students as problem-prone and distinct from an assumed normal, traditional, or mainstream student.

Second, official texts often focus on the individual-level traits of students while ignoring the broader social context of inequality within which students are positioned. The most prominent decontexualizing strategy is the continued use of deficiency tropes as I have traced throughout this chapter—or what Valencia (1997) calls "deficit thinking." For example, in *Phi Delta Kappan*, Conrath (2001) writes, "Alternative education can catalyze America's unrealized hopes by helping poor, discouraged youngsters overcome their most debilitating handicaps: rampant pessimism, failure to trust in effort, and mistrust of societal institutions" (585). Here, students are framed as responsible for their own failures and as suffering from "debilitating handicaps" and "rampant pessimism"—terms clearly intended to conjure negative and undesirable connotations. While most scholars use significantly more nuanced language, this statement nevertheless reflects the dominant perspective that last chance high schools exist to remediate the problems and shortcomings of defective students. In other words, deficiency theories locate the causes of educational failure inside the students themselves rather than in the larger structures and practices of schooling and society (Valencia 1997). In this framework, the educational system is presumed to be neutral and objective, so if students fail, it must reflect a problem with *them* rather a problem with the system. Such theories do not account for the possibility of systemic or institutionalized discrimination, or the paradox of getting ahead (discussed in the introduction), as viable explanations for school failure.

A second decontextualizing strategy is the mismatch frame, which was popularized during the alternative schools movement of the 1970s. This frame explains school failure not in terms of students' deficits but in terms of a mismatch between dominant practices of schooling and the unique or special needs of particular students (see, for example, McGee 2001; Knoeppel 2007; Raywid 1994; T. Young 1990; Khan 2008). Reflecting this frame, Price (2008) describes typical high schools as a "one-size-fits-all educational environment" in which many students "flounder" (42) but notes that "students who formerly failed in traditional school environments often succeed in [alternative] programs" (44) due to the ability of these programs to meet students' individual needs. Along these same lines, Knoeppel (2007) writes, "Studies have found that we all learn differently and at varying rates. The students who attend continuation high schools typically have fallen behind in their credits, developed a serious truancy problem and often have issues with large class sizes, where they receive little in the way of teacher assistance" (36). She goes on to say that continuation high schools are "successful in helping these students" due to smaller class sizes and "the philosophy of educating the whole child" (ibid.). While the mismatch frame is an improvement over the deficiency frame, it also tends to ignore broader issues of educational and social inequality, including institutionalized discrimination, racism, and social class, and therefore obscures the important role of the sociopolitical context (Nieto and Bode 2012) in accounting for educational achievement disparities.[14]

The third theme to emerge in my review of official texts is the defini-

tion of continuation students in terms of the number of high school credits they possess, and their level of risk for dropping out of high school.
Terms such as "credit deficient" (California Department of Education)
and "over-aged and under-credited" (Ruiz de Velasco et al. 2008) exemplify the role of credits and diplomas in describing continuation students and the purpose of continuation schools. The framing of these students as "'undercredited' relative to their age group" (EdSource 2008, 2)
is consistent with the dominant developmentalist framework that char-
acterizes much of the contemporary professional discourse on adolescents (Lesko 2001; Stevens et al. 2007). In this framework, success and
failure, deviance and normality, are intricately connected to notions of
time, as youth are considered "slow learners," "lagging behind," "devel-
opmentally delayed," or "growing up too fast." As Bashi (1990) argues,
"The school's cultural core comprises the concept of *time*; the school's
attitude toward time is crucial. In every curriculum, method and pattern
of interaction, students are expected to learn certain material within a
given time period. Those who fail to do so are defined as weak students
and referred to various remedial settings outside their regular classes"
(132–33). Inbar (1990) writes that the entire "cultural pattern" of schooling is dominated by "relationships between time and standards" (9), and
no doubt this relationship between time and standards has become intensified in the current era of standards and accountability. Today, continuation students are at least partly defined as those who challenge normative ideas about the proper pace in accumulating high school credits.
Ironically, while the reformers of the 1920s worried that continuation
students were growing up too fast by joining the workforce, educators
today worry that these same students are progressing too slowly in their
acquisition of credits.

Together, these themes constitute the outlines of the *discourse of
these kids*—the dominant discourse defining who last chance students
are, how they are unique, and what the purpose of schooling is (or should
be) for them. As in the past, "these kids" continue to be defined largely
from a deficiency perspective, and in a way that *decontextualizes* their
experience from larger social structures of power such as racism and social class. The purpose of schooling for "these kids" is defined primarily in terms of enabling access to a high school diploma, although little
is said explicitly about the meaning or purpose of that diploma, or the
knowledge that it symbolizes. Today, the continuation high school resembles the regular high school in many ways—with credits, diplomas, aca-

demic subject area courses, and a full school day that matches the traditional high school schedule. And, like Jackson High, most continuation high schools in California have long since removed the word *continuation* from their names, even though the state Department of Education still maintains a division called the Office of Continuation Education to oversee these schools. While continuation high schools do indeed have the benefit of smaller size and more favorable student-teacher ratios, their basic structure, curriculum, and instructional practices largely reproduce what is found in the lower-track classes of regular high schools. Rather than providing an alternative for students, continuation high schools arguably function as a bottom track in a highly stratified secondary school system, distinct only for having a student body that is roundly viewed as deficient, problematic, and at risk.

Conclusion

This chapter has examined the history of continuation education in California with a focus on showing how the *last chance student* was constructed, in tandem with the *last chance high school*, as a new and distinct kind of kid requiring a new and distinct kind of schooling. The history of the continuation high school in California reveals two key insights. First, rather than offering a genuine alternative, continuation high schools have in fact reproduced many of the same structures, practices, and assumptions of mainstream schooling (Kelly 1993a). Instead of providing a "safety net" or "second chance," they may instead offer a "ritualistic second chance" (Inbar and Sever 1989)—an illusory second chance that merely reproduces the first-chance system and, in so doing, reinforces the initial designation of its students as failures.

Second, continuation schools have played a role in creating popular conceptions of a mainstream, traditional, or normal student as well as a deficient, deviant, or troubled one (Kelly 1993a). This has occurred in part through the ever-expanding category of "these kids," which began as a "juvenile worker" and evolved into a grab-bag list of characteristics and traits that presumably defined one as maladjusted, delinquent, or at risk. As the meaning of the continuation student expanded to include more and more categories of students, what remained constant was its definition *in opposition to* an invisible and untheorized normal, adjusted, mainstream, or regular student. In these definitions, the "normal" high school student was routinely invoked but never adequately defined or theorized. In addition, when new categories of youth were added to the ever-expanding grab-bag list of traits—such as unadjusted students or pregnant and parenting girls—these too became markers of difference bestowed with educational significance where none had existed before. Rather than being a *response* to the different needs of different students, we could argue that last chance programs help *construct* particular kinds of differences as educationally relevant, and define the boundary between different/deficient and regular/mainstream kids. In this way, the two categories of mainstream and deviant are mutually co-constructed in and through the discourse of these kids.

As we have seen, throughout the past century, the continuation high school has consistently pursued the goal of keeping more adolescents in school for longer periods of time. But beyond achieving more seat time for kids, it has struggled to define the precise purpose of the education it provides. Each new era saw a redefinition of purpose—from vocational guidance to citizenship training, psychological adjustment, and most recently to a traditional academic curriculum leading to a high school diploma. This struggle to define the purpose of the continuation high school reflects our society's more general struggle to define the purpose of education for adolescents who have already landed at the bottom of the educational hierarchy, and are already on a path toward low-wage, low-status, and low-rights occupations (Imber 1985; Kantor and Tyack 1982; Kelly 1993a). Helping "these kids" prepare for a future, without appearing to unjustly and irreversibly confine them to subordinate social positions, has long posed an uncomfortable challenge for educators. This is what I refer to as the dilemma of hierarchy. The history of the continuation high school provides a window into this historic dilemma, because its stated purpose roughly reflects the dominant answers of the time.

The discourse of these kids builds from and extends historical narratives associated with the establishment and maintenance of last chance high schools, and more broadly, with the processes of educational hierarchization. In tracing the emergence and development of this discourse and of the last chance high school in the context of increasing educational hierarchization, my goal is not just to provide interesting background for the story of PARTY but also to situate Jackson High and the PARTY project in their complex social, cultural, and historical contexts. As we shall see in the chapters that follow, "concepts, methods, and viewpoints come with a history of use and interpretation, and this history matters" (Blommaert 2005, 3–4). In the next chapter, I consider how the history of this social category—the deficient and maladjusted continuation student—bleeds through to the present. I begin the story of PARTY with a discussion of how the youth participants interacted with the discourse of these kids, illustrating its continuing significance in their/our sociocultural worlds.

Being Professional: Figured Worlds and the Construction of Self

On a late September afternoon, the original PARTY group convened around the hexagon-shaped table in a conference room at the local city college for our weekly meeting. Our group consisted of three recent Jackson High School graduates—D, Lolo, and Louis—and myself, a former Jackson teacher. In previous meetings, we had decided to recruit two current Jackson students to bring our size up to six members. We had visited the school with flyers to tell students about the project and had invited those interested to attend an interview, on the basis of which we would select two new students. Our task for today was to develop interview questions and decide how to structure the interview process. Louis suggested we start by reading sections of the grant proposal I had written. With an orange highlighter in hand, he studied the document for a moment. "I got it," he announced, and started reading aloud from the middle of the methods section:

> The Youth Research Team brings together students who have been low-achieving and disengaged from school, and places *them* in the position of experts—

"Whoa, whoa, whoa!" Lolo and D cut him off in almost perfect unison. Once again, the familiar tropes of "low-achieving" and "disengaged" youth had turned up in my writing, even as I self-consciously struggled to challenge those tropes in my approach to the project. This was, in fact, the very same proposal from which I had read aloud just one week earlier, when D claimed my portrayal made the youth participants "look like fuckups" (introduction). Even after revising the proposal's language with D's critique in mind, I had managed to reproduce the same discourse. The immediate cry of "Whoa, whoa, whoa!" emerged like a reflex, in sync, the moment Lolo and D heard those words pronounced out loud and as a description of themselves. The speed and urgency of their response suggested the depth of injury submerged beneath those words.

This recurring exchange with the youth over my proposal illustrates how pervasively deficit-oriented tropes saturated my writing and formed the guiding frame through which I justified the PARTY project to an academic audience. It was all too easy for me to operate inside the frame of educational underachievement and disengagement, for it occupies a central place within dominant educational discourse. My use of this frame in academic writing seemed (I believed) to increase the project's legitimacy in the educational research and practitioner communities. But it also reflected and reinforced a dominant and problematic discourse—what I refer to as the *discourse of these kids*. In chapter 1, I examined the nature, scope, and reach of this discourse, characterizing it as a *dominant* discourse in the sense that it is ubiquitous in research, policy, and practice texts about last chance high schools and their students. In this chapter, I show how Jackson students and PARTY members employed the logic of this discourse to represent themselves and others as particular kinds of kids. I examine their use of discourses and artifacts from the "figured worlds" (Holland et al. 2001) of work and schooling to position themselves and construct identities as deserving, capable, and professional young adults.

This chapter employs a microethnographic approach (Bloome 1993) focused on the sequence of interviews and subsequent debriefing session through which PARTY members selected two new students to join the project.[1] The interview sequence and the debriefing session that followed it reveal how the discourse of these kids formed part of the landscape for interaction among the youth, constraining and enabling particular forms of meaning making and identity making. Just as I unwittingly employed this discourse in my academic writing about the PARTY project, so too did the youth participants rely on it as a framework for distinguishing different "kinds of kids" and positioning themselves. Specifically, this chapter shows how youth participants mobilized, reproduced, and con-

tested the discourse of these kids by alternately positioning themselves
in *opposition* to it (as if to say "I am not one of these kids!"), in *accordance* with it (as if to say "I am proudly one of these kids!"), or by *contesting* certain aspects of it (as if to say "I am one of these kids, but we're
not what you think we are!"). The story illustrates the power and reach
of the discourse of these kids in shaping everyday interactions and identities of youth at Jackson High.

The Interviews: Mobilizing the Discourse of These Kids

Louis, a thin Filipino American graduate of Jackson, convened the first
interview with James, an African American freshman, by introducing
himself tentatively, as if asking a question: "Hello. I'm Louis?" And then
in conclusion, with a bit more confidence: "Jackson High, class of 2000."
He spoke with an air of formality that was unfamiliar in our meetings,
his voice quivering with nerves as if *he* were the one being interviewed.
His shyness was a marked contrast from his bold hip-hop style of dress—
two layered, oversized T-shirts and baggy pants worn low on the hips,
exuding an air of toughness and hypermasculinity. Lolo proceeded with
similar formality. "I'm Lolo," she began confidently, flashing a disarm-
ing smile at the newcomer student, "Jackson High, class of '99." She re-
shuffled her long braided hair extensions and let them drop again over
her shoulders before turning her head toward D, who was seated beside
her. Slouched in his chair and buried beneath an oversized, puffy black
jacket, D adjusted his weight and continued to look down at his hands
as he mumbled, almost under his breath, "D. Class of 2000." Finally, I
introduced myself as a former Jackson teacher and a graduate student
in education. Then all eyes focused on our interviewee, James. Tall and
slender, he sat with a straight spine, fidgeting slightly. Despite the intimidated look on his face, his words came out with confidence and poise:
"My name is James and I'm a freshman at Jackson." His deep and pen-
etrating voice sounded more mature than that of a freshman in high
school, yet his face looked boyishly young, as if it had yet to catch up
with his body's growth spurt.

Louis, Lolo, and D took turns explaining the purpose of the PARTY
project and the nature of the work involved. "The responsibilities of the
job are basically to show up on time and be dedicated," Lolo offered in
summary. Then Louis directed the first question to James: "What qual-

ities do you bring?" For a moment James appeared stunned to be put on the spot, but quickly offered, "Um . . . I like the news," and named a news radio station that he listened to. The room fell silent as Louis, Lolo, and D made brief eye contact with one another. No one acknowledged James's answer or asked a follow-up question about his interest in the news. Instead, Lolo moved on to the second planned interview question: "If you could change something about Jackson High, what would it be?" James responded that the lunch period should be longer. The interviewers exchanged barely perceptible nods and turned their eyes toward me for the next question. We proceeded in this formal manner for nearly fifteen minutes, following a strict question-answer format with little additional conversation. At the end, James rose from his seat and extended his right hand toward D for a handshake. D smiled, appearing pleased by this gesture, which seemed to encourage James to repeat it with Louis, Lolo, and me. When James had left the room, D remarked with a satisfied grin, "I *like* that, I *like* that! He reminds me of *myself*! My grandma taught me to do that [shake hands] too."

The remaining four interviews were similarly formal. Throughout the process, PARTY members appeared to be as nervous as the students were. They adhered strictly to the interview questions and refrained from side conversations, digressions, and jokes. Their comportment gave the interviews an air of seriousness that caught me by surprise, for it was a marked departure from the relaxed feel of our regular weekly meetings. In addition to James, two students—Yolanda and Leila, both sophomores at Jackson—reciprocated with an equal degree of formality. In their interviews, these two students appeared to work hard to convince PARTY members they were capable young adults and deserving of the job. To do so, these young women evoked the discourse of these kids but positioned themselves in opposition to it—as if to say "I am not one of these kids."

"I Am Not One of These Kids"

A shapely young woman with round eyes and a young face, Yolanda wore her hair unstyled in a short pony tail, and no makeup or accessories. Her verbal style of self-presentation was as unadorned as her physical appearance: Yolanda spoke plainly and directly, without smiling, embellishing, or humoring her listeners. She did not appear to be nervous, but neither did she seem entirely at ease as she fidgeted in her chair, shoulders raised and hands tucked underneath her thighs. When asked what qualities she would bring to the group, Yolanda gave a one-word answer: "Dedication." When asked what she would change about Jackson High, she elaborated in some detail about how she would expand the school to take over the vacant building across the street; she would offer more classes and get more students into the internship program at the local hospital. She herself participated in the hospital program, which helped her realize she wanted to become a nurse. She had a nine-month-old son, she added, and she was currently a sophomore in high school.

When asked what changes she would like to see in society, Yolanda thought for a moment and then replied simply: "Black kids." I asked her what she meant by that, and she explained, in the very same matter-of-fact tone, "Black kids who sit up there on the street all day and complain like 'The white man's takin' everything from us and whomp-whomp-whomp . . . ,' but they ain't doin' anything about it." With the hope of turning the conversation toward political solutions, I asked, "What do you think you could do to change that?" Yolanda answered there was nothing she could do; she said, "*They* need to change. Stop complaining and get a job." For the first time, her comment provoked a reaction from one of the interviewers. D shot back without missing a beat. He said, "I relate to these kids you're talkin' about. The only reason I went to school was 'cause I had my head on straight, and because of my grandma. But a lot of these kids ain't got their head on straight, and when they mess up, they don't get no second chance."

In this brief verbal encounter, Yolanda and D had given voice to and contested dominant constructions of "these kids"—these "black kids" who "complain" but "don't do anything about it"; who should "get a job"; who "ain't got their head on straight"; and who "don't get no second chance." What we see here is Yolanda mobilizing the discourse of these kids in order to position herself in opposition to it, as if to say "I am not one of these kids." But in distancing herself from the discourse in this way, she succeeds in reproducing it—and many of its racialized images or tropes. D responds by contesting certain aspects of the discourse of these kids. He insists the kids are not at fault for their situation, because they don't get second chances as do other kinds of kids. He also explicitly identifies with these kids, stating, "I relate to these kids you're talkin' about," but he challenges the way Yolanda has constructed them.

In short, D attempts to reshape the terms of the discourse: He seems to be saying, "I am one of these kids, but we are not what you think we are."

One week later, when the second group of Jackson students had their interview appointments, we met Leila. One of a handful of white students at the school, Leila had entered with the first cohort of voluntary freshmen in the year Jackson was renamed Maytown Alternative Program (MAP, discussed in chapter 1). She arrived to the interview with an olive-green scarf tied around the back of her head, out of which a bundle of thick, chestnut-colored dreadlocks emerged and fell past her shoulders. A beaded, choker-length necklace with a silver pendant in the shape of a marijuana leaf was plainly visible against her neck. She wore a long, flowing skirt in a flowery print and a fitted white T-shirt, along with black combat boots. Leila sat with a stern expression on her face as she introduced herself as a sophomore at Jackson. Upon hearing the description of the youth research project, her hazel eyes immediately lit up. "That's so cool!" she exclaimed with visible excitement. "I've actually thought about doing something like that before."

When Louis asked what qualities she would bring to the project, Leila replied that she brought an interest in politics, and she wanted to know what was going on in the world. She added that this project was important because "the students at Jackson really don't know or care what's going on around them." Her voice was flat as she made this claim, her tone conveying both the assurance and emotional detachment of an expert on the topic. When Lolo asked what changes she would make to Jackson High, Leila replied, "Better teachers." She added that classes at Jackson were too easy, and there was "not enough discipline" at the school: "The kids are crazy," Leila said unflinchingly. "I think it's the way they were raised. Sometimes I'm embarrassed to be the same age as them." She maintained a stern facial expression as she spoke with presumed authority about Jackson students' home lives and behaviors. When I asked Leila what she would change about society, she said she would change the news because it was biased. She said she was thinking about starting her own newspaper so she could "get the information out there," especially to other teens. Throughout the interview, Leila spoke with an air of certainty and entitlement about her interest in politics, her critique of Jackson and its students, and her ideas for making change. She did not hesitate to tell the group that she had already thought about ways of educating Jackson students better, or starting her own newspaper to bring better information to her peers. Perhaps it was this assuredness that enabled her depiction of Jackson students as apathetic and undisciplined to go unnoticed or unchallenged, at least for the time being.

Like Yolanda, Leila actively positioned herself in opposition to the discourse of these kids, as if to say "I am not one of these kids." She attempted to distinguish herself as different from the others—and therefore worthy of a job with the PARTY group—by labeling Jackson students as "crazy" and locating the causes of their dysfunction inside their families or in the "way they were raised." Both Yolanda and Leila worked hard to position themselves as different "kinds of kids" from the presumably troubled, at-risk, irresponsible, and deviant kids at Jackson. As they did this, they reproduced the discourse of these kids and many of its racialized images and tropes. But these young women were not acting and speaking in a social vacuum, nor did they pull their responses out of thin air. Instead, they drew from existing social discourses or public meaning systems that were widely available to them, discourses with robust histories in American social and educational thought. These provided the conceptual frames and linguistic tools that enabled the young women to select and perform these particular social identities. I have referred collectively to these as the *discourse of these kids.*

In contrast to Yolanda and Leila, two other student interviewees used body language and interaction styles that seemed to affirm the identity of "these kids" proudly. These two students, Sherry and Na'ilah, made no explicit attempts to differentiate themselves from other Jackson students or from the discourse of these kids. Instead, their actions, gestures, and language seemed to reclaim this discourse—as if to say "I am proudly one of these kids."

"I Am Proudly One of These Kids"

Sherry was a fragile-looking African American sophomore whom I had met previously through my work as a substitute teacher at Jackson. Scarcely five feet tall with a diminutive frame, Sherry made up for her small size with an exaggerated sassy attitude. As I started to introduce myself at the beginning of the interview, Sherry interjected midsentence, "*I* know *you!*" in a voice dripping with insult. When asked what strengths she would bring to the project, Sherry replied, "*I* don't know!" Her voice was part sarcasm, part anger, part humiliation. When asked what she would change about society, she offered a lengthy answer that included her concerns about the wars in Afghanistan and Iraq ("Innocent people have to go and fight"); her fear that the government would introduce a draft ("I'm glad I'm not a man 'cause I wouldn't go fight in no wars"); and President George W. Bush ("a bad, bad man"). At the end of the interview, when Louis said one of us would call with our decision, Sherry rolled her eyes and exhaled forcefully with a dramatic sulking motion. She pulled herself up from her seat with what appeared to be a great effort, dragging her feet as she exited the room and slammed the door behind her with a surplus of force.

In the last interview, an African American junior named Na'ilah spoke in a barely audible voice and fidgeted in her seat as she twirled a long braid of hair around her index finger. Her responses were succinct—anywhere from a single word to a brief sentence in length. She named "talking to people" as the quality she would bring to the job; "teachers" as the thing she would change about Jackson High; and "the war, all the killing" as the thing she would change about society. When asked to elaborate on her answers, she shook her head and drew a blank. About two minutes into the interview, she laid her head down on the table and closed her eyes, continuing to answer questions from this position. The last question, as always, came from Louis, who asked Na'ilah if she had any questions for the PARTY group. With her forehead resting on her folded arms, flat on the table, she lifted her head just about one inch, scarcely enough to shake it side to side indicating "no." The entire interview lasted just over five minutes.

The Debrief Session: Race, Representation, and Authenticity

No sooner had the last student left the conference room than Louis, Lolo, and D resumed their relaxed postures and easy conversational style, diving into a discussion about the five Jackson students they had interviewed. We had established selection criteria in a previous meeting and verbally agreed on the intention to select one male and one female student to join the group. Of the five students interviewed, Leila emerged quickly as the first choice. She was described as "the most professional," according to Lolo; the "most likely to get the job done," according to D; and "smart," according to Louis. Yolanda emerged in a close second place, with Louis describing her as the "most responsible." Sherry and Na'ilah were quickly disqualified on account of being seen as "unprofessional," "disrespectful," and "ghetto." Despite Sherry's comments about the US military involvement and her willingness to voice an opinion about politics, PARTY members did not discuss the content of her responses during the debriefing session. Instead, their discussion focused solely on her comportment and "attitude," with Louis beginning, "She was rude." Lolo agreed: "Really disrespectful." D laughed as he remarked, "She *was* ghetto, though." Lolo then wondered aloud if she was "being too harsh," but quickly answered her own question with confidence: "It's just the way she interrupted Kysa like that. It was *rude*. She shouldn't be like that in an interview. It's a *job* interview. She should put on her best face." Louis said it was important for new members to be "someone we can get along with," and expressed doubts about Sherry on this front due to her "attitude." With no further comments on Sherry, they turned their attention to the next student, Na'ilah, whom they also disqualified quickly on the basis of being "unprofessional." When I probed for more detail, Louis recalled that she was "playing with her hair" and "taking a nap" during the interview. When I suggested that Na'ilah had given some thoughtful answers, I was met with curious silence and quizzical stares before Louis brought the conversation back to Yolanda, reiterating his view that she was the "most responsible."

The first student, James, was hardly discussed at all, presumably because he was the only male student to show up. D commented only that "I liked James. He reminded me of *me*." He recalled how James had shaken our hands at the end of the interview, and nodded to show his approval. D's comments, left uncontested, confirmed that James was qualified enough to fill the slot of "male student." With these conclusions established, the final decision came down to a debate between Yolanda and Leila—the two who had positioned themselves in opposition to the discourse of these kids—for the slot of female student. PARTY members appeared to be leaning toward Leila, the white student, as the superior choice largely because she was seen to be "smart." Leila's "smartness" became a theme that wove throughout the debriefing session, and she was the only one of the five students ever described with this adjective. Given the brevity of the interviews, there was little basis on which to make evaluations of "smartness"—even if a mutually agreeable definition for the term could be found. One reason for Leila's perceived smartness may have been her unequivocal assertion that Jackson classes were "too easy" (a claim that no other student made). But of more importance, I believe, was her capacity to speak assertively and with a sense of entitlement—as if she knew her opinions were valid and deserved to be heard. Her tacit assumption of authority and expertise evoked the image of smartness and lent credibility to her implicit claim that "I am not one of these kids." Her positionality as a white student and her use of Standard English dialect likely undergirded both her ability to demonstrate confidence and the PARTY members' interpretations of that confidence as smartness. Like all forms of cultural capital, Leila's capacity to speak with assuredness and in Standard English dialect appeared to be something "natural"—based on innate "intelligence"—rather than a product of social privilege acquired through a lifetime of enculturation (Bourdieu 1994; Bourdieu and Passeron 1990).

Just as a consensus was building in favor of Leila, Lolo recalled something that gave her pause. "I didn't like how Leila said, 'I'm embarrassed to be the same age as them' [Jackson students]," she told us. Lacking the words to explain why the statement troubled her, Lolo nevertheless wore a demoralized look on her face as she recalled it. This time, it was Lolo who identified and challenged Leila's use of the discourse of these kids, but, like D, she lacked the linguistic and conceptual tools to articulate exactly why and how Leila's words had injured her. Louis said it was a sign that Leila was an outsider who would not represent Jackson students. His comment prompted an intense discussion of whether Leila was a "real" Jackson student, given that she was white, and that her style—the dreadlocks and combat boots combination—did not reflect any identifiable Jackson student subculture.

Conceding that Leila might not be representative, D asserted, "It don't matter if Leila don't represent the school 'cause we got *James* for that!" Louis countered that Yolanda and James "*both* represent the school." D replied, "Yeah, but did you see those *dreads*?" His question was met with silence. Louis shrugged and Lolo cast an apologetic glance in his direction, suggesting that D had possibly scored a winning argument. The question "Did you see those *dreads*?" was clearly rhetorical; few observers would fail to notice her dreadlocks. Instead, the question was posed as an assertion of her legitimate claim to insider status: Leila *could* represent Jackson students, and her dreads offered the evidence. The basis for D's claim is somewhat curious given that no other women at Jackson High, of any race, wore their hair in dreadlocks. But by asserting her dreads as a claim to (partial) insider status, D exercised voice over how the group identity of PARTY was to be defined and where its boundaries would be drawn. The association of dreadlocks with marijuana usage, with a rejection of white middle-class aesthetics and sensibilities, and with blackness combined to make Leila a real-*enough* Jackson student—as long as her outsiderness was balanced out by a *really* real Jackson student such as James.

Exactly what made James such a *really* real Jackson student remained implicit throughout the debriefing session. The assumption that he would get one of the two available positions was not challenged; indeed, it was not even stated explicitly. That this assumption could be so obvious as to remain unsaid, and yet shape the choices so clearly, reveals the deep-seated gendered and racialized conceptions of what a real or representative Jackson student was and looked like. The actual student body at Jackson reflected a nearly equal gender balance. And yet the image of a prototypical Jackson student was most certainly black and male. This assumption was so strong that I myself operated within it, never once raising a question about James or posing the option to consider the combination of Leila *and* Yolanda as the two new PARTY members. To the degree that gender was discussed at all, it was only to bemoan the lack of (black) males to take an interest in PARTY. When only two boys signed up for interviews, everybody blamed D for refusing to take time off from work to visit the school to recruit students. When one of those male students did not even show up for his interview, we shook our heads with disappointment and wondered aloud why more young men did not take part, again blaming D for not doing enough to be a "role model."

In all of these ways, our conversation around gender reproduced dominant narratives. Rather than interrogate our gendered and racialized notions of what a "real" Jackson student was, who could be one of "these kids," and how these assumptions reflected and reaffirmed tropes of "at-risk," "troubled," and "criminal" youth—all embodied in the young black male—we instead took this imagery for granted and engaged in talk about scarcity and tokenism, reifying notions of the young black male as an "endangered species" (Ferguson 2001) and pressuring D (who is black) to do a better job of "role modeling." It is important to point out that Louis (who is Filipino American) was never called upon to be a "role model" in this way. Explicitly, Louis was let off the hook for the fact that he had designed the flyers, thus making a contribution to the recruitment of students. Louis was never implicitly blamed for the lack of male student candidates (as D was), nor was he teased for being a slacker for not making time to visit Jackson to recruit (as D was), even though Louis did not have a job that would have prevented him from visiting the school during the day. Only D had the privilege of being seen as the most authentic and representative Jackson student/graduate, and the concomitant duties of such authenticity. In one meeting, Lolo had pleaded with D to "be a role model" by joining her on a campus visit. In response, D had tilted his head to the side with a smirk and muttered softly, "I ain't no role model." The words sounded matter-of-fact but lightly subversive; it was as if not being a role model was, simultaneously and somewhat paradoxically, a source of great pride and quiet shame.

In the end, after an intense debate and many changes of mind, the PARTY group chose Leila, and not Yolanda, for the female student slot. Leila's perceived greater intelligence outweighed concerns about her representativeness as a Jackson student. But it was D's claim-disguised-as-a-question ("Did you see those *dreads*?") that had pushed the group over the edge. Neither Lolo nor Louis offered a sufficient counterargument on this point. In fact, it was perhaps because D was recognized as the most authentic or representative Jackson student in the group that his approval of Leila carried significant weight: as an unquestionably "real" Jackson student himself, D had power to determine who was, and wasn't, worthy of this label. Thus, when the final vote was taken, Leila emerged unanimously as the group's first choice. Notably, although racial and gendered meanings were embedded throughout the debriefing discussion, they were not explicitly named; group members resorted to color-blind and gender-blind discourse as they considered who could and should represent Jackson High in the PARTY group.

On Being Professional

What is striking about the debriefing session is that the only two students who were seriously considered and discussed, Yolanda and Leila, were the two who had reproduced the discourse of these kids and explicitly positioned themselves in opposition to it. They were seen as more responsible and professional, while the other students were seen as disrespectful and ghetto, or—in the case of James—merely as unremarkable. During the debriefing session, there was almost no discussion of the content of students' answers; instead, discussion of their behavior took center stage, and the ability to perform dominant notions of professionalism and politeness became the primary qualification for membership. James's hand shaking and Leila's presumed "smartness" served as evidence of their ability and commitment. Likewise, Sherry's interruption of me in a tone coded as rude and Na'ilah's laying of her head on the table served as evidence of deficiency—a lack of ability, commitment, and professionalism. In this way, the interview and selection process carried out in PARTY reproduced dominant discourses and mirrored the "real-life" processes of labor market gatekeeping and cultural reproduction, more than perhaps any of us realized at the time.

Why did this occur? Almost a year later, in a meeting with all three original PARTY members, I asked them about it:

Kysa: When we were talking about the interviews, you guys were saying things like "Oh, so-and-so just didn't act professional." Do you remember saying things like that?

Lolo: I remember saying that. About, are you talking about the one, the one who laid her head on the desk? [*laughs*]

Kysa: Probably.

Louis: I know that's who I was talking about bad most. [*laughter from Lolo*]

D: I was talking about both of them, just that they came late.

Louis: Yeah, that too. That wasn't professional. I think that's what, that's what y'all was talking about unprofessional. Yeah, that's not cool.

Lolo: And then one of them said something smart to Kysa in the interview. I was like, what!? [*laughter from all*]

Louis: What did she say?

We recounted the incident in which Sherry had interrupted me to state "*I* know *you*!" at the beginning of her interview. As PARTY members replayed her response with some laughter, I continued with my line of questioning:

Kysa: But . . . , you know, what did you mean by unprofessional? Are you going by, like, society's definition of unprofessional?

D: You'll never get a job like that. You'll *never* get a job like that! Never!

Lolo: Just, in general, everybody should think that way. This is not even nothin' personal. It's like, even if I knew you, even if I knew D or Louis and I hadn't seen 'em in a while, and he forgot that he met me, and he was like "Hi. My name is D," I ain't gonna say [*mimicking Sherry's tone*] "*I* know who *you* are!" I'm gonna say—

D: [*talking over her*] Especially when I'm interviewing you! When you—

Lolo: [*continuing*] —I'm gonna say, "Oh, I believe we may have met," you know?

Louis: [*responding to D*] When you're in front of other people—

D: —Yeah, the other people that's interviewing you too! You know, in a group interview, you go [*high voice, snappy*] "*I* know *you!*" [*laughter from all*]

Lolo: That just wasn't right at all. That's saying "Don't hire me."

What had bothered PARTY members about Sherry's statement—"*I* know *you!*"—was not the information it contained but her style of communicating it. Lolo even went so far as to rephrase Sherry's statement as a hedged claim, complete with a Standard English inflection: "Oh, I believe we may have met." The hedged rather than emphatic claim signals deference to authority, even though the information contained within the statement is the same. When Lolo offered the hedged claim as the "professional" way to speak in an interview, she used her most polished Standard English accent, not her everyday vernacular.

This reflection on the student interviews shows how PARTY members coded certain behaviors as unprofessional: putting one's head on the desk, arriving late, and responding to one of the interviewers in a voice deemed inappropriate. Not only did PARTY members code these behaviors as unprofessional, but they also revealed disapproval, even scorn, toward the students who had behaved this way in the interview setting. "Professional" behavior, they suggested, was the behavior necessary to get a job; it included arriving on time, showing deference to authority, and using "polite" forms of Standard English dialect. The PARTY group's debriefing session points to a theme that would reemerge later in the project: that of making evaluative judgments about the intelligence, competence, and achievements of other similarly positioned youth based not on the content of their verbal or written statements but rather on the form of their behaviors, body language, dialect, and "attitude." Educational researchers have documented how teachers' judgments of student ability are powerfully shaped by perceptions of their "attitude" as read through outward signs of behavior, body language, and dialect (Ferguson 2001; P. Gilmore 1985; Lopez 2002). Such assessments may be influenced by race and class of the students and teacher, and typically have the effect of reinforcing existing race/class hierarchies of achievement. This body of research illustrates the significance of cultural displays and cultural capital in the micropolitics of schooling and the reproduction of social inequalities in and through schooling.[2]

While this finding is not novel in educational research, it is striking to see how quickly PARTY members adopted similar practices and cultural scripts, deploying these against other similarly positioned youth, in the course of the interview sequence. The moment "these kids" were positioned as gatekeepers to a scarce opportunity, they drew on an array of dominant cultural scripts and assumptions about being "responsible," "respectful," and "professional," with notably reproductive results. These outcomes suggest that such cultural scripts are extremely generalized and well known, even by students who are often framed as lacking this knowledge.[3] It is also noteworthy that PARTY members employed dominant and reproductive cultural scripts in the interview process, even though they also embraced alternative and resistive scripts when acting and interacting in other contexts (as we will see in chapters 3–4). How are we to interpret this apparent inconsistency? The concept of "figured worlds" (Holland et al. 2001) offers a useful analytic tool.

Figured Worlds and the Construction of Self

Holland et al. (2001) define a *figured world* as "a socially and culturally constructed realm of interpretation in which particular characters and actors are recognized, significance is assigned to certain acts, and particular outcomes are valued over others" (52). Examples of figured worlds in the literature include those of romance (Holland and Eisenhart 1992), Alcoholics Anonymous (Cain 1991), academia (Holland et al. 2001), classroom settings (Boaler and Greeno 2000; Jurow 2005), and schools (Rubin 2007a). Each of these "worlds" can be conceptualized as a shared frame of reference—similar to the concepts of "fields" (Bourdieu 1993), "communities of practice" (Lave and Wenger 2008), or "big-D Discourses" (Gee 2005). In these (figurative) cultural worlds, particular discourses are shared, cultural scripts are recognized, categories of people exist, and kinds of activities "make sense." For example, in the figured world of (heterosexual) romance, women's choice to dedicate tremendous time and money toward personal beautification "makes sense," since physical attractiveness to men is valued currency in this world (Holland et al. 2001, 56). Each of us interacts within multiple and overlapping figured worlds, some of which are more generalized (like the figured worlds of schooling or romance), and some of which are more local, specific, and concrete (like the figured world of Jackson High School or the PARTY group) (Wortham 2006).

Figured worlds are not just abstractions that exist "in our heads."

Rather, they are always shared and (re)produced socially and culturally through the mundane, day-to-day activities of people. They are invoked through discourses or artifacts (Holland et al. 2001): items with a shared symbolic meaning in the context of the figured world—for example, poker chips in the world of Alcoholics Anonymous or report cards in the world of schooling. Figured worlds contain internal hierarchies of power and status, along with cultural scripts and cues for signaling status or making claims to social position. Holland et al. (ibid.) conceptualize identity formation as occurring within figured worlds; in fact, some identities can only exist in the context of a figured world where a particular identity category is recognized and given meaning. Figured worlds are a useful construct for theorizing about identity because they underscore the significance of social and cultural context, and allow us to draw connections between micro-level interactions and macro-level discourses and power relations.

In the PARTY interview sequence, two figured worlds were potentially relevant: that of work and that of the continuation high school. Although both were potentially applicable, Louis, Lolo, and D used the discourse of professionalism and the embodied practices of stiff demeanors, stern facial expressions, and formality of speech to invoke the figured world of work. Like all figured worlds, that of work contains a set of characters and roles—in this case, bosses, employees, and prospective employees. The job interview is an artifact that evokes the figured world of work. The interview follows a recognizable script and rules of interaction that govern the exchange between bosses and prospective employees. In this world, the power hierarchy between bosses and (prospective) employees is real and consequential: the boss has the power to hire and fire, and this decision has material consequences (i.e., the giving or withholding of money) for the employee. Operating within this figured world, PARTY members (perhaps unconsciously) expected these roles and rules to be obvious and looked for them accordingly. Students who failed to conform—due either to willful defiance or to simply not recognizing the relevant figured world—were coded as deficient.

It was the interview performances of Sherry and Na'ilah that PARTY members coded through this lens of deficiency. In analyzing the young women's interviews retrospectively, we might choose to see them as small acts of resistance—to the dominant cultural scripts being enacted, to the interview process itself, to the institutions of schooling and higher education that were clearly represented in the project. An equally possible and likely explanation is that Sherry and Na'ilah simply misjudged the situation—interpreting the interviews as if they were unfolding in the figured world of the continuation high school rather than that of work. The world of the continuation high school has its own set of actors, roles, rules, and status hierarchies. Instead of bosses, employees, and prospective employees, we find teachers, counselors, students, and dropouts. If Sherry and Na'ilah were "reading" the interview process as if it were unfolding in the figured world of the continuation high school, they would see a teacher (me) and three students (the youth PARTY members) rather than four prospective employers. I had, in fact, worked as a substitute teacher in Sherry's classroom earlier that year. Interrupting a teacher—especially a substitute—in a tone of voice heard as confrontational "makes sense" in the figured world of the continuation high school. In this world, insulting speech is a routine form of interaction between students and teachers (which goes in both directions), and talking back to a teacher is a claim to social status among students (see chapter 4; see also Rubin 2007a). Unlike a boss—who has real and consequential power vis-à-vis employees—the only power that teachers have vis-à-vis students is the power to give high or low grades, which have little currency for students at the bottom of the educational hierarchy (Rosenbaum 2001, 1–12; Kelly 1993a).

Holland et al. (2001) argue that social positioning occurs every time people interact: "The dialect we speak, the degree of formality we adopt in our speech, the deeds we do, the places we go, the emotions we express, and the clothes we wear are treated as indicators of claims to and identification with social categories and positions of privilege relative to those with whom we are interacting" (127). All of the participants in the interview sequence—the student interviewees, youth PARTY members, and myself—engaged in this form of social positioning. But we invoked different figured worlds when making our claims to social status, thus leading to a miscommunication. Each of the activities that PARTY members coded as signs of deficiency in the interview context may be seen as claims to social positioning in the figured world of the continuation high school: talking back to a teacher, showing visible disengagement (e.g., putting one's head down on the desk), and exaggerated gestures like sulking, rolling the eyes, and slamming the door.

The potential for miscommunication of this sort was relatively high, because the PARTY group in general and the interviews in particular were a different kind of social context—not quite school, and not quite work. This ambiguous and unfamiliar situation made improvisation necessary: "the sort of impromptu actions that occur when our past, brought to the present as habitus, meets with a particular combination of circumstances and conditions for which we have no set response" (Holland et al. 2001, 17). Certainly, the interview sequence represented a set of "conditions for which we ha[d] no set response," and we improvised accordingly. For PARTY members, this meant treating the interviews as if in the figured world of work, mobilizing its discourses, artifacts, and identities while "trying on" the role of boss/employer. Holland et al. argue that improvisation offers the possibility (though not the guarantee) of altered subjectivities and acts of agency. In the case of PARTY, this opportunity to play the role of employer was experienced as an altered subjectivity that PARTY members later described as exciting, strange, and fun. Almost a year after the event, they recalled:

Lolo: The hiring process was fun.

Louis: Yeah! Oh yeah! That was the funnest thing! That was the funnest thing!

[*laughter from both*]

Louis: I was like [*acting out*] "Oh, you know, we're just thinking about hiring a few people. . . ." [*trails off to laughter*]

[*increasing laughter from both*]

Kysa: So why, why was that so fun?

Lolo: It was just fun to be in the position of doing the hiring—

Louis: Power!

Lolo: —and not havin' to be hir*ed*.

[*laughter*]

Kysa: Uh-huh.

Louis: I can see doing *that* for a while!

Lolo: It was just fun being the, the . . . [*searching for word*], the *elite*.

The interview process was a rare opportunity to be in a position of real institutional power. The job with PARTY was a paid position, which meant the interviews were consequential for the distribution of real resources. Being in power—the "elite"—was a new and exhilarating experience that afforded an opportunity for altered subjectivity and acts of agency. Opportunities to exercise agency were present throughout the interviews, but so too were opportunities to reproduce the very discourses and cultural expectations that had excluded PARTY members in the past. How did PARTY members exercise agency in this process? And in what way was their agency limited?

Identity, Agency, and Structure

The PARTY group interviews afforded opportunities for altered subjectivity and the possibility of agency. But the outcome of the process, as we have seen, was largely reproductive rather than transformative: Leila and Yolanda affirmed the discourse of these kids in order to differentiate themselves from it; PARTY members followed suit by selecting these two students as the best and most "professional" candidates; dominant discourses of race and gender blindness were unwittingly reproduced as PARTY members considered the meaning of a "real" Jackson student; and the debriefing session reproduced dominant assessment practices by focusing on students' comportment and "attitude" rather than the content of their answers. In all of these ways, the interviews and debriefing process reproduced dominant educational discourses. Where was agency in this process? Were all of us merely powerless pawns mimicking the cultural logics of dominant groups? Had we so thoroughly internalized these logics that they simply moved through us unaware?

My answer to these questions is both yes and no. I first consider the interview strategies of Yolanda and Leila, who mobilized the discourse of these kids in order to position themselves in opposition to it. In using this strategy, Yolanda and Leila exercised agency (as do all individuals) to construct their own identities and craft their own styles of self-representation. Yet their choices were also constrained (as they are for all individuals) by the discourses to which they had access (Bettie 2003). At Jackson High—and in the more generalized figured world of the continuation high school—the discourse of these kids is the backdrop against which students must forge an identity and define a place for themselves in the social world. This backdrop makes some subject positions more readily available than others (Bettie 2003; Holland et al. 2001). For Yolanda and Leila, positioning oneself in opposition to this discourse was a rational and viable option, and it was easy to accomplish because it kept familiar social categories intact. To convey "I don't belong at Jackson" was the most straightforward way to communicate they were people of value, people with abilities, and people deserving of the job as PARTY member.

Yolanda and Leila did not have to understand the historical significance and political implications of the discourse of these kids in order to make use of this strategy. It is not necessary to have such an under-

standing of a discourse to mobilize and use it as a framework for interpreting and explaining the social world. It is precisely the point of critical sociocultural analysis to uncover how specific systems of meaning
become naturalized such that they are reaffirmed as a matter of course
in everyday life, "taken on" voluntarily and even unconsciously by individuals and groups. As Holland et al. (2001) explain, "The discourses
and categories dominant in a society . . . are 'inscribed' upon people,
both interpersonally and institutionally, and within them. Selves are socially constructed through the mediation of powerful discourses and
their artifacts" (26). As young people construct identities and selves,
they employ social categories (such as the category of "these kids") that
originate outside themselves but are "imposed upon [them], through re-
current treatments and within interaction, to the point that *they become
self-administered*" (62, emphasis added). In the interview sequence, we
were able to catch a brief glimpse of this process.

In emphasizing the power of discourse to shape identity and agency,
I do not wish to portray the youth as powerless pawns merely ventrilo-
quizing for a dominant class. Rather, I hope to shed light on some of the
ways that power inequalities are reproduced through discourse, not only
within bodies of "official knowledge" but also in face-to-face actions and
interactions among individuals that occur every day. Power operates not
only through the maintenance of material inequalities (such as access to
resources) but also through the maintenance of "regimes of truth" that
naturalize and legitimize existing structures of power (Foucault 1980).
As seen in chapter 1, the discourse of these kids contributes to this legit-
imization by obscuring or ignoring patterns of social-structural inequality and pathologizing and blaming the victims of inequality for their own
apparent "failures." This chapter illustrates how young people captured
by this discourse interacted with it by resisting, reproducing, and contesting it. In the PARTY interview sequence, the final result was reproduction—but it was not without small acts of contestation and resistance,
nor was the reproductive outcome predetermined.

The interview sequence and debriefing session did not just show us
youth captured by harmful discourses and categories; it also showed
us examples of everyday resistance[4] and the possibilities for exercising
agency. When D contested Yolanda's use of victim-blaming discourse,
he attempted to claim and reshape the category of these kids. In this instance, D took the beginning steps toward articulating a critique, per-

forming a small act of resistance against the debilitating discourse of these kids. His actions are an example of agency—conceptualized as the act of imagining and creating new ways of being (Holland et al. 2001, 5). But while D took these initial steps, he lacked the conceptual and linguistic tools to articulate a full-blown critique, advance an alternative discourse, or shift ways of talking and interacting within PARTY. Indeed, all of us lacked these tools, and instead we fell back into the familiar social-cultural categories and meaning systems that "made sense" to all of us in that particular time and place.

This example helps us see how agency is "embedded always in collective meanings and social relations," even as possibilities for agency are present in every moment (Holland et al. 2001, 5). Throughout the interviews and debriefing session, we saw how agency was always possible, *and* how it was limited at every turn by constraints that were largely *discursive-ideological* (Kim 2000) rather than purely material.[5] In other words, we might think of the constraints on agency not only in terms of the material elements of structure—such as institutionalized inequalities in labor markets, educational opportunities, wealth, housing, health care, and political voice—but also the discursive, ideological, or cultural elements of structure such as the social categories we use and the meanings we attach to them in our lived cultural worlds. In addition, we must consider how the material and discursive dimensions of structure are linked to each other and embedded in social relations. While possibilities for agency are always present, an individual's power to exercise agency is nowhere near comparable to the power of dominant social groups to shape public meaning systems, expectations, and assumptions through the control of mass media and other cultural institutions (such as schools). Possibilities for individual agency are even smaller when the individuals in question are young, low-income, last chance high school students and graduates.

As we will see in the coming chapters, Jackson students and PARTY members performed countless small acts of resistance, and the possibilities for agency were ever present. But the constraints of institutionalized structures, practices, and discourses weighed heavily on the PARTY project, shaping its course and outcomes in ways that became evident to me only after our work together concluded. Moreover, many of the actions and activities of PARTY—such as those of the youth featured in this chapter—cannot be readily classified as wholly reproductive or re-

sistive. Indeed, the experience of PARTY reveals that acts of agency, resistance, and reproduction are messy and complex. A single act—such as
positioning oneself in opposition to the discourse of these kids—might
be interpreted as an act of resistance or of reproduction. And that single
act may in fact be both resistive and reproductive at the same time.

Conclusion

This chapter offers one example of how youth PARTY members wrestled with a discourse that was all about them—the discourse of these
kids. We saw instances in which the youth did and did not "take on"
this discourse as their own, and we saw various strategies through which
they mobilized, reproduced, and contested it. The interview sequence
and debriefing session illustrate how the externally imposed social category of "these kids" shaped the social and cultural worlds of Jackson students and graduates. In speaking with and about themselves and other
Jackson students, these young people continually bumped up against familiar discursive tropes—packaged images of, and assumptions about,
certain kinds of kids, which are deeply racialized, classed, and rooted
in dominant social discourses. At times the group members contested
these discursive tropes that construct them as problems and failures, as
when D confronted Yolanda on her depiction of "black kids." At other
times they employed these tropes wholesale, as when Sherry and Na'ilah
were disqualified on the basis of being "ghetto." But always, group members effortlessly employed these tropes as a framework for talking about
other students as well as positioning themselves. As they struggled with
and against the discourse of these kids, PARTY members alternately positioned themselves in opposition to this discourse (as if to say "I am not
one of these kids!"), in accordance with it (as if to say "I am proudly one
of these kids!"), or by contesting it (as if to say "I *am* one of these kids,
but we're not what you think we are!"). I contend their actions cannot
be readily classified as either wholly reproductive or resistive, but rather,
reflect the messiness of the structure-agency dialectic, the power of discourse as a dimension of structure, and the constraints on agency.

In the process of interviewing and selecting Jackson students for the
group, PARTY members were constructing a collective identity, defining and negotiating the boundaries and meanings of group membership.

This process offered opportunities to reimagine and recreate the category of "these kids," and the youth took some important steps toward that end. But they ultimately chose to position the group *in opposition* to the discourse of these kids in much the same way that Yolanda and Leila did—as if to say "We are *not* a group of these kids!" Certainly there were internal negotiations, compromises, and contradictions, but the debriefing session and the final decision it ended with revealed a deep desire within the group to be seen as *professional* above all. PARTY members deployed discourses and artifacts from the figured world of work as a means of positioning themselves and the group as professionals in opposition to the discourse of these kids and in opposition to the figured world of the continuation high school.

The interview sequence and debriefing session illustrate the complexities and challenges of constructing a positive group identity around a shared attachment to a stigmatized and marginalized institution such as Jackson High while preserving a sense of dignity, self-worth, and deservedness. The belief that school performance provides some measure of an individual's worth—in terms of intelligence, ability, and entitlement to society's resources and political voice—is quite strong in American culture, and alternative discourses offering a different set of meanings and explanations are lacking (Rose 2005b). Given the association between continuation high schools and school failure (both academic and personal), Jackson students had to find ways to justify their presence there while preserving their sense of self-worth as capable human beings deserving of the good things life has to offer. The most readily available responses are to accept the discourse of these kids wholesale— which means accepting oneself as a certain kind of failure—or to somehow differentiate oneself, as if to suggest "I don't really belong there." Indeed, this last strategy was the one that Leila and Yolanda chose, and PARTY members not only recognized their cue but followed suit. By reproducing the discourse of these kids, Yolanda and Leila succeeded in getting recognized as responsible, professional, and deserving of opportunities. PARTY members also reproduced this discourse as they forged a collective group identity as representatives of Jackson High engaging in serious participatory research. With the PARTY team now assembled—Louis, Lolo, D, Leila, James, and myself—we were ready to begin our work as participatory researchers. In the next chapter, I turn to an examination of that work, and continue to explore practices of identity, agency, and resistance. In particular, I show how weekly PARTY meetings were a space that enabled the deepening of critical consciousness and the construction of an oppositional political identity among youth PARTY members. This emerging political identity informed their decision to design and teach a social justice class at Jackson High.

PART II

Theorizing Identity and Agency

People Have the Power: Critical Consciousness and Political Identity in PARTY

On the day of our first meeting with the full PARTY team, I arrived early to the small conference room I had reserved at the local city college, wrote an agenda on a large sheet of butcher paper, and taped it to the wall. D arrived a few moments later with a friend, both of them on bicycles. His companion was a familiar face—a graduate of Jackson High named Suli, and a former student of mine. "Suli's gonna sit in today," D announced as they walked their bikes across the room and leaned them up against the opposite wall. "I didn't think you'd mind." I had not expected this, but I smiled and invited Suli to join us.

The full PARTY group now consisted of three graduates (D, Lolo, and Louis) and two students (Leila and James). I opened the meeting by welcoming Leila and James to the group and introducing Suli as a guest for the day. Then Louis, who had agreed to facilitate the first portion of the meeting, led a "check-in" during which everyone shared how their day was going, followed by "current events" to discuss what happened in the news that week and how it affected our lives. We spent about a half hour on these before moving to the main agenda item: intro to critical theory. I told the youth that our first four meetings would involve basic training in critical theory and educational research methods, but thereafter, we would develop a research project together and make decisions collectively. To get us started, I passed out copies of a three-page article on pop culture pedagogy (Mahiri 2000), which we read aloud, defining four key terms as we encountered them: *pedagogy, discourse, dominant discourse,* and *counterhegemonic discourse.* We discussed the author's argument that hip-hop could be used as a form of counterhegemonic pedagogy. I then invited D to demonstrate a lesson using hip-hop, a plan we had discussed previously.

D rose to his feet and almost cracked a smile as he stood facing the group, his body language conveying an even mix of pride and self-consciousness. He slipped a CD into a boom box and played a song by the hip-hop group Bone Thugs-n-Harmony called "Change the World." James was elated, exclaiming "I have that CD in my Discman right now!" The song played for about a minute when D hit Stop. Then he asked, "What do y'all think: Dominant? Or counter?" A brief silence ensued before Suli called out "counter" and others quickly followed suit. "Why did y'all say counter?" asked D. They discussed passages from the song and concluded that its message was about making the world a better place for the next generation. They contrasted this with what they considered the dominant messages of pop culture: "girls" and "flossin'" (showing off one's possessions). They laughed as they tried to say the full word *counterhegemonic* without tripping up the syllables. Suli was the first to say it all the way through without laughing. He beamed with pride as he repeated it over and over again. We discussed other music they liked and what made a message dominant or counterhegemonic. At the end of the meeting, Suli exclaimed, "I learned more in the last two hours than I learned in my whole last year of high school!"

Over the next two years, the PARTY group developed research questions, administered a survey to Jackson students, conducted interviews and participant observation, attended lectures and conferences and political demonstrations together, visited other youth PAR groups in the region, and invited guest speakers to present their research to us. We continued to meet every week and to begin each meeting with a discussion of current events. The youth often arrived eager to share news stories they had read or facts they had learned during the week, making these current events discussions the most animated part of our meetings. Toward the end of our first year, we moved our meetings from the local city college to my home, which was within walking distance of Jackson High and offered a more relaxed, comfortable space to work. At the beginning of our second year, we decided to design and teach a social justice class at Jackson High. From that point forward, our work focused on preparing for, teaching, and reflecting on the class.

The PARTY group experienced significant turnover in these two years. Halfway through our first year, Lolo left to attend community college in a rural part of the state. We invited Yolanda (chapter 2) to replace her in the group, but after just three meetings, she stopped coming back and explained that she was too busy with schoolwork, a hospital internship, and being a mother. Lolo returned to the group briefly after moving back to Maytown, but again dropped out citing time commitments to work, church, and her new (local) community college. Louis also stopped participating in the second year, as he became increasingly active at church (the same church that Lolo attended). James moved to another city with his father, and so did not return to the group or to Jackson High for the second year. D continued to bring friends to our meetings, especially Suli, who attended so many times that we all treated him as a full group member. Leila also brought occasional friends, one of whom briefly joined the group, but dropped out because she did not feel a personal connection to Jackson High. D's friend Suli, however, kept coming back, so we eventually invited him to become an official (paid) member of the group. Around the time that Suli joined PARTY, we began pursuing the idea of teaching a social justice class at Jackson High. D, Suli, and Leila were the three PARTY members who stayed on to teach the class.

In this chapter, I show how weekly PARTY meetings facilitated the deepening of critical consciousness and the formation of a collective, oppositional political identity among the youth participants. This, in turn, enabled the exercise of political agency. I argue that this deepening of critical consciousness was not primarily a result of the formal "research" we did in the group, but rather, of the dialogic process of open-ended critical reflection that occurred in weekly meetings. As I will show, PARTY meetings were a place in which youth participants shared personal stories and experiences, as well as information they had learned in the newspaper, at political events, or in their classes. In these meetings, they shared about and reflected on their lived experiences with civic institutions that affected their lives, particularly the educational and criminal justice systems. They wrestled with and sought to articulate theories of society and of social change. And they forged a collective political identity in order to exercise some (partial) agency as social justice educators at Jackson High. For the three youth who taught the social justice class (D, Suli, and Leila), it was seen as a political intervention with explicitly political goals. Their aspirations for the class reflected their emergent critical consciousness and resonated with Labaree's (1997) "democratic equality" goal of schooling (see introduction for discussion).

PARTY Meetings as a Space of Critical Consciousness

Paulo Freire (2000) describes critical consciousness (or *conscientization*) as the realization that structures of oppression are social constructs that are built—and potentially changed—through collective action. According to Freire, this realization on the part of the oppressed leads to a sense of empowerment and agency because the possibility of change becomes visible. With critical consciousness, people "perceive oppression not as a closed world from which there is no exit, but as a limiting situation which they can transform" (ibid., 31). Freire's concept of conscientization has inspired countless educators, theorists, and activists who have built on and extended it in ways far too numerous to count. Despite the enormous heterogeneity of theories, all of them share a basic set of assumptions about the social world: that relations of inequality exist between dominant and subordinate groups (e.g., men and women, whites and people of color); that these inequalities result from institutionalized oppression; and that dominant ideologies function to obscure and legitimize them. The first step toward critical consciousness is the recognition of this injustice (Mansbridge 2001)—that is, when the oppressed see their subordinate social status as a product of historical and institutionalized oppression rather than their own (or their community's) inherent inferiority.

PARTY meetings were a space in which this type of critical analysis was nurtured. In these meetings, the youth shared many personal experiences as well as new information from their individual research, their classes, and the news. The stories they shared, and the discussions they fostered, often revealed *disjunctures* between the ideals and realities of US democracy (Rubin 2007b). These disjunctures were especially visible in the youth's encounters with the education and criminal justice systems—the two civic institutions with which they had the most sustained and intimate contact. Group discussions of these two institutions facilitated the development of a systemic critique of inequality and an increasingly oppositional political identity. I explore these processes more deeply in the two subsections below.

Critique of Education

In the opening check-in at one weekly meeting, Lolo brought up an article she had read in her English class at community college. "It reminded
me of the stuff that we were talking about in the [PARTY] group, about
the education you get in different areas, and the unequal education."
Louis (who was in the same college class) recognized the text she was re-
ferring to and jumped in to explain:

Louis: There was one essay we read in class. I was, like, this made me
think about the education system—

Lolo: For me specifically Jackson High.

Kysa: What was the essay about? What was it called?

Lolo: "The Seven-Lesson Schoolteacher."

Louis: Yeah, the seven lessons. It was about him being a schoolteacher
in New York. It was about what he *actually* teaches, you know. He talks
about [how] the school system doesn't need to be reformed because the
school system that they want is active and it is doing its job. It is teaching
kids how to follow orders, how to look for a grade for satisfaction.

Lolo: And not to think independently. Not to think for themselves.
If you go to elite, like an elite area or community, they teach their little
fifth graders, they take them out on trips [*laughs*] and have them measure things on their own, you know, and have them create a problem in
their head and then create a solution. Instead of a handout saying "Do
this," "Do that," "The directions is on the paper and all you have to do
is follow those directions and you'll be able to get the answer or come up
with something." You know.

Lolo and Louis had read "The Seven-Lesson Schoolteacher" by John
Taylor Gatto (1992) in their English class. Lolo explained that the seven
lessons in the title were called the hidden curriculum, and the essay reminded her of PARTY because "it [the hidden curriculum] was something we were trying to change, it's something we are trying to make different at Jackson."

Gatto's essay identifies seven lessons that constitute the hidden curriculum of American schooling, describing this as a de facto national curriculum that is "universally taught from Harlem to Hollywood Hills" (1).
The lesson that resonated most with Lolo and Louis was the second one,
called "class position." This lesson, according to Gatto, involves teaching students to stay in the same social class as the one into which they

were born, and to accept this fate as natural, inevitable, and legitimate. Gatto writes, "If I do my job well, the kids can't even *imagine* themselves somewhere else because I've shown them how to envy and fear the better classes and how to have contempt for the dumb classes. Under this efficient discipline the class mostly polices itself into good marching order. That's the real lesson of any rigged competition like school. You come to know your place" (5).

As she narrated the themes of Gatto's essay, Lolo implied that reading it allowed her to become conscious of a truth she had already known, but had yet to put into words. She explained, "It's like you already feel that way. Then it's like, from reading the essay it's like, 'OK' . . . [*trails off*]." She tried again, explaining, "It's eye-catching, it's, like, it applies . . . [*trails off*] It's about what is going on in their [Jackson students'] lives." I asked if she thought Jackson students would enjoy reading the essay, and she replied affirmatively, adding:

Lolo: When they read it, it's gonna open up their understanding to how they're feelin'. You know, I mean, those words, what is written in the essay is gonna be like their personal feelings that they probably haven't even spoken yet, or just something they are thinking inside their head that's gonna open up an understanding.

This was the impact that reading the essay seemed to have for Lolo: to "open up an understanding" by giving her the words to express facts about schooling and inequality that she had already learned from experience. Gaining access to a discourse that gave meaning to her experience led to a deepening of critical consciousness. This discourse, or rather *counter*discourse, on schooling offered Lolo a new lens through which to interpret her experience as an involuntary transfer student to Jackson High, a struggling community college student, and a young adult settling into a life of working poverty much like the working lives of her family members. This new, more critical, lens allowed her to interpret these lived experiences as the result of something other than her own deficiencies. With a somber voice that betrayed more pain than anger, Lolo reflected:

Lolo: I just feel like I was robbed of my education, real education, me being able to think independently. In the essay [that she wrote for class later], I said that I struggle in college now because of this, because I wasn't taught to think independently or on my own, you know what I mean? I don't know, that's what I feel. If the education system was the same, like the elite everywhere, and even in the poor neighborhoods and the not-so-populated areas, then everybody would have a chance to equal education. But it's not like that. It's not those kids' fault that they can't think independently like those children that are in elite schools. It is the system; it is how the system works.

Lolo's rendering of "The Seven-Lesson Schoolteacher" revealed a "disjuncture" (Rubin 2007b) between the ideals and realities of the US educational system. The ideal of equal opportunity is central to American public schooling, and Lolo alluded to this ideal when she commented that "if the education system was the same, like the elite everywhere, and even in the poor neighborhoods and the not-so-populated areas, then everybody would have a chance to equal education." But what she had observed and experienced in her own life was a highly unequal system: one in which kids "in the poor neighborhoods and the not-so-populated areas" were not afforded the same opportunities to grow and develop as "the elite." Recognizing this disjuncture, she began to articulate a *systemic* critique of education—emphasizing "it's not those kids' fault" because "it is the system; it is how the system works."

Many scholars have argued that low-income youth and youth of color are more likely than their privileged counterparts to experience this type of disconnect between the ideals and realities of US democracy (e.g., Epstein 2001; Ladson-Billings 2004; Sánchez-Jankowski 2002; Rubin 2007b; Rubin and Hayes 2010). For example, Rubin (2007b) examined how high school students reacted to social studies curricula, and found that those from more privileged backgrounds were more likely to experience "congruence" between their own experience of civic institutions and the ideals of US democracy learned in social studies class. As such, privileged students were more likely to accept the institutions of US democracy at face value and to believe that the government upheld the ideals it espoused. In contrast, students from marginalized backgrounds were more likely to have direct personal experiences with civic institutions that ran counter to the espoused ideals of US democracy. For many marginalized youth, these experiences of disjuncture formed the basis of a critique that recognized systemic inequalities and countered dominant narratives about individual or cultural shortcomings of disempowered groups.

For PARTY members, weekly meetings provided a space not only to share their own experiences of disjuncture but also to reflect on them, draw connections across different stories, and practice articulating new analyses. For Lolo, exposure to a counterdiscourse in her college class provided an alternative, critical frame for interpreting her lived experiences of disjuncture. But PARTY meetings then provided an additional place in which to reflect on this new frame and to practice articulating a new *systemic* critique of educational inequality in the supportive and affirming company of peers. By sharing many such stories and analyses in the group, the youth could identify recurring themes and develop or try out new theories to explain and interpret them. Due to PARTY's focus on educational issues from the beginning, disjuncture in the educational system was the most salient theme to run through our meetings. But a significant and related theme to emerge was disjuncture in the criminal justice system, which I explore below.

Critique of Criminal Justice

"The prison guards be whuppin' my uncle," Suli said during the opening check-in. He sounded nonchalant, with just a hint of irritation as if complaining about traffic or the weather. D was quick with a response: "Prison guards got the *right* to whup your uncle." And after a pause, D continued, "So-called. [*pause*] Technically. [*pause*] They got the power." Suli answered back in a sarcastic tone, "Lightweight." D continued, "They [prison guards] got more power than police officers, though. 'Cause they be, they be—" Suli cut him off, defending his uncle: "Hey, a couple of inmates tried to jump him [the uncle]." D continued to defend the guards: "They can whup *anyone*, blood! *Anyone!*" The rest of the conversation proceeded as follows:

Suli: Nah, listen, listen, a couple inmates tried to jump my uncle. And he whupped, he whupped two of them, and he was wrestling with another one of them, you feel, when the prison guards came. They didn't whup dude. They whupped my uncle!

D: Because they seen your uncle act aggressive, you feel, 'cause he had dude wrestling.

Suli: But he was getting *jumped*, though!

D: They didn't see that part, you feel me? They didn't see that. They just seen your uncle on top of dude.

Suli: They broke his jaw! They broke his jaw, though!

D: But they cannot get fired for that. 'Cause they doin' their job. You feel me? The uncle was aggressive, you feel me? So they have to use all force necessary.

As Suli narrated his uncle's story, he appeared to be pleading for a

sense of outrage against the prison guards, while D refused to display
outrage and proceeded to defend the guards' behavior as just "doing
their job." Suli's tone grew more frustrated as D maintained a detached,
matter-of-fact posture.

Suli: Hey, they whupped him 'cause he won't pick a color.

D: They can whup your ass for that too, nigga!

Suli: Why?! 'Cause he won't choose to be black or Mexican?

D: Yup. Hell yeah!

Suli: [*sounding outraged*] You can't whup me because of my ethnic
background! Blood, you *can't*, blood! They can't force you to choose [a
race]!

In this excerpt, Suli suggested his uncle's beating resulted from his refusal to claim a racial identity as either black or Latino—because he was
both, a biracial identity that Suli also shared—in a prison where inmates
were segregated by race. D responded calmly, in a voice one might use to
read to a small child.

D: A prison guard can do anything he want to, blood. He got that
right. You feel, we ain't talking about if they got the right to whup you
because you didn't pick a color. We talking about they got the right
'cause that's their *job*!

Suli: So it's their job to whup you because you're in a cell by yourself?

D: It's they—it's the police's job to be assholes! You feel? You gonna
complain about that?

Suli: [*defiant*] We *do* complain about it!

D: We can't do nothing about it. We can't do nothing about it.

Suli: You really can't, though.

D: The government gave them that authority. This country gave
them people the authority so we gonna have to work with it in the system. Your uncle shoulda just picked a neutral color, you feel, he shoulda
picked Asian and fucked their head up, you feel me? And then said
"Fuck y'all!" You feel me? Or he should just get his ass whupped! Or he
should just pick a color.

D continued speaking but shifted his tone, now sounding conciliatory.

D: I ain't saying it's right to be whupped, though. I find that fucked-up.
You feel me, when they jump on you, for no reason, they be, like, five,
ten deep, you feel me, on one person, that's not right. And about them
breaking the jaw, you feel, shit, man. He shoulda got him a lawyer or
something, blood, and tried to prove his case, man. Because, they *broke*

his jaw, you feel me? They just didn't hit him, you feel me? He got physical proof now, you feel? Like—

Suli: They just wired him up and took him to the hole.

D: That's even *more* fucked-up! You feel me? Shit!

Suli: He on twenty-four-hour lockdown right now.

This exchange between D and Suli draws our attention to a lived experience that many Jackson students shared—that of having a loved one behind bars. Suli was not merely aware of his uncle's incarceration; rather, it provided him an intimate encounter with state power. This encounter brought the opportunity for him to reflect on the workings of the state, as when he and D wrestled with questions about the use of violence by guards in a prison. While Suli wanted to hold the prison guards personally responsible for violence against his uncle, D insisted the guards were simply doing their job, noting, "The government gave them that authority." D's argument advances a systemic analysis that portrays violence by guards as part of a *system* that relies on violence—"They got the right 'cause that's their *job*!" Their conversation also addresses the role of racism and racial categorization in the exercise of state power. Suli believed his uncle was punished because he did not fit into a single state-sanctioned racial category (either black or Latino). His story alludes to the power of state disciplinary institutions, such as prisons and schools, to label, categorize, sort, and rank individuals (Foucault 1995), even when its official categories do not reflect the complex individuals captured by them (Pollock 2005). As Suli wrestled with the meaning and implications of his uncle's experience, his tone shifted from moral outrage to resignation about a system he saw as unjust but inevitable. In a moment of outrage, he appealed to a higher standard of justice beyond the legal rights of prison guards and police, insisting to D that "we *do* complain about it!" Yet almost the moment he made this appeal, Suli adopted a position of resignation, agreeing with D that "you really can't [do anything about it], though."

The expansion of the prison and criminal justice systems is an important part of the sociopolitical context of Jackson High, shaping both the material and discursive world of students and PARTY members. Since the 1980s, the United States has seen a major expansion of the prison system, growing its prison population and criminal justice infrastructure to historically unprecedented levels (Parenti 2000). These trends disproportionately affect communities of color and the poor (Alexander 2010; R. Gilmore 2007; Mauer and Chesney-Lind 2002b; Black 2009), as well as youth (Ginwright and James 2003; Kwon 2006; Hirschfield 2008). The dramatic expansion of the prison system has been accomplished, in part, by the passage of laws that extend sentences and criminalize behaviors that previously were not considered punishable by jail (Mauer and Chesney-Lind 2002a; Black 2009). These legal changes have been accompanied by an intensification of policing and surveillance within communities of color and low-income areas (Kwon 2006; Parenti 2000). All of this is occurring as funds for social services, including public and higher education, are being cut and social programs are scaled back or eliminated. As Mauer and Chesney-Lind (ibid.) point out, "Corrections costs have been the fastest growing segment of state budgets, and this has meant that virtually all other aspects of spending, including funds for education and social welfare, have been affected in order to accommodate prison expansion" (11).

Given this sociopolitical context, it is not surprising that the criminal justice system was a powerful frame through which PARTY members developed their understanding of the state. Far from being an isolated event, Suli's story about his uncle reflected a pattern of storytelling about criminal justice encounters; stories such as these were a mainstay of PARTY meetings. We learned, for example, about a time when Suli was pulled over, taken to the police station, and held for several hours for making an illegal left turn, an infraction that should have prompted no more than a traffic citation. On another occasion, he was handcuffed and brought to the station for suspected robbery, and then released with no charges many hours later. D recalled a time he was stopped, searched, and brought to the station for not having a light on his bicycle. Another time, he claimed that police officers pulled guns on him while he was walking in his own neighborhood, simply because he was not carrying a photo ID. Both young men recalled a time they were walking with a group of friends when a police officer, according to Suli, "threw [the friend's] head into the gate, and it knotted up immediately," provoking the youth to call for an ambulance. Louis shared about being harassed in parks and public places when hanging out with friends. Lolo shared about her eldest brother, who was shot and killed by a police officer in the year before PARTY started. Leila, who was white, did not share a similar repertoire of intimate criminal justice encounters, but she participated in producing and reproducing criminal justice narratives by complaining about police officers clad in riot gear at the many political demonstrations she attended.[1]

Within PARTY, then, the criminal justice system was experienced as intimate and real (rather than abstract). Much research suggests that PARTY members were not unique in this respect: in marginalized communities of color, police harassment and abuse are commonplace (Flanagan and Gallay 1995; Kwon 2006; Lopez 2002; Rubin 2007b; Black 2009), and stories about these encounters may be shared over and over among friends, families, and neighbors. For PARTY members, these stories were a key point of reference used to justify their mistrust of the state and to position themselves as members of subordinated racial or class groups. Their belief that the state worked against their interests and the interests of others like them was reaffirmed and reproduced through the stories told about the criminal justice system. Like their discussions of schooling, the criminal justice narratives that wove through PARTY meetings revealed a disjuncture between the ideals and realities of US democracy. In particular, the ideal of equal protection under the law was one that youth saw regularly violated through racial profiling and unequal sentencing practices, leading D to conclude that "people with money get different laws, different punishments, than people that's broke."

In PARTY meetings, the youth not only shared and reflected on their civic experiences but they tried out new theories to interpret them, and gained practice articulating a systemic critique in the supportive company of the group. By sharing personal stories with one another, they could connect *individual* experiences of disjuncture to a *collective* experience and therefore support the development of a group oppositional identity. As Mansbridge (2001) writes:

> The experience of daily indignity at the hands of the dominant group *cements group identity* [emphasis added], fuels anger against the dominant group, prompts attention to a host of injustices, helps locate the source of those injustices in a system of domination, and encourages the thought that all members of the group have an identity of interest in overthrowing the system. (251–52)

This set of processes was evident in PARTY, as the youth shared their own experiences of "indignity at the hands of the dominant group" with one another and, through reflection on these, began to forge a collective political identity that was *oppositional* to the state and to dominant social groups.

When reflecting on the project at the end of our first year, all of the youth described it as an experience that was both educational and politicizing. "I'm a lot more antigovernment now," remarked Louis, "'cause the job they're doing now is not effective. It's effective for them, but it's not effective for all the millions of people out there struggling." He added, "I also learned that society doesn't just change when you just sit there. You can't just say 'Things need to be changed.' You actually have to *do* something to make a change." Leila said she "became more aware" in PARTY, and had a new desire to learn history and economics so she could do "something major" in the political arena: "I mean, I know the basics [about history and economics], but I actually wanna get, like, really deep into it and just kind of, like, bring that to the present day and kind of connect that together." She noted that participation in PARTY had "gotten me into, like, just wanting to learn and learn and learn. Nonstop." Even D, who was typically constrained with his praise, described PARTY as a space of learning: "I learned there's two sides to every story. Two opinions to everything. [. . .] And [you have to] read between the lines. Don't just read that stuff that's printed. Basically, learn your history. Learn everything. Don't just listen to whatever people say."

In short, the youth emphasized the political learning they had done and their increasingly politicized perspective on the social world. However, this learning appeared to be grounded in the free-flowing, unstructured, critical dialogue and reflection that occurred in weekly meetings, rather than the process of formal research that I had tried to facilitate. In fact, in their reflection on PARTY's first year, the idea of research scarcely came up at all. The only hints of the formal research component were D's comment that "when we were going over them little surveys and stuff like that, that kinda got kinda boring," and Lolo's that "I liked the meeting when we was brainstorming for the questions that we was gonna ask for the survey." Noticing that research had not figured prominently in the youth's recollections of PARTY, I asked, "Did we learn anything from the survey?" A pause of many seconds ensued. "Um . . . ," began Leila, trailing off to silence. Another achingly long pause followed. "We tallied them," offered Louis, sounding conciliatory. More silence. Then Leila continued, "We did [learn something], 'cause, like, we have a list of what they were saying and the average of students [who] wanna do this or are going to go to college or something like that. But I actually don't know, it's not in my memory, so it's like . . . [*trails off*]. But I mean we did, we concluded." A similar pattern followed with regard to the research interviews. When I asked if we learned anything from them, D responded, "We did 'em!" Leila agreed that we completed some interviews but worried about whether the information was valid because "the kids probably weren't taking them so seriously." In short, the youth offered few words about the formal research activities conducted in PARTY: the developing of research questions, selection of methods, implementation of those methods, and analysis of the results. Rather than learning from these, Louis's observation that "we tallied them" and D's that "we did 'em!" may be the most accurate representations of what occurred. Below, I reflect further on the process of formal research in PARTY, and what it reveals about the youth's developing critical consciousness and oppositional political identity.

Reflections on Research in PARTY

In PARTY's first year, we had faithfully followed a sequence of steps that I had defined as our "research." We read and discussed excerpts from hooks (1994), Freire (2000), and Woodson (2006) as an entryway to theorizing the role of education in the reproduction and transformation of social inequalities. I led interactive activities designed to teach the youth about different research methods used in the social sciences, such as surveys, interviews, focus groups, and participant observation. We visited two other youth-led PAR groups to learn about their research projects and get ideas for ours. Next, we brainstormed research questions, agreed on four, and discussed what methods could help us gain insight about each one (see table 3.1). We decided to start with a survey because it could reach the broadest number of Jackson students. Each PARTY member wrote his or her own survey questions, which we pooled and then eliminated or merged redundant questions. Louis typed and formatted the survey on his home computer. James made an appointment with the principal, Mr. Galo, seeking permission to administer the survey during the school-wide thirty-minute homeroom period. I simply made a follow-up call to confirm it was really happening and made one hundred hard copies of the survey. We got responses from sixty-one students—about half the school's official enrollment but only slightly lower than the number present on any given school day. We then held a series of "working meetings" in which PARTY members paired up to manually enter survey results into an Excel spreadsheet.

TABLE 3.1. **Research questions brainstorm**

Research question	Related questions	Research method
1. What interests and motivates Jackson students?	What are their hobbies? What do they like to do in their spare time? What do they like/dislike about school?	• Interviews • Surveys
2. What are the hopes and dreams of Jackson students?	What are their goals? What do they want to do after high school? What careers do they want? Do they want to have a family? How could school be more connected to their goals?	• Interviews • Surveys
3. What are the social, political, and economic issues that affect the lives of Jackson students?	What obstacles do they face? What issues interfere with their coming to school? Do they have adult responsibilities? What happens in their daily lives? What are the root causes of these obstacles? What communities are they from, and what are these communities like?	• Interviews • Surveys • Library research • Newspapers, news magazines, and the Internet
4. What teaching strategies are most effective for Jackson students?	What classroom activities do they enjoy most? In what classes do they learn the most? In what classes do they remember the most? In what classes and activities are they most engaged in learning? What have been powerful teaching/learning experiences in their past?	• Surveys • Interviews • Participant observation

When data entry was complete, I compiled the results and printed copies of the totals. I wrote some questions on a large sheet of butcher paper taped to the wall: "What can we learn from this? What does it mean? What is surprising in this result? How can we interpret it? What other questions does it lead to?" I asked each PARTY member to facilitate a discussion of results for a group of survey questions, and D volunteered to take the first five. He looked down at his copy of the tallies and read directly from the page: "One. What grade are you in?" He looked up at the group and said simply, "That one say what grade they're in." He looked back down at the page and read aloud: "Two. Do you enjoy going to school?" Looking back up at the group, he repeated: "That one says if they like school or they don't like school." Then he summarized: "Most of 'em said three, [for] 'It's OK.'" He added, "Hey, that's what I woulda said too!" And as if having a conversation with a friend who had just asked whether he liked school, D responded, "It's all right, you know. It ain't *great*, but it ain't too bad, you feel, it's just all right." He nodded and produced a satisfied grin, as if to show approval for this reasonable answer. The other youth remained silent as D proceeded to the next question: "Three. What is your favorite class?" He made it through all five questions in this manner, then nonchalantly placed the paper on the table and looked up to conclude, "That's it." With the exception of one comment from Louis, there was no additional discussion.

We had nearly made it through all twenty-two survey questions in this fashion when James interrupted to announce that some "girls" from a nearby university had given a survey at Jackson earlier that very day. "They were just like us!" he exclaimed, grinning proudly. His statement transformed the mood in the room from dull boredom to curiosity. James said the survey was so long that most students did not have time to finish it. "But," he added, "it was the same two questions over and over again: Do you cut school, and do you do drugs?" He gave examples to demonstrate: "When do you cut school? Where do you go when you cut school? What do you do when you cut school? Do you do drugs when you cut school? Where do you go to do drugs? . . ." As he rattled off this list, the other group members showed increasing interest, and James appeared to enjoy being the center of attention. Then he remembered the survey had also included a comparable set of questions on the theme of "Do you have sex?" He started reciting a list: "When do you have sex? How often do you have sex? Who do you have sex with? . . ." Then he added, "They gave us cookies afterwards too."

D mumbled, "Hey, man, that survey [is] reinforcin' stereotypes, though." His comment prompted Leila to say, "West side kids [the wealthiest section of Maytown] do way more drugs and have way more sex!" Louis chimed in, "But you don't see *them* getting a survey like that." After some more discussion of sex, drugs, and other joys of skipping school, D brought our attention back to the survey, exclaiming, "Man, that [survey] ain't gonna make Jackson a better school!" His voice was seething with anger. Louis said the university students were probably only giving the survey "for a grade." His tone was disapproving. D went on, raising his voice, "That is stupid! How is that gonna make Jackson a better school? Tell me how!" Before I knew it, our time was almost up, and I called attention back to our own survey. Louis raced through the remaining questions with no participation from the group. My attempts to bring our discussion back to the questions I'd written on the butcher paper were met with blank stares or evasive answers. During checkout, James said it was a "cool meeting" and that "we did a good job analyzing our survey." After that, we never returned to the survey again.

Interpreting the Survey

How are we to make sense of D's angry response to James's story? And of our own haste in abandoning a survey we had spent many months working on? At least two factors likely played a role. First, it may be common for academic researchers to seek out continuation high schools as a convenient place to locate pools of "at-risk" youth with whatever sort of problem-coded characteristic they are studying (see the appendix for a discussion of this point). As such, it is likely that many continuation students—if they attend regularly and live relatively close to a major university—will become subjects in some sort of research study. Jackson students in fact participated in at least one school-wide survey each year, administered by graduate students in a nearby social work program. We might expect many of the surveys given at Jackson High to be like the one James described—focused primarily on the deviant-coded behaviors of students themselves—for, as we saw in chapter 1, much of the research published about continuation students is centered precisely on these issues. Even though research on these topics can potentially contribute to creating better programs and policies for youth, the youth who are repeatedly *subjected* to such studies—that is, who become research subjects—may only be reminded of the negative stereotypes and stigma by which they are captured. D's visible anger in response to the survey James described suggests the psychological injury that repeated subjection to this type of research may inflict on continuation students. And it raised the possibility of our own complicity in this process.

Second, one week after the meeting described above, PARTY hosted a guest speaker who inspired a change in direction for our research. Guest speakers were a regular part of PARTY, as I periodically invited scholars of color to present about their own research and their thoughts on doing research for social change.[2] On this day, our guest was an African American doctoral student named Brenda, who was discussing her research on racial equity in education when Louis interjected, "What will it take to fix the schools?" Brenda replied that the solution would be complex and multilayered, but tried to explain how her research offered some insight about achieving greater equity. Louis persisted, "But what can *we* do to fix it? How can we get involved?" He mentioned the current budget cuts affecting Maytown schools, citing rumors that hundreds of teachers would be getting "pink slips" and programs such as art and ethnic studies were in jeopardy of being eliminated. D said that cutting those programs would harm the very students who needed them most, recalling, "Those was the only classes I ever wanted to go to in the first place!" Agreeing with D's point, Leila asked why students weren't allowed to vote on which programs to save and which to cut. "That's right!" shouted D, getting excited now. "How come the *students* don't get a vote?"

The youth's indignation grew pronounced as they pondered these questions and lamented the looming budget cuts. I jumped in to ask Brenda what advice she might have for us, as a group, in channeling this passion toward a research project at Jackson High. She suggested we decide what changes we wanted to see at Jackson and then figure out who had the power to make it happen by learning how decisions were made in the school district. James suggested we talk to the school board. Louis said the superintendent was the boss so we should interview him instead. Brenda explained that if we started investigating how decisions were made, we would discover that the superintendent works for the school board, and the school board works for the voters because they are elected. Then she asked, "Do you know anyone who voted for the school board?" The youth responded with blank stares. Brenda asked, "Who votes?" Leila answered, "The rich."

In the very next PARTY meeting, I wrote "Continue survey analysis" on the agenda, but Louis wanted to skip to the following agenda item: "Discuss next steps." D jumped right in: "I wanna know what's the problem with this whole school system. How can we change it?" He continued without waiting for a response: "I also wanna talk to the school board and ask them, do you really think this system is correct?" The conversation proceeded with each PARTY member calling out in a fast, lively rhythm:

Louis: I wanna ask them why are they cutting down on programs—

Leila: —why didn't they keep better track of the money?

Louis: Don't the parents have a say in the money? They should get a vote.

Kysa: They *do* have a vote. The whole city votes. But remember what Brenda said about who votes?

Leila: Yeah, but if we advertised it enough, like, got the word out, like, what is really happening, a lot more, I think, like, more people would vote and overturn it.

D: Voting shouldn't even just be the adults, though. It should be the kids. You feel, if you put a vote to the kids, they would never vote to cut art!

I proposed revisiting our four original research questions in light of our emerging interest in budget cuts and the school board. The youth shrugged, showing no enthusiasm. But when I asked them to share their own personal questions, they had no shortage of ideas. Spontaneously, I wrote on a large sheet of butcher paper: "What do you *really* want to know?" James shared first: "I wanna know why." "Why what?" I asked. "Why everything," he answered. "Why the funding—" D cut him off: "Why the system is the way it is. Why certain different cities, different people, got different kinds of education. I'm not gonna say it's a race thing, but, when you look at it, you feel, it *is* a race thing." D explained that his friend recently moved to a predominantly white suburb in the area. He told us the schools were better there, and after some discussion about the town, he continued, "I wanna know why is it like that. If minorities gonna get less education, then come up and say it! Don't keep hidin' it. We can take it! We can handle being on the bottom! It's been that way for years, generations! The problem is y'all hidin' it!"

D's impassioned plea was buried as Leila and Louis jumped in with their own questions: "I wanna know why private schools are better than public" (Leila); "I wanna know how can we be more effective in changing the system" (Louis). D exclaimed, "School should teach people to empower theyself!" while Louis wondered aloud, "How can we spread the information that we gather?" At the heart of their questions was a clear and deep concern about educational inequality, a desire to understand why it persisted and how it could be changed. They talked about interviewing students, teachers, the superintendent, and the school board. James suggested we ask students what they would want to ask the school board. Leila said she wanted to focus the research on "education generally and why it's unfair." D insisted that we "focus on the root." As I wrote their ideas up on butcher paper, I smiled and said to D, "I like that. Focus on the root."

Focus on the Root

In the following months, the PARTY project grew less structured as each individual member pursued his or her own questions. Each week, the youth volunteered to do things they were especially interested in: attending lectures, conferences, and protests; interviewing friends, family members, and teachers; conducting participant observation at public events and in schools. We also attended two conferences together as a group—one academic conference about social justice education at a nearby university, and one community-based conference about youth organizing held at a local high school. In weekly meetings, everyone reported back on what they had done and learned during the week, while I wrote notes on butcher paper trying to capture the important themes. The youth took this work on with enthusiasm. They were animated and engaged during meetings, and they all volunteered for new research activities every week. Nevertheless, at the end of our first year, it was still not clear what the outcome of PARTY's work would be. Although we had engaged in many research activities—a survey, interviews, guest speakers, lectures, readings, conferences, participant observation—they had not seemed to generate momentum toward a specific project or action. The survey had felt more like an empty exercise than a meaningful research endeavor. The interviews and other activities were taken up with enthusiasm but disconnected from one another. As the summer approached, I was not certain whether PARTY would continue into a second year.

I reconvened the group in the fall, still uncertain about whether it would be our last meeting or the start of a new phase of the project. As we ate pizza in my backyard, D described his vision for what he then called a "PARTY class" at Jackson High.

D: Basically we go, and just get the kids, Jackson kids, voicing their opinions. You feel, bring in little issues to the class. You know, how this government is fucked-up, how the schools is fucked-up, just get them to voice their opinion and show them that their voice is power. Basically. You know, like, you got your, you got a opinion, you know, basically. And don't be scared to say what you gotta say. You know, as long as you can talk, somebody can hear you.

Louis: Showing them how to formulate and express their opinion?

D: Yeah, you feel, just don't stand down and be like—

Louis: —like, "*You're* the boss—"

D: Yeah!

Leila picked up on D's idea and responded: "I think the best way to learn is through other people's opinions. So I mean, like, I'm sure they'd learn a lot about the issues that way." She suggested we might visit different Jackson classes to lead discussions about current events and social issues, much like the guest speakers did for us in PARTY. D insisted that more time was needed to reach Jackson students than a single class period. We would need our own class entirely. Louis agreed: "In a class, see, a real class, we'd have time to teach, to teach this, about the United States, and to show people how to be more politically aware so that they can, you know, vote on the issues that affect their lives."

Leila had reservations. She was "really iffy about doing the class thing," adding, "I would love to, like, gather the information and, like, setting up the curriculum, but actually teaching it would be a challenge for me." Lolo countered her with, "I mean it's a challenge, but it's a challenge that you wanna jump on!" Lolo grew visibly excited and smiled as she turned to D to ask "So are we committed?" D answered, "I'm down. I'll teach a class." I felt the excitement in the room as the youth began visualizing their class at Jackson High. I asked how serious they were about doing this, to which D declared resolutely, "I'm down to teach. I'm down to teach a class." Lolo added, "I feel like that would be doing something great." The mood was positive as we decided to meet again and resume our discussion of the PARTY class.

Despite their initial excitement, Lolo and Louis discontinued their participation in PARTY shortly thereafter, as both became more deeply involved in a new church. The group continued on with D, Suli, and Leila. From that point forward, our work focused solely on designing and teaching a social justice class. Though we continued to discuss current events at the beginning of each meeting, we dropped the narrative that we were doing "research" and instead focused on the immediate task of preparing to teach. Our roles shifted such that I was now the only member of the group explicitly doing formal research, despite my effort to integrate action-research (Pine 2008) and participatory-evaluation (Estrella and Gaventa 1998) into the work of teaching.

At the time, I felt somewhat defeated by our inability to persist with more explicit collaborative research. However, it is evident from my subsequent analysis of PARTY meeting transcripts and field notes that these youth were drawn to PARTY, and persisted in it, not primarily because they wanted to do research in the way I had defined it. Rather, they came because the group provided a meaningful opportunity to engage in critical dialogue, develop new ideas, and participate in making change. These are the things they remembered, talked about, and claimed to like the most. In short, they participated in PARTY because it was a space of meaningful learning, for deepening critical consciousness, and exercising political agency. This is precisely the experience they hoped to re-create in the social justice class at Jackson High.

The Social Justice Class as Political Agency

A few days after receiving permission from the Jackson principal and so-cial studies teacher to teach the social justice class, D, Suli, Leila, and I gathered in my living room for our weekly meeting. I taped a piece of butcher paper to the wall that read "Brainstorm: Topics and themes" and asked the youth to share any ideas for the class that came to mind. "I wanna teach why the United States produces more waste than any other country," offered Leila. D said, "I wanna teach about the war, [about] who really benefits from going to war." After a pause, he added, "And the prisons, what we was talking about with the prisons." Suli added "ed-ucation," and then elaborated: "how it doesn't really prepare you for col-lege and how the system is set up to keep you down." Within minutes, we had generated a list of topics for the class: waste, the environment, war and foreign policy, prisons / criminal justice, education / educational in-equality, police brutality, racism, global trade, poverty, welfare, health care, capitalism.

I asked the group how our list of topics could be synthesized into one or a few broad themes to organize the class. D responded immedi-ately: "Power. They all got to do with power." The room fell silent for a moment before D continued, "That's a class that can go on and on for years and never run out of topics." Another brief silence ensued as Suli and Leila considered D's words. "I like that!" D concluded for himself. "Yeah, that's really good," agreed Leila. "I agree," I chimed in. I said that power could include both the coercive power of "the system" as well as the transformative power of knowledge and the collective power of or-ganizing. "Yeah, that people have the power," D summed up. "Exactly,"

I said, writing "POWER" in capital letters on the butcher paper and, under it: "People have the power."

In the next few weeks, we developed a written statement of our learning goals to share with Ms. Barry, the social studies teacher.

> Students [in the social justice class] will learn:
> - Why things are the way they are;
> - How all of this affects their life;
> - To question why it is the way it is;
> - What they can do about it: People have the power.

These learning goals emphasize orientations and habits of mind that are consistent with Freire's notion of critical consciousness, such as the questioning of taken-for-granted truths ("to question why it is the way it is") and the recognition that social change is possible through collective action ("people have the power"). In individual interviews with each PARTY member in the days leading up to our first class, I asked each of them what they hoped students would learn in the class. They replied:

D: Basically, I want to teach [students] that it's power in numbers. If you come, you feel, millions and millions and millions, they not gonna be able to stop us, you feel, even the National Guard. If *everybody* in this country believed in *one* thing, you feel me, and actually stepped up to the plate, you feel, we're unstoppable. Even if minorities just come together, you feel? And we just on different sides, minorities, and then high-class rich people, they're on the other side. We're unstoppable! Nothing can stop us!

[separate interview]

Leila: I want [students] to know that we really do, like, the lower-class people really do have the power. [. . .] I would do *so much* if everyone would work with me on that, you know? Like, 'cause I really feel like we should just, seriously, shut down the system. We could.

[separate interview]

Suli: The main one [goal of the course] is, like, voting. And just, like, if they wanted to go to a public, you know, speaking or like when they pass, like, certain laws they're open to the public. And a lot of people don't know that. Like they could just go and voice their opinion. And, you know, not necessarily say it in a manner in which they look at you and it's like, "OK, he doesn't know what he's talking about, he's just talking." You know, they'll actually know what they're talking about and have learned something about it to where they can speak in a manner that is, like, will be heard, rather than going in there and speaking like some person, you know, they look at you like you're just some person off the street, you don't know what you're talking about. And they can speak about it and know what they're talking about. You know, have the proof.

These responses suggest that PARTY members shared a vision for the social justice class as a political intervention with explicitly political aims. In their own way, each PARTY member emphasized the civic purposes of education and the skills of democratic citizenship, from protesting and engaging in civil disobedience to voting and attending city council meetings. The vision they articulated resonates with the educational goal that Labaree (1997) calls "democratic equality" (see introduction for discussion). Rather than take present social structures for granted, PARTY members wanted students to see change as possible and to see themselves as change agents. They wanted to involve Jackson students in the same process of critical dialogue and reflection for conscientization that they had experienced in PARTY. But even as the youth embraced the liberatory potential of education, they remained critical of schooling. An implicit and sometimes explicit goal of the social justice class was to create an alternative model of education to empower Jackson students, in contrast to what they perceived as the silencing and disempowering practices of mainstream schooling. As D said:

D: This country is ran off of followers. They never go in deep and have their own opinion. They follow somebody else. You know, but schools, it's all about schools, though. What schools teach today is they teach you how to be followers, instead of teaching you how to have your own opinion.

Unlike this dominant model of schooling, the social justice class would empower students to speak. As Suli emphasized, "*We* give them an opportunity to speak their mind. It's not about being right, just say what you want to say. *We're* giving you a chance to speak your mind. You can say 'Fuck [President] Bush' if you want to, and you can say the school system is a bunch of bullshit." Likewise, D observed in a separate meeting, "I just want them [students] to voice their opinion. On all the topics and issues we be talkin' about. And don't bite your tongue, you feel? Don't bite your tongue just 'cause the teacher don't let you speak. Or the principal don't let you speak." The youth's explicit disidentification with mainstream schooling became more evident as we began teaching at Jackson High—a theme that I explore further in chapter 4. At the same time, the theme of "voicing your opinion" emerged within the PARTY group as the central purpose, method, and measure of success of the social justice class. Suli reflected in one meeting about Jackson students: "They've *got* opinions, but sometimes they just don't voice it. They might think these topics we're talking about don't affect them. But they *do* affect them. And they might start to see that [in the social justice class]."

Because the class was framed in political terms, and pursued explicitly civic goals, the choice to teach it can be conceptualized as an act of political agency on the part of D, Suli, and Leila. The youth's goals for the class reflected a deepening critical consciousness and a faith in the liberatory possibilities of education. Their collective identity as social justice educators was a political and politicized identity, as well as an oppositional one: the youth saw themselves as change agents and teaching as an act of social change. D even drew an explicit connection between his own teaching and the work of building a social movement.

D: My only goal is to get the issues in their [students'] head. Whatever they do with them is totally on them. 'Cause I got the issues in *my* head, and I chose to do whatever I did with them. And I'll teach them. And that's the only way the cycle will keep going. That's the only reason why we actually know Martin Luther King and Malcolm X and every other black activist and white activist, because somebody taught them, you feel me? They decided to *talk*, and tell other people. And if people keep on doing that for another hundred years, we *will* see some change.

Here, D discursively connects the work of teaching to a larger process of social change and a cycle of teaching and learning for collective political empowerment. In conceptualizing the class this way, D and the other PARTY members hoped to implement an alternative vision of teaching and learning that, unlike traditional schooling, would offer opportunities for meaningful voice and political empowerment. In short, PARTY members rejected schooling but embraced liberatory education rooted in the assertion that "people have the power."

Conclusion

In this chapter, I examined weekly PARTY meetings as a space of mutual learning and deepening critical consciousness. This was not pri-

marily due to the formal research activities we carried out but rather to the organic and unstructured critical conversations that occurred there. These conversations included the sharing of personal stories, "current events," and other information learned during the week, and were punctuated by the insights of occasional guest speakers. Through these processes, the youth PARTY members revealed and analyzed their own lived experiences and personal encounters with civic institutions, especially in the education and criminal justice systems. Their encounters with these civic institutions revealed disjunctures between the ideals and realities of US democracy. PARTY meetings offered a space to name these disjunctures and to theorize them, leading the youth to articulate an increasingly systemic critique of social inequalities as well as a collective oppositional political identity. This emergent critical consciousness and identity informed their choice to teach a social justice class at Jackson High and the way they approached their teaching. The three youth who taught the class—D, Suli, and Leila—conceptualized it as a political intervention with explicitly political goals. They discursively connected it to images of social movements and transformational social change, identifying themselves as change agents through their work as social justice educators.

Though not explicitly stated as such, their approach to the class assumes a degree of faith in the power of education as the practice of freedom. They brought passion to this work and incredible optimism about the potential of the class to inspire social change. It is noteworthy that these three young people embraced this belief in education's promise so decisively. All three had personal histories of "failure" in school. They had been rejected, stigmatized, and disempowered by schooling, and yet they had not given up on the belief that education could be meaningful, empowering, and affirming. This apparent "contradiction" will not surprise conscientious educators who have worked with other thoughtful, motivated students at the bottom of the educational hierarchy. But it is worth emphasizing here, because it challenges two widely held assumption about "these kids." First, it challenges the assumption that school failure reflects a failure to value to education. Second, it challenges the assumption that "these kids" lack political interest, knowledge, and analytical skills needed for civic engagement. The actions of all PARTY members, even those who did not eventually teach the social justice class, demonstrate a commitment to their own learning and to that of their peers and future generations. All of them cared deeply about what they saw as the unjust inequalities of the educational system and wanted to change them. They embraced the opportunity for deep, meaningful, self-directed learning that weekly PARTY meetings provided. In all these ways, we see a group of young adults deeply committed to education for its own sake. As well, PARTY members were informed about current events, followed the news with interest, voiced a desire to learn about history and social issues, and demonstrated a real passion about issues of social inequality and justice. Their words and deeds throughout the two-year project suggest a yearning to take action for social change, but they lacked mechanisms for exercising meaningful voice, and they believed (perhaps rightly) that their voices would not be heard.

For D, Leila, and Suli, the desire to engage in some form of political action translated into the choice to design and teach a social justice class at Jackson High. Obviously, this choice was not made in a vacuum. It was made possible by the structure of the PARTY project, which provided both the support and the expectation of taking action, as well as the natural link to Jackson High. When given this chance, these three youth selected an action that reflected a deepening critical consciousness and a belief in the liberatory potential of education. And they stayed with the project—doubling and even tripling their weekly time commitment without any corresponding increase in their weekly stipend. As they approached the first day of teaching at Jackson High, they expressed optimism and excitement about the work and a sincere expectation that the class would make a difference. In the next chapter, I examine the trajectory of PARTY as we moved from theory to practice—and actually started teaching at Jackson High. With this shift, our work moved from an out-of-school PAR project into the "figured world" of the continuation high school, marked by a new set of discourses, roles, rules, and identity categories. The next chapter explores the significance of this shift and the ways in which PARTY members constructed distinct teacher identities within this new figured world. As we will see, the distinction between the ideals of education and the imperatives of schooling became more pronounced, and undermined our ability to implement the liberatory vision of education we had hoped for.

From Theory to Practice: Teacher Identity, Agency, and Reproduction at Jackson High

A week before teaching our first social justice class at Jackson High, I received an email from Ms. Barry, the US government teacher in whose class we would be working. It explained that she was "interested in developing the social/behavioral/academic skills of these kids," and along these lines, she hoped the social justice class would emphasize the teaching of "self-control, self-awareness, self-respect, anger management, etc." She requested that PARTY assign, collect, and evaluate a written assignment every week. She closed by reiterating that we would be "teaching students who have been trained to be phobic around academics and whose value system oftentimes reflects some of the worst aspects of street life." I shared the email with the group at our subsequent PARTY meeting. Suli's response was swift:

Suli: Man, she is dumping on her students! It seems like she wants to give us more work so she can give less work. And she just be dumping on all her students!

Leila: Personally, I kind of feel like she wants us to enforce the oppressive laws that come from school in general. Like trying to change their whole mentality towards learning. We're not there to be like the teacher of everyday, like that's kinda different, like I don't know.

Suli: She wants us to be her puppet. That's an interesting way to look at it, though, right? I'm not a puppet, man!

Leila: Damn.

Suli: I think we should stick to our game plan. What is she fucking talking about? She's trying to mold us into herself. She's trying to mold us into her little robots.

Leila: It kinda seems like she wants to change our whole reason for coming in and teaching these kids into something completely different.

In this scene, Leila and Suli distance themselves from Ms. Barry and the work of schoolteachers. As they prepared to teach their first social justice class at Jackson, Leila insisted, "We're not there to be like the teacher of everyday." Implicit in this "everyday" teacher was a deficit view of Jackson students, suggested in Ms. Barry's email, which Suli had rejected in anger: "She is dumping on her students!" In contrast to the "teacher of everyday," Leila and Suli positioned themselves as a different kind of teacher. They were, in other words, making a claim to teacher identity.

In this chapter, I draw from sociocultural theories of teacher identity (e.g., Battey and Franke 2008; Freedman and Appleman 2008; Olsen 2008) to explore how PARTY members constructed teacher identities in the social justice class and in weekly PARTY meetings in which they reflected on their teaching. As the youth transitioned from researchers in a PAR group to teachers in a real school, they entered into a new figured world (Holland et al. 2001), marked by a new set of rules, roles, expectations for behavior, and opportunities for identity. This figured world of schooling was significant in shaping the trajectory of the PARTY project and the emerging teacher identities of its members. As we negotiated this new terrain, the youth PARTY members and I adopted distinct teacher identities—acting and interacting as particular *kinds of teachers* (Gee 2000),[1] both inside the classroom and through our reflections on classroom practice. This chapter argues that the sociocultural context of Jackson High—and the broader figured world of schooling of which it is a part—made some teacher identities readily available while rendering others more elusive, with significant implications for teacher agency and social justice. It also shows that despite PARTY's goal to implement a liberatory educational intervention, the social justice class largely reproduced dominant practices and discourses of schooling. Before embarking on this discussion, I present a typical day in the social justice class.

The Social Justice Class

D, Suli, and Leila taught the social justice class every Tuesday for one semester as part of Ms. Barry's third-period US government class. The third teaching day was a relatively typical one. When the second bell rang at twelve twenty signaling the beginning of class, there were exactly zero students in the room. As usual, about twenty desks were arranged in a semicircle facing the whiteboard at the front. Windows along one wall faced an interior courtyard at the center of the school, and were open to let the warm breeze circulate into the classroom. Ms. Barry announced, "I'm going to round up the kids" as she walked toward the door and disappeared into the courtyard. Shortly thereafter, students began to trickle into the classroom, one or two at a time, taking seats as they talked with one another in pairs or small groups, often consuming the rest of their lunches from the brief lunch period before. A full ten minutes after the official beginning of class, I motioned to Suli that we should get started. There were twelve students in the room: six boys and six girls.

Suli walked to the front of the class and stood facing the students. He inhaled deeply as if to begin speaking but stopped short, hesitating perhaps because students were still talking among themselves and none showed any sign of noticing his approach to the front of the room. Even Ms. Barry was talking to a student at her desk. When a few moments had passed, Suli inhaled again and this time spoke in a commanding voice that caught most students' attention: "All right, everybody, we're gonna get started." Ms. Barry was still talking to a student. In the rest of the class, a continuous soft buzz of side conversations never completely died down, although most students looked up in Suli's direction. Suli continued to speak: "I'm gonna read you this fact of the day." He gestured to the whiteboard, where a sentence was written across the top: "One in three African American men will serve time in prison during their lifetime." Suli turned back to the students and asked, "Do you think this is true?" Several answers came out at once: "It's higher than that!" said one; "I think it's *two* out of three!" said another; "No, it's two and a *half* out of three!" came the next. Then Frank, a student who often played the role of class clown, called out, "No, it's *three* out of three! 'Cause if they're not in jail now, they've *been* there!"

Suli had planned to engage the class in a discussion of the fact: its root causes; its effects on students' lives, families, and communities; its relation to other social issues and to social structures of power. We had prepared a few discussion questions in our previous meeting, but the actual class discussion focused on other things: "Do you smoke?" "Do you drink?" "Have you been in jail?" students called out to Suli. To each of these questions, Suli offered responses: "If I'm not old enough to buy it, then I'm not old enough to drink it!" he said; and "No, I haven't been to jail." Frank called out to Suli, "Maybe that's because you're light skinned." Another student corrected him: "No, Suli is *mixed.*" The class discussion quickly dissolved into several cross-conversations, with Suli in one corner of the room explaining to Frank and others that although he was mixed race, "to the cops, I'm just as black as you are." Close to five minutes passed as the class relaxed into separate group conversations—some, but not all, of which were loosely related to the issue of criminalization and incarceration. The other PARTY members observed the action, but no attempt was made to restart the class discussion or move on to the next item of the lesson plan.

When it became clear that Suli was not going to resume the whole-class discussion, I signaled to Leila to start the second activity, known as "the news." Leila rose from her seat and assumed Suli's position at the front of the class. She held up a local newspaper and pointed to a story on the front page about an antiloitering law that had just passed in a neighboring city, which civil rights groups had criticized on the grounds that it would increase racial profiling. Immediately, students called out comments: "This is a stupid law!" and "This ain't gonna stop drug dealing!" Leila said the city council would review the law in one year to assess its impact on racial profiling, and encouraged students to register formal complaints with the city for this purpose. "Nobody's gonna make a formal complaint!" called out Frank, adding, "Real talk, tell me *who* is gonna make a formal complaint?" Then he added, as if it just occurred to him, "Hey, why don't we know about this law anyway?" Frank's questions were potentially provocative entry points for a critical discussion of local legislative procedures, available pathways to political voice (and their limits), and information flow. But they never led to any such discussion; instead, the chorus of student comments branched off into simultaneous side conversations, despite Leila's call for students to talk "one at a time."

After the fact of the day and the news discussions, the remainder of class time was dedicated to the main lesson plan—usually an activity, debate, or project carried out in small groups. On this day, we broke students into groups for a discussion of the prison-industrial complex, and each PARTY member led a group. By this time, three additional students had arrived to class, bringing the total attendance for the day to fifteen (there were twenty-eight students on the roll sheet). To anchor the small-group discussions, PARTY used a lesson plan developed by the Prison

Activist Resource Center, an advocacy organization that fights prison expansion. Toward the end of the period, groups were asked to present back about what they had discussed. Each group selected a spokesperson who shared back to the class, and students watched intently as their classmates presented. The small-group discussions and presentations were the one time during this class period in which most students appeared to be engaged in ways I had anticipated and hoped for.

As soon as the last group had presented about their discussion, we directed students to write their reactions to the activity in their journals. No sooner had the announcement of journals been made than a student called out, "We don't have time! Class is already over!" I corrected the student that there were still fifteen minutes remaining in the class, and this was plenty of time to write a thoughtful journal response. Frank stood up from his seat and announced in his loudest possible voice, "Class ends at one thirty-five! It's a new schedule!" The room quickly filled with sound and motion as students rose to their feet, joined their friends in conversation, whipped out makeup and mirrors, or repositioned themselves closer to the classroom door. Suli and D disappeared from the room, which prompted Frank to insist, "If the *teachers* are leaving early, I think *we* should leave early too!" Ms. Barry—the classroom teacher, who had been at her desk the whole class period—called out to students, "This is not chill time. You should be working on your journal assignments." Nobody acknowledged her directive.

As the sound and movement in the classroom escalated, Frank's voice rose noticeably above the rest: "I'm done for the day!" he announced confidently. I approached him and said, "In that case, could you at least lower your voice so that others can write in peace?" He answered me in high volume, "No one is working! Look around!" He was right. Few students were even seated anymore; no journals were open, and certainly no one was writing. A few moments later, Suli was outside the classroom popping his head through the open window and ruffling the plastic blinds. This sent Frank into an uncontrolled laughing fit that propelled him from his seat. He walked in circles around the room, punctuating his laughter with exaggerated, overdramatic body movements. When I (instinctively) asked Frank to quiet down, he replied, "Kick me out so I can leave early! I'm ready to go!" I ignored his request. Somehow, in the midst of all the activity, four students managed to scribble a few sentences into their journals and hand them in. When the bell finally rang at one forty, only eight of the fifteen students were still in the classroom; the others had quietly slipped away in the last fifteen minutes of class—a common phenomenon at Jackson High.

The journals I brought home read as follows:[2]

Journal 1

I think the story we read about the 40 year old man who was a truck driver and was taking a package for his friend and he didn't even know what was in the package and when he got pulled over and it was drugs, he got put in jail for 15 years to life.

I don't think that's a true democracy, he got put in jail for something that wasn't his and he didn't even know about it, he was trying to do something nice.

Journal 2

Story.

The story that I read with my group is about a 40 year old portorico man who was a truck driver.

He live in Bufflo and he was on his way home from new York, and his friend told him to take a pakage with him, turns out it was dope. once the cops caught him he was sentence to 15 to life for having something that he didn't know.

Journal 3

I read the article of "Lionel Tate"

I think that its wrong and not fair to little boy that's only 14 he was just wrestling w/ a little girl that's only 6 he committed the "crime" when he was 10 but mentally he wa 6 the same mind. everybody plays & wrestles at a yong age and wishes they could be a proessional wrestler Im pretty sure he was just playing and didnt mean no harm to the little girl. I don't think his entention was to kill the girl. I don't think that the boy should of got life especially in a penintentury?

Journal 4

I think that it is really mest up what his penalty was. He was twelve but his brain was four years behind. They are basically sending an eight year old to a grown men prison. He didn't know what he was doing so I think they couldv'e at least send him to juvinile hall or some special place.

Interpreting the Typical Day: Identity, Context, and Power

What is striking about this typical day is just how "typical" it really is—in the sense that it resembles countless other typical days in countless other typical classrooms, reproducing many of the dominant (and problematic) practices, discourses, and rituals of schooling. Despite PARTY's goal of implementing an alternative vision of education, the social justice class was in fact structured and carried out much like "typical" classes at Jackson and many other schools, from the "fact of the day" warm-up activity to the obligatory small-group lesson and the required writing assignment (to be collected and evaluated by the teachers for a grade). The basic structure, routine, and message of schooling stayed the same. Only the messengers had changed.

The typical day described above suggests how the sociocultural context of Jackson High shaped the trajectory of the social justice class and the emerging teacher identities of PARTY members. Existing school and classroom norms, which preceded PARTY's entry on the scene, constrained possibilities for identity and agency of all participants: students, PARTY members, Ms. Barry, and me. Power relations within the classroom, PARTY group, and school formed overlapping points of tension that set the stage for classroom conflict. As we saw, students' participation in organized class activities and discussions could not be taken for granted; it had to be negotiated and cajoled at every moment. When cooperation was achieved, it was temporary and fragile, ready to disintegrate at any moment. When it disintegrated, widespread noncompliance and a feeling of disorder prevailed. The room erupted into exhilarating noise, movement, and play. As with other classes at Jackson High, students routinely arrived late and left early, rendering the first and last fifteen minutes of every class session "chill time." The eighty-minute class period was thus reduced to forty-five or fifty minutes of instructional time, and those remaining minutes were frequently interrupted by students' highly skilled and well-executed displays of "active not-learning" (Kohl 1995), or "the conscious effort of obviously intelligent students to expend their time and energy in the classroom actively distancing themselves from schoolwork" (Ferguson 2001, 99).

Perhaps the most notable example of active not-learning occurred when the journal assignment was given. Every week without fail, the announcement of journals spurred an identical student reaction: collective, determined noncompliance, which seemed both spontaneous and expertly coordinated. Students' refusal to complete this assignment was tacitly supported by PARTY members, who failed to enforce it and, as in the typical day above, sometimes left the classroom altogether. Although I had taught at Jackson and experienced this type of reaction to many assignments, I still found myself bewildered by the emphatic nature of student resistance to the journal, which seemed out of proportion to the demands of the assignment itself. I thought to myself, "It is a free-writing assignment in which they can write *anything* they want, and for which they receive full credit simply for writing a paragraph, regardless of the quality of their response. No doubt they expend more energy *avoiding* the journal than they would spend writing something—anything—to receive credit for the assignment."

My reaction, which I held for so long that I published it in those terms (Nygreen 2010), reflects my own bias as a classroom teacher who is fluent in school-based academic literacies. It also reveals my inability to interrogate the perspectives of students, even when D and Suli worked hard to expose them to me. I failed to consider how assignments such as the journal were not only meaningless and boring, but could also, for some students, be a source of injury and pain—for they would inevitably render their (lack of) academic literacy skills visible and problematic. In my frustration, it was difficult to understand why students might find it easier to spend fifteen minutes avoiding the work than to spend five minutes getting it done. But why? In my own life, I certainly found it easier to spend hours surfing the Internet for useless trivia than to spend fifteen minutes on a treadmill. Blinded by my own perspective and bias, I cast the students as well as D and Suli in a deficit frame and wondered silently, "Why won't they work with me?"[3]

At our next PARTY meeting, I brought up the events that had occurred in the last fifteen minutes of class.

Kysa: I talked to Ms. Barry about the whole thing that happened with the journal on Tuesday, so I just want to talk about it.

D: [*innocently*] What happened with the journal?

Kysa: Well. What happened was that there was fifteen more minutes left of class, and I said, "Let's do journal," and [*hesitating*] no one wanted to do it, and [*hesitating*] Suli and D left the room a couple times, and, um [*hesitating*], I just felt like that delegitimized, you know I felt like, um, by us, as a group, not taking the journal assignment seriously, it gave students permission to not take it seriously either. And so, you know, and at one point I heard students, they were trying to leave early, right? And Frank yelled out, "Well, if the *teachers* are leaving early, *we* can leave early too!" and that's when I noticed that you guys were out of the room. And, um, so it made them think, like, "Oh, this, we don't really have to do this, 'cause the teachers aren't even gonna be around." And if the teachers aren't even making it look like it's important, then they're especially not gonna want to do it.

Leila jumped in immediately to justify D and Suli's exit from the classroom:

Leila: But the thing is, after they said that, someone [else] was, like, "The teachers already did their job, blah-blah-blah." And so I think they're just kinda using that as an excuse, and they don't necessarily think, because they . . . I think we sort of do have like a . . . I think we should stay in the class, but I don't think it was that bad that they left. And, like, it's kinda like, well this is your job now. It's like, yeah, we did finish our job. [. . .] I kind of felt like maybe I should have been, like, encouraging them more? [. . .] But I felt like I didn't want to pressure them too much, because it's kinda like, if they're fixed on not doing it, they're not gonna do it.

Here, Leila suggests that enforcing the journal is not part of PARTY's job: once it has been assigned, PARTY's work is over ("We *did* finish our job"). Although she tried to find a middle ground—"I think we *should* stay in the class"—she was careful to place the blame on students, not PARTY, if they failed to complete the assignment. She denied that PARTY had a responsibility to compel, or even to actively entice, students into completing the written work, claiming that if they are "fixed on not doing it, they're not gonna do it." In this way, Leila distanced herself and the group from those aspects of teaching that involved persuasion or a perceived need of coercion. She wanted to lead engaging lessons and discussions, but "to pressure" students to do a writing assignment against their will was not what she signed up for.

Indeed, PARTY members often implied that the exercise of "pressure" in the classroom too closely resembled the coercive work of schoolteachers, not the liberating work of educators. All PARTY members worked to distance themselves from this aspect of teaching. Following Leila, Suli justified his actions in leaving the classroom during the journal assignment:

Suli: See, in my opinion, for me personally, I don't feel like we should necessarily even be forcing them to *do* the journal. That's just my opinion. I wasn't, I mean, [to Kysa] I understand where *you're* coming from where it's, like, you want to see if they're getting something out of the class on a day-to-day basis, so it's cool for you to give the journal. [. . .] I don't like the journal. I never did.

Kysa: So, why . . . explain more why you don't like it.

Suli: I just don't think, personally I just don't think anybody wants to do it. And that's before we actually went in there and assigned it, though. I mean I didn't feel like they would want to do it anyway. It's like, it basically just makes it kinda like, after they enjoy, like, I guess, say enjoy the class, last fifteen, twenty minutes, then it's just like "Aww, they givin' us *work*." 'Cause I know if I went there, I wouldn't do the journal.

Leila: I completely see what you're saying—

Suli: [*resolutely*] Right or wrong. Right or wrong. I wouldn't do the journal.

Suli echoes Leila's suggestion that the journal requires a kind of co-ercion—"forcing" students to do an assignment against their will. Even though all PARTY members agreed to the journal when Ms. Barry requested we assign, collect, and grade a written assignment each week, Suli now placed responsibility for the journal on me ("I understand where *you're* coming from"), implying that I alone had demanded it. The fact that Ms. Barry had requested a weekly writing assignment, that I had supported it, and PARTY had consented to it revealed the disproportionate power that the "real" classroom teachers exercised in shaping this supposedly "youth-led" class. I had interpreted the youth's consent to the journal as approval, as if we had developed the idea ourselves through a process of equitable dialogue and consensus. In truth, a superficial consensus had been reached. The youth had not protested, but neither did they take ownership of the decision.

When defending his position on the journal, Suli actively identified himself with the students who refused to write it and claimed with pride, "I wouldn't do the journal. Right or wrong. Right or wrong. I wouldn't do the journal." This explicit identification and solidarity with students was a strategy that both Suli and D employed to distance themselves from the role of teacher. Both young men worked hard to disidentify with teachers while identifying with students and romanticizing their own "disruptive-student" histories and identities. After our very first day in the classroom, Suli expressed pride that some of the "cool guys" in the class had participated in the discussion, as this gave symbolic permission for others to participate as well. As Suli and D recalled the comments of these "cool guys" in our subsequent meeting, they were overcome with laugher.

Suli: I'm telling you, it's like they gotta get the approval of the cool guy. They gotta get the approval of the gangster to speak up in class. If he doesn't learn, nobody learns. There's a couple of 'em [*cool guys*].

D: Jabari's cool.

Suli: No, it was Tommy, though, 'cause he was *on* one![4] [*mimicking Tommy's comments in class*:] "Whatever happens happens, man! Man, I ain't thinkin' 'bout this stuff. But in a couple years I might be thinkin' about it." [*resuming his own voice*:] Man, you too hard, blood!

D: That *is* hard! [*laughing*]

Suli: Man, he be like, [*mimicking*:] "Man, I'll be out there on the picket line, just give me, like, thirty blunts!" [*laughter from both*] Man, he was *on* one!

D: [*through laughter*] Yeah, he was on one!

Suli: Yeah, he was! [*uncontrolled laughter*]

D: [*through laughter still*] He had me rolling!

It was with a clear sense of approval that D and Suli replayed Tommy's comments in class, identifying both Tommy and Jabari as "cool guys," "gangsters," and "hard." The behaviors exhibited by Tommy and Jabari in class that day were, by my estimation, anything but "professional" as previously defined by PARTY members (chapter 2): they called out comments that were off topic and random; made obvious references to illicit activities such as smoking thirty blunts (marijuana) on a picket line; and engaged in a playful side conversation, replete with inside jokes and underhanded insults of the teachers, loudly enough to disturb the class discussion and derail the lesson plan. Despite all this, D and Suli recounted the class fondly while I tried to raise the issue of classroom authority.

Suli: The hardest part is not laughing along with them!

D: [*still laughing*] They *is* hard, though!

Suli: [*collecting himself*] It's not good to laugh, though. You gotta kinda keep that to yourself.

Kysa: What did it feel like, you guys, being in that teacher position?

Suli: Remind me of myself. Like, Jabari and Tommy, they sit next to each other. That remind me of, like, when I had Ms. Peabody's class, I used to sit next to D, and [*starting to laugh*] we used to be *on* one! But it used to be funny.

D: [*through laughter*] That is true, though, we used to be on one! Ms. Peabody, though . . . [*trails off to laughter*]

Suli: [*through laughter*] With her haircut, remember . . . ? [*trails off to laughter*] And the shirt, with the little pocket? [*both laughing*]

Once Ms. Peabody's class had been mentioned, D and Suli embarked on a new chain of memories, recounting and reliving their own disruptive-student practices. Several minutes of the meeting passed as D and Suli replayed memories of getting in trouble in Ms. Peabody's class.

D: She didn't like me.

Suli: She didn't like me at all. She used to kick me out every day.

D: Every single day.

It became clear that D and Suli could identify with the "cool guys" in the PARTY class since they too had been "cool guys" in their own time at Jackson. Their identification with the young men who had enacted the most visible disruptive-student identities in the class made it difficult for D and Suli to simultaneously identify as teachers. For cool guys were, almost by definition, against and opposed to teachers, while teachers were against and opposed to cool guys.

Like all figured worlds, the figured world of schooling contains a recognizable cast of characters and relations among them. This world is populated by teachers, counselors, principals, and students—including good students, bad students, disruptive students, class clowns, and so forth. These roles constitute the range of readily available identities to assume in the world of schooling. In the specific figured world of Jackson High, cool guys and teachers were mutually exclusive and oppositional categories. This created a difficult situation for PARTY members (including myself) because we had to negotiate conflicting identities of student/teacher, youth/adult, ally/enemy in a context marked by conflict and a perceived need for coercion. As we moved from the informal setting of PARTY into the figured world of schooling, we all assumed new roles—both because we chose them and because we were assigned them by others. Identity always involves recognition work (Gee 2000): we may act and interact as a particular kind of person, but we must also get recognized by others as that particular "kind." As others act and interact with *us* in particular ways, they affirm some aspects of our identity while deterring others. Identities are fashioned out of this constant dialectic between our own practices and those of other social actors in response to us (Tatum 2003). At Jackson High, I was immediately recognized as the "teacher" in charge of supervising PARTY youth, while D and Suli were quickly recognized as "cool guys." These patterns of recognition from other social actors at Jackson did not *determine* our teacher identities or erase our capacity for agency, but they made some identities more readily available and easily accessible than others, thereby placing considerable constraints on agency.

Kinds of Teachers

Reflecting his allegiance to "cool guys," Suli often joined with students in practices that many teachers would code as disruptive. In one class, his small group dissolved into chaos as he and a student ran around the room yelling at the top of their lungs. According to Suli, the student, Shannel, had been passing notes to her friend during the group activity. Suli asked her for the note, but she refused to hand it over. He snatched it from her hand, at which she released a horror-movie-quality scream and tried to snatch it back. Suli quickly stood from his seat and ran away, as Shannel chased after him in pursuit of the note. The two of them ran laps around the classroom for almost a minute before Ms. Barry and I intervened. At our next meeting, Leila brought it up:

Leila: [*to Suli*] You shouldn't, um, perpetuate Shannel's, um, flirtation.

Suli: Oh, me? That was my fault.

Leila: Yeah. No, no, it's cool, it was cool. I know you were getting the letter from her.

After replaying what had happened in the class, Suli went on to explain:

Suli: She [Shannel] was flirting.

Leila: Anyone that she can, like, mess around with, she will. I don't know, I noticed that.

Suli: I mean, 'cause technically I'm not a teacher, you feel. I can't totally reprimand her. It's kinda like, "Who are you?"

Leila: No, no, it's totally cool, you should hella,[5] like, I just think that, specifically her, like, having her chase you around the room was kinda like, you should just put it in your pocket and be like "You know it's over, I'll give it to you after class." I don't know, that might be teacher-like.

Kysa: That's a good question. Maybe we should be more teacher-like in times like this?

D: I say we shouldn't be teacher-like.

Leila: We shouldn't be teacher-like, but then we shouldn't, like, perpetuate their distracting other groups, you know, messing around.

Suli: Yeah, that was my bad. I didn't mean to distract you.

D: You didn't distract me, though! I found it kinda funny.

Leila: No, I thought it was funny, I thought it was funny. But then everyone, like, it took like five minutes for my group to get back in order. They were all just hella staring at her. I was like "C'mon, you guys!"

Here, Leila insists they should not act teacher-like, but strives to find a middle ground between being teacher-like and enabling "messing around" or "distracting other groups." Leila seems to long for a classroom environment that is orderly enough to enable the serious engagement with content she desires. But even as she seeks this middle ground, she works hard not to appear too committed, reassuring D that "I thought it was funny, I thought it was funny." In contrast, D refuses to characterize the chase as problematic and insists it was funny rather than distracting. Here again, he asserts his "cool guy" identity. Suli attempts to present himself in the reasonable middle by apologizing about the chase ("That was my bad. I didn't mean to distract you"), but his actions in the classroom consistently belied his true allegiance with "cool guys" and against teachers.

Leila occupied a unique position in the PARTY group. Unlike D and Suli, she could not rely on a sense of identification with Jackson students. Although she had been tracked into Jackson during the school's attempt to recruit white students (chapter 1), Leila had transferred out during her sophomore year to the more academically rigorous independent studies program, and aspired to attend a four-year college. Rather than common experience, Leila found social distance between herself and Jackson students, and this was exacerbated by her raced-classed-gendered self as a white woman performing a middle-class (upwardly mobile) student identity (Bettie 2003). While D and Suli reminisced fondly about their days at Jackson, when they were "cool guys" having fun at teachers' expense, Leila's memories were distinctly negative: "I was frustrated with Jackson, and, like, going there I just was really, like, let down. Just 'cause the environment's really negative and no one really cares and no one's really, like, aware of stuff. And the school, in general, like, it's really, like, it didn't challenge me at all, like, the work. And so I was frustrated with that." At another meeting she recalled, "I really hated that school. I kind of felt really demotivated and stuff. [. . .] That whole environment and stuff just really brings you down."

Despite her negative feelings about Jackson, Leila tackled the social justice class like a determined student eager to succeed. She came armed with statistics, background research, and rehearsed talking points about the topics at the center of the day's lesson plan. She prepared vigorously for each class, researching supplementary information on the Internet and often bringing her own handouts to distribute. For one class, she made twenty photocopies of a newspaper article and used a purple highlighter to mark key sentences on each copy. She worked incredibly hard, but often expressed a sense of failure and a lack of efficacy as an educator, employing self-deprecating language as she narrated her experiences of teaching. A typical report back from her small-group activity was like this one:

Leila: It was good, but me personally, I don't know, I think that I sucked.

Kysa: Why do you think that?

Suli: Something went bad in your group?

Leila: No, no, no, the group was good, but like I said, I was kinda really having to, like, I felt like, certain parts, like, it was quiet for like two seconds and I had to think of something to, like, trigger the conversation or whatever. And so I kinda felt like maybe they were thinking, like, "She doesn't really know what she's doing." Or, like, I don't know. And then, like, I was kinda flipping up when I was presenting, and they weren't really responding to me, like, when I was, like, you know about . . . [*trails off*] It's like, you [*to Suli*] kinda had to step in with the social issues song 'cause, like, they weren't really responding to me at all.

Kysa: Uh-huh. Like, which part did you feel like they weren't responding?

Leila: I don't know. I was just, like, I don't know. Maybe it's 'cause they can tell that I'm not that confident when I'm, like, presenting things? I don't know, 'cause, like, you [*to Suli*] got up on the board and you were like [*authoritatively*], "OK, what is a social issue? Blah-blah-blah," and they started, like, actually responding. But, like, for a while I was just kinda like, "Anyone?" and no one was saying anything. So I just felt really lost.

Leila expressed similarly harsh self-criticisms and lack of confidence as a teacher in almost every weekly PARTY meeting. Though she put her heart and soul into preparation for the class and cared deeply about the topics we were addressing, she often felt that students did not "respond" to her as they did to Suli and D. She felt unable to engage them in the course material at a deep enough level. "I want them to be able to explain it [course content] more," she said of students. "I want them to be able to teach other kids. [. . .] I think they actually *do* understand it on some level, but they can't articulate it to other students necessarily."

Leila's experience resonates with that of many novice white teachers in high-poverty urban schools (Cochran-Smith and Zeichner 2005; Hollins and Guzman 2005; Saffold and Longwell-Grice 2008). She was motivated by a strong helping instinct and genuine political commitment, but not a deeper sense of identification or solidarity with students. Although she desperately wanted to help and "empower" Jackson students, she had difficulty relating to them or understanding them on their own terms. When her sincere efforts to teach went unappreciated, she expressed a loss of confidence and even signs of burnout. In her frustration, she alternated between blaming herself ("I think that I suck") and blaming the students by activating deficit frames. In one meeting she said of students, "I don't know, it's just disrespectful. People at that age, I really think that they should be, you know, at that level or something, where they should be, like, mature and respectful with other people, and value their education." At another meeting she said of students, "They're, like, totally disrespectful. It's, like, how do you expect to survive in the world when you're sitting there goofing off when we're talking about something really important?"

As the semester wore on, Leila increasingly distanced herself from Jackson students and actively identified with me and Ms. Barry. In an interview halfway through the semester, Leila explained:

Leila: I'm just not in the same mind-set as the students who go to that school. I'm not saying that it's better, but they have a different mind-set. They don't think the same way as me. There's different cultures, and I can relate to you [*to Kysa*] a lot because we're aiming for the same kind of stuff and we act in the same kind of way. And Ms. Barry too, the kids don't like her, but don't they see she is trying to help? Making a conscious effort to empower you?

For my part, I found myself empathizing with Leila on many occasions. My past experiences as a high school student, doctoral student, and Jackson teacher formed part of the filter through which I made sense of classroom dynamics. These experiences afforded me a sense of entitlement in the figured world of schooling and filled me with an inflated sense of my own expertise, even as I skillfully employed the progressive language of egalitarianism. I could relate to Leila's sense of frustration with the class, and I privately shared her deficit view of students, sometimes applying this view to Suli and D. These alliances and cleavages within the group became especially visible in our discussions of student behavior and achievement. The next two sections address two examples of this: our interpretation of Emily and our assignment of final grades.

Interpreting Emily

When Emily transferred to Jackson in the middle of the semester, she became the only white student in the social justice class. During class, I often noticed Emily rolling her eyes, sulking, and shaking her head in frustration. She sat as far from other students as possible and killed the time by drawing comics and reading novels. (In one class, I noticed she was reading *A Clockwork Orange*.) Emily quickly became a topic of conversation in PARTY: D and Suli categorized her as disrespectful, while Leila defended and justified her behavior, often with my support.

Leila: Actually, like, *what* we're teaching, she [Emily] actually knows a good amount about it. And she'll comment on it too. And then the other kids are not understanding, and I explain it and she gets all frustrated—

Suli: A lot of them *do* [understand], though—

Leila: No, like, they take it *in* well, but I don't think . . . I think they understand the main things, but they're, like, actually learning. And [Emily]'s just kinda like "Oh yeah." And then she kind of gets this attitude because the kids don't get it or something.

Here, Leila describes Emily as intelligent and well informed, someone who "actually knows a good amount" about the content of the social justice class, while suggesting that other Jackson students lack this understanding. When Suli challenges her deficit framing of the other students, she partially takes it back by conceding that other students understand "the main things" but they are still learning in the class, while Emily already knows everything being covered. In this way, Leila depicts Emily as more advanced than the others.

In another meeting, Suli noted that Emily didn't participate in class. Again, Leila rushed to her defense, this time with my help:

Suli: She [Emily] don't participate either.

Leila: The thing is, I feel like she has a shitload to say but she doesn't participate 'cause she actually, unfortunately, I don't think she feels like the other students are worth her, like, you know. . . .

Kysa: She does participate in small groups—

Suli: That's a bad attitude, though.

Kysa: She doesn't participate in the *whole* class [discussion], I think, because maybe she's intimidated, or she's—

D: She don't even pay attention with the whole class, man.

Kysa: [*conceding*] She reads, huh.

Suli: Yeah! Just like today during the presentations, I came over there and was, like, "Man, we're gonna start. Can you just show at least a little bit of respect? Put the book away." And she put it away for a second, right, and then we started, and then, you know, five minutes later she's back in the book!

Leila: Uh-huh. But I know how that is, 'cause that's how I was at Jackson, though. I would just read books.

Suli: I mean if you don't respect your classmates, you feel, enough to even listen to what they got to say, why are they gonna respect you?

D: She think she's just too good for everybody.

Suli's description of his exchange with Emily over a book is striking for how closely it resembles the language and tone of a classroom teacher describing a perpetually difficult student. The fact that Emily complied with Suli's directive to put the book down only to start reading again within minutes is also typical of "disruptive-student" behavior as I have experienced and observed in my own teaching and research. The antagonistic relations between teacher and student were reproduced; the only differences were the players and the offending behavior of the student.

For Suli, Emily's choice to read a book while other students were giving class presentations was interpreted as willful defiance. For Leila, it was understandable. Leila noted that she also used to read in her classes. She could relate to Emily's sense of alienation from the classroom and her need to escape its stifling environment by losing herself in a book, or at least hiding her face there. At the time, I shared Leila's perspective and interpreted Suli's position as a double standard, writing the following in an analytical memo:

> Suli defines Emily's reading as disruptive and disrespectful, but has no problem with other students who carried on loud and distracting side conversations during the student presentations. To say this reflects the application of a double standard would be a gross understatement, as Suli (and D) regularly justified other student behavior that could arguably be coded as disruptive (e.g., talking during presentations, cracking jokes, running around the classroom, throwing wads of paper across the room during class). They routinely denied my claims that such behavior was disruptive by justifying it and say-

ing it was "funny" or that "at least they were into the conversation." To code Emily's reading of a book as disrespectful is beyond any rational logical standard that I can see.

While I immediately identified Suli's perspective as a double standard, it took years of analyzing transcripts to see my own perspective in the same light. But if Suli's selective definition of disrespectful behavior was "beyond any rational logical standard," as I had written, then so too was my own. For just as with other disengagement strategies, reading is a way to make a monotonous and uninspiring class pass by faster. It also displays clear disengagement from official class activities. Instead of asking myself why the social justice class was so monotonous and uninspiring—indeed, so much so that I empathized with Emily's choice to disengage—I simply coded her disengagement as acceptable.

In our roles as teachers, all PARTY members made regular choices about which students and behaviors to label disrespectful or disruptive, and which to ignore or encourage. For all of us, the ability to empathize and identify with a student appeared to lead to a more permissive stance: We ignored or justified displays of active not-learning when we could understand the logic of the behavior and felt that we too would have behaved the same way. When we experienced empathy and understanding, we rationalized displays of active not-learning as reasonable responses to the unreasonable circumstances of the classroom. When empathy and understanding were lacking, we interpreted these displays as willful and punishable acts of noncompliance (Ferguson 2001).[6]

These patterns resonate with a wealth of research literature on disciplinary and assessment practices in the classroom. Much research has demonstrated disparities in punishment practices, according to which certain students of color—in particular, African American boys—are punished more frequently and more severely than other students, even for comparable behaviors exhibited in the classroom (Ferguson 2001; Lopez 2002; Monroe 2006; Noguera 2003). Scholars have shown that teachers tend to interpret the noncompliance of African American boys as more hostile and threatening than noncompliance by other kinds of kids (Ferguson 2001; Lopez 2002). Others have shown that common disengagement strategies of girls (such as applying makeup, looking at photo albums, braiding hair, reading) are more likely to be quietly condoned or ignored by teachers than the disengagement strategies of boys, which tend to be more boisterous and loud (Bettie 2003; Kelly 1993a; Lopez 2002; Sadker and Sadker 1995). Others have documented how teachers often interpret students' body language, gestures, dialect use, and "attitude" as signs of their inherent level of intelligence and deservedness of school rewards (Ferguson 2001; P. Gilmore 1985; Delpit 2002; Delpit and Dowdy 2002). In examining how teachers use "attitude" to make academic assessments, both Ferguson (2001) and Perry Gilmore (1985) argue that interpretations of bad and defiant attitudes are powerfully shaped by the racial meanings attached to particular forms of speech and body language.

If we consider the research findings above in light of the fact that white women constitute the vast majority of the teaching force (Cochran-Smith and Zeichner 2005), then PARTY's labeling practices are consistent with broader patterns. These patterns suggest that our own cultural frameworks, past experiences, and identities are intertwined with how we interpret the behavior of students and where we place them on a continuum of deserving/undeserving of rewards or punishments. Our raced, classed, and gendered selves do not *determine* the meanings we attach to student behavior, but they shape our own past experiences and identities, thereby contributing (perhaps unconsciously) to our ability to empathize with students who look like, and remind us of, ourselves. In PARTY, these dynamics contributed to the reproductive outcomes of the social justice class. But perhaps no moment in PARTY captures the ironies of social reproduction as poignantly as the assignment of final grades, discussed below.

Final Grades

Just one week before the last day of school, Ms. Barry asked the PARTY group to give a grade to each student in the class. We had not previously discussed giving grades but did not question Ms. Barry's request. Instead, in a two-hour meeting that followed immediately after our last class at Jackson High, the youth PARTY members and I read through the class roster, discussing each student and assigning him or her a grade. There were two notable outcomes of this conversation. First, it reproduced the tendency to emphasize the form over the content of learning, rewarding students for going through the motions of schooling rather than engaging deeply with course material. Second, it produced a hierarchy of achievement that included students who failed and others who succeeded.

"Knock It Out"

D: I gotta give Jamar an A, man. I don't know. He was pimping the situation.

Kysa: What?

D: He was pimping the situation, you feel me?

Kysa: What does that mean?

D: It just means he was doing what he had to do, you feel me? On top of the game. If he had to talk, he would talk. And if he actually, he didn't bite his tongue, put it like that. He remind me of myself. If he had an opinion about something, he'll give it to you. And if he need to come to this class to graduate, and do this project to graduate, he's gonna do it. So, I say A.

Kysa: Do you think it matters that he came, usually, like, almost every single day, like, fifteen minutes late?

D: [*resolutely*] It has no . . . It does not matter. It does not matter at all. You feel me, 'cause I used to the do the same thing. As long as you come to your group and knock it out.

D: Jamar was a tall and slim African American male, a senior, and a popular "cool guy" with a boyishly handsome face. According to my field notes, Jamar had a perfect attendance record in the social justice class, had arrived between ten and twenty minutes late to each class, and had completed a total of one journal assignment during the semester (which was two sentences in length). In class, Jamar participated in group discussions, often contributing comments that were humorous and playful in nature. Above, D notes that Jamar "remind[s] me of myself," suggesting that his ability to identify with Jamar may have contributed to his positive evaluation of Jamar's performance. But he also emphasizes a particular quality of Jamar's that he codes as valuable: his ability to "knock it out," or do the minimum amount of work required to pass the class and graduate from high school. D elaborated on this point further in an interview held one week later.

D: Jamar was just trying to knock shit out the box. By all means necessary. Coming to school just about every single day, but still having the same life, you feel me, still doing the same thing. Like all the aspects of coming to class. He used to come to class late. He used to go take his little smoke break, but *still* came back to school. He used to knock out the work. And that's it, you feel me, that's *it*. You know, after school he's gone. Shit, before school he ain't there. You know, but he *come* for first period, or second period, whenever they start. And just come every period, maybe ten minutes late, in every class. But he'll come. And he never really, truly, truly clown around like that, you feel me? He knocked that work out, voiced his opinion in our class. [. . .]

D: So I say he remind me of myself 'cause I was on the same page senior year. By all means necessary. I take whatever class it took, you feel me, knock that work out, you feel me, and leave. Period. I used to take my little smoke break at the store, you feel, but I still used to show up, five, ten minutes late. And whatever, it's nothing. [Jamar] did, he was open to learn new stuff. He was cool. He was cool.

Once again, D notes that Jamar reminds him of himself and that he likes Jamar. But he especially admires Jamar's ability to "knock shit out the box" in order to graduate "by all means necessary." Jamar's grade of A was justified precisely on the grounds that he had done the minimum amount of work needed to get a passing grade and graduate. That he did so without sacrificing his identity as a cool guy, including his regular smoke breaks, was perhaps his greatest accomplishment of all.

The concept of "knocking it out," or doing the minimum amount of work necessary to pass, is a rational response to the structure of schooling and the mobility paradigm that has come to dominate it. This paradigm, in fact, may encourage students to find ways of doing the minimum amount of work for the desired grade, since getting ahead of others is framed as the most important goal of education (Pope 2003; Demerath 2009; Labaree 1997). Many scholars have demonstrated the pervasiveness of such behavior at the highest levels of the achievement hierarchy, where cheating, plagiarizing, bargaining for extra credit or grade changes, and other questionable practices are a routine part of pursuing high grades for personal advancement (Pope 2003; Demerath 2009; Callahan 2004). Denise Pope (2003) refers to these behaviors as "doing school," or "going through the correct motions" of schooling but without "learning and engaging with the curriculum" (4). "Knocking it out" and "doing school" place emphasis on the *form* of education (grades, credits, diplomas) rather than its *content* (substantive learning and engagement with ideas) (Labaree 1997).

For students at the higher end of the achievement hierarchy, "doing school" may include learning some of the course material, even if much of it is forgotten immediately after the test (Labaree 1997; Pope 2003). At the lower end of the achievement hierarchy, on the other hand, learning is significantly less relevant. For non-college-bound students, having a high school diploma is clearly favorable in the job market compared with not having one. But employers of work-bound high school graduates rarely examine students' high school transcripts or consider the learning done in high school classes when making hiring decisions (Rosenbaum 2001; Royster 2001). At Jackson, then, it really *is* the diploma that counts and not the learning it represents. Work-bound students have a strong incentive to do as little as possible to squeeze out a grade of D—or as Kelly (1993a) describes it, to minimize unpaid labor while receiving the same paycheck of the diploma (172)—and to have some fun in the meantime. Jackson students had by and large perfected this skill to an impressive degree.

This emphasis on the instrumental (rather than civic, social, or intrinsic) purposes of education has been labeled *credentialism* (Labaree 1997). There is nothing new about credentialism, of course, but many scholars have argued that it is growing more pervasive as the competition to secure individual advantage grows more intense (ibid.; Demerath 2009). Demerath (ibid.) suggests the increasingly fierce competition for individual advantage may be attributable to factors associated with neoliberalism, such as middle-class fears of downward mobility and a renewed cultural emphasis on competitive individualism. In the new postindustrial economy (discussed further in chapter 5), middle-income jobs are diminishing and income is being concentrated at the top and bottom of the occupational hierarchy. These changes create fewer "winners," more "losers," and a longer distance to fall for those in the middle. As long as schooling is tied to labor market outcomes, these conditions increase the tendency toward credentialism and intensified competition for educational advantage. Arguably, students at the bottom of the achievement hierarchy are less affected by this intensified credentialism because they, for the most part, have always opted out of the rigged competition of schooling (Labaree 1997; Kelly 1993a; MacLeod 2008). But as practices such as "doing school" and "knocking it out" become increasingly naturalized in the broader culture, it simply becomes harder and harder to imagine how meaningful forms of engagement, commitment, learning, and discovery might occur at all inside an official school classroom. Yearning for this type of educational experience may even

appear quaint. In PARTY, this disjuncture between the ideals of education and the imperatives of schooling became evident.

(Re)Constructing Failure

Just as PARTY members described students we liked as deserving of
good grades, we did not hesitate to label others as undeserving and assign
them low grades. In making these determinations, our process mirrored
the interview sequence that had initiated the PARTY project (chapter 2).
As with the interviews, in which "being professional" emerged as the
primary qualification for the job in PARTY, the grading conversation
focused almost exclusively on students' behavior and "attitude" rather
than the content of their work or the quality of their learning. In all but
one case, failing grades were justified on the basis of a "bad attitude." Of
a girl named Akiliah, Suli remarked, "Ah, man, she gotta get a F, man,
I'm sorry! I just ain't feeling her attitude. 'Cause she got that same type
of negative attitude. She don't contribute nothing." When suggesting an
F for a student named Maya, D added, "I never did like Maya's attitude."
Of a boy named Jonny, Suli said, "Jonny got an F. And if it was up to me,
I'd give him an *extra* F *minus*." D concurred: "Jonny, man, I don't like
his attitude, so I'm the wrong person to ask about him. 'Cause I give that
nigga a F. That's some bullshit. I had to tell that nigga today, 'Man, like,
what you doin'?' He was, like, 'Shit.' Well that's how your grade gonna
look, then, you feel me? Like shit!"

The imperative to rank students into a hierarchy of achievement remained implicit throughout the two-hour grading conversation. We determined fine gradations of deservedness and undeservedness by comparing students against one another: "I would think that you would have
a problem with [giving Danyelle a B], 'cause you just were talking about
Jamar and *his* attendance, and being late. But, see, at least Jamar came
every day. She [Danyelle] didn't come every day," noted Suli. And D:
"But she did more than Jamar. [. . .] I say she did more than Jamar 'cause
she did all that unnecessary shit. She made up journals. She did her journals every week." It is noteworthy that D describes the journal assignment here as "unnecessary shit" but still wants to reward Danyelle for
having done it every week. In this way, he simultaneously trivializes the
assignment and reifies its instrumental value—exemplifying the practice
of "doing school." Moreover, by comparing Jamar and Danyelle to each

other, Suli and D determined "better" and "worse" performances and produced a ranked hierarchy of achievement within the class.

At one point, D seemed to recognize this relationship between grading and gatekeeping with some discomfort, noting, "I wouldn't give nobody no grade that's gonna fuck up them graduating. Period. Seriously. That's not what *I'm* here for. That's defeating my whole point." With this assertion, he positioned himself as refusing to participate in gatekeeping. He would not contribute to denying any of his peers a high school diploma. And yet, in the very next sentence, Suli brought up Jonny—who was previously assigned a grade of F (or "*extra* F *minus*," in Suli's words)—and D quickly reaffirmed the fairness of Jonny's failing grade even if it prevented him from graduating.

D: Jonny fucked up!

Suli: That's on *him*, though.

D: That's on him. Totally.

Despite D's previous resistance to individual assessment and gatekeeping, he quickly changed course in this instance, interpreting Jonny's failure as the result of individual choices rather than unfair circumstances. Once again, the youth simultaneously resisted and deployed dominant discourses of failure—sometimes interpreting it through an individualistic lens of agency and choice, and other times through a structural lens of unreasonable or unfair circumstances.

The above examples illustrate that, as with the student interviews discussed in chapter 2, PARTY members easily adopted dominant, reproductive discourses when placed in the unfamiliar position of gatekeeper. Opportunities for agency were indeed present: we might have rejected Ms. Barry's request for final grades; explored the implications of her request or the impacts of individualized assessment on the practice of liberatory education; redefined the meaning and purpose of grades; or at least critically reflected on these issues as a group. But just as in the interview debriefing session, the grading conversation was ultimately reproductive. Like much of the grading done in schools everywhere, our process emphasized the form over the content of education, privileged "attitude" over other evidence of learning, and sorted students into a hierarchy of achievement.

The practice of assessing individual student achievement is an essential and valued component of American schooling (Tyack and Cuban 1997); it is also the linchpin of what Varenne and McDermott (1999) call "the success/failure system" (see also McDermott 1997; Varenne,

Goldman, and McDermott 1997). Even when done with the best of intentions—such as to inform and improve teaching practice, or remediate deficiencies in students' understanding—the practice of individualized assessment colludes with the larger project of ranking, sorting, and identifying students as failures or successes on the basis of competence displays. As Varenne and McDermott (1999) show, it is precisely through the taken-for-granted, routinized, daily practice of individualized assessment that failure and success are made visible, documentable, and consequential in schools. In precisely this way, the youth PARTY members had themselves been identified and labeled as school failures for the majority of their school lives. Now we reproduced this category as soon as Ms. Barry requested individual grades. Once the request was made, we went looking for failure and success in the social justice class—and found them. Through these processes, the grading conversation was an instance in which micropolitics of educational and societal gatekeeping were reproduced on a small but significant scale.

A Parody of Schooling

The grading discussion exemplified a familiar ritual of schooling—the assignment of consequential course grades—but in a manner devoid of intrinsic meaning. We showed that we could go through the motions; we had learned the rules of schooling and could easily apply them. But we did so with surprisingly little reference to actual student learning, or to the political goals that had initially motivated the social justice class (chapter 3). The process looked more like a parody of schooling than an example of liberatory education. Much of this reproduction occurred without conscious awareness or at least without explicit recognition. How did we arrive at this place?

Tyack and Cuban's (1997) analysis of the grammar of schooling offers a useful perspective for interpreting these outcomes. According to them, the grammar of schooling—meaning the basic form and organization of schools, classrooms, and instruction—is held in place by a combination of structural-institutional constraints (e.g., policies, curricular frameworks, standardized tests, and interdependence with higher education and labor markets) and widespread cultural beliefs about the definition of a "real school." On the latter point, the authors note that teachers, parents, and the general public have all learned the basic grammar of schooling from their own experience of being students, and take it for granted as "the way schools are" (Tyack and Cuban 1997, 85). These widespread cultural assumptions go largely unnoticed, while "it is the *departure* from customary school practice that attracts attention (as when schools decide not to issue student report cards)" (85). In fact, programs and classrooms that depart too far from the basic grammar of schooling are often accused of having low expectations for students, failing to uphold academic standards, and allowing students to goof off (Tyack and Cuban 1997, 96, 105–6; see also Swidler 1980). This last point is essential and connects back to the history of the last chance high school told in chapter 1. As I will discuss further in chapter 5, close adherence to the grammar of schooling—through written assignments, individual grades, the traditional academic subject areas—is one of the ways that schools, particularly those serving low-income students and students of color, have tried to maintain the appearance of standards.

Tyack and Cuban's analysis of the grammar of schooling provides two insights that help shed light on the reproductive outcomes of PARTY. First, it highlights the discursive dimension of structure by emphasizing how taken-for-granted cultural assumptions about schooling serve to regulate teacher agency and prevent alternative educational approaches from taking root. Although PARTY enjoyed substantial freedom over how to organize and teach the social justice class, we nonetheless reproduced many aspects of traditional classroom instruction. In most cases, PARTY members mimicked dominant practices of schooling, not because we had to but because it seemed to "make sense." Our actions were constrained by the inability to imagine alternative ways of being educators in the context of a "real school." A second insight provided by Tyack and Cuban's analysis is the connection between the grammar of schooling and the discourse of academic standards. As noted above, straying too far from the grammar of schooling is often perceived as a *lowering* of standards. Two elements of the grammar of schooling that seem essential to the notion of standards are individual assignments and individual assessment. But in the social justice class, these two elements—reflected in the journal assignment and the final grades, respectively—were the most reproductive and the least educative of our pedagogical choices. The next chapter explores this apparent paradox further.

Conclusion

This chapter has focused on PARTY members' emerging teacher identities as enacted in the social justice class and weekly PARTY meetings. We all struggled to balance conflicting identities as student/teacher, youth/adult, and ally/enemy in a context in which students and teachers were framed as mutually exclusive and oppositional. We used different strategies to negotiate this terrain, with varying implications for the quality of teaching and learning that unfolded in the class. This chapter has shown how the existing school and classroom norms at Jackson High, as well as the more generalized figured world of schooling, powerfully influenced the teacher identities that PARTY members (including myself) constructed and the teacher identities that were readily available for each of us to assume. It has also interrogated how macro relations of power, particularly those rooted in race, became manifest in the micro interactions of the PARTY group and within the social justice class. And as we saw in the student interviews (chapter 2), PARTY members, including myself, often reproduced dominant cultural scripts when placed in gatekeeping positions, with notably reproductive results.

As argued in chapter 3, PARTY members had once envisioned the social justice class as a liberatory educational intervention for collective political empowerment. The ideals that animated our work resonated with the "democratic equality" role of schooling articulated by Labaree (1997). But for all its lofty rhetoric, the social justice class did not embody a real alternative. As this chapter has demonstrated, the class largely reproduced dominant discourses and practices of traditional schooling rather than challenging them. At no moment was this more apparent than the two-hour grading discussion at the end of the school year. In assigning final grades, the PARTY members and I were led to isolate, quantify, and assess individual displays of competence in the class. The purpose of this practice was not to build collective power or even to educate students, but, rather, to determine and make visible which students had completed the course "better" and "worse" than others. Failure, once again, was (re)produced.

The grading process arguably brought the PARTY project full circle: from a vision of alternative education to a parody of schooling. At the moment of assigning grades, the imperative to identify and measure individual displays of competence for the purpose of evaluating, la-

beling, and ranking students was winning out over the ideals of collective empowerment, meaningful dialogue, and consciousness-raising that
had once motivated the project. PARTY's experience illuminates how
the figured world of schooling can undermine the practice of social justice education. The characteristics of this figured world are so deeply in-
grained in our consciousness that when the youth and I sought to implement an alternative vision of education, we fell back into familiar
approaches and discourses—with the same familiar results. Ironically,
many of the most reproductive aspects of the social justice class were
justified on the grounds of upholding academic "standards." In the next
chapter, I elaborate on this argument and examine the apparent paradox
it suggests.

PART III
Dilemmas of Social Justice at the Last Chance High School

Paradigms of Educational Justice: Contested Curricular Goals in the Social Justice Class

D: The whole point of the class was to empower people. That was the first lesson, you feel me?

Kysa: Well, what does that . . . I don't understand what empowering people means. That's something that, like, everyone in education wants to do. What's that? I mean, what does it mean?

Suli: Everybody gets something different out of that, though. It's, *his* vision of empowering people isn't the same vision that you have or I have or Leila has. [. . .] Everybody's, everybody's opinion of power and empowering people is different.

Suli's statement captures a challenge that PARTY faced as we designed and taught a social justice class at Jackson High. While all PARTY members wanted to empower Jackson students to become agents of social change (chapter 3), we often disagreed over how to translate this abstract principle into specific curricular goals. Chapter 4 showed how the class reproduced many dominant practices and discourses of schooling. It was also fraught with tension, as teaching raised new questions and forced new alignments within the group. Debates within PARTY emerged over issues of discipline, assignments, grades, and "attitude." This chapter examines another significant debate: over the meaning of academic "standards" and the relative importance of academic versus vocational preparation for Jackson students.

From our first days of planning for the social justice class, Ms. Barry

and I had encouraged the youth PARTY members to stress the importance of academic achievement and use their position as teachers to promote college-going aspirations. From my perspective, these goals were
central to the very idea of social justice education. But the youth remained divided and ambivalent about these goals. D, and increasingly
Suli, rejected them outright. My immediate reaction to this was to label
their perspective as a kind of false consciousness, a reproductive critique
that merely reinforced their subordinate social class locations rather
than challenging them. As I began data analysis, I found myself searching for explanations of what went wrong: How and why had PARTY
failed to convince these young men of the "truth" about college? Why
had the development of their critical consciousness been stifled? Eventually, I abandoned this line of questioning and refocused the analytic
gaze on my own expectations for the project.[1] Instead of asking what was
wrong with the young men, I began to ask how and why I had acquired
the assumption that a social justice class at Jackson High must be about
college preparation. And why did I equate agreement on this point with
evidence of a more developed critical consciousness?

   In this chapter, I answer these questions while examining PARTY's
intragroup debates over the curricular goals of social justice education
at Jackson High. I argue that although we employed similar terms, such
as *empowerment* and *social justice*, these had different meanings de-
pending on the paradigm of educational justice that informed our work.
The competing paradigms that emerged in PARTY reflect, in significant
ways, national debates about the "academic" versus "vocational" mission
of the high school, especially for youth at the bottom of the educational
hierarchy. In current parlance, this debate is often framed as a choice between "college for all" on one side and vocational, career, or technical
education on the other. This chapter shows how these two paradigms—
college for all versus vocational education—emerged within the PARTY
group and considers their implications for addressing broader questions
of social justice in the context of the last chance high school. But, first,
I explore the history of the so-called vocational-academic divide as a
means of situating the debate over college for all historically, particularly as it pertains to the last chance high school and the education of
youth at the bottom of the educational hierarchy. The debate over college for all has gained renewed attention in recent years, but the issues at
stake are not new; they are a current manifestation of long-standing un-

certainties about the purpose of education for adolescents at the bottom of the educational hierarchy (an issue introduced in chapter 1).

The Academic-Vocational Divide[2]

College preparation and a traditional "academic" or liberal arts–based curriculum have always been the primary education offered to privileged students, and this fact has not been particularly controversial. Controversies, instead, have centered on the proper curriculum for the rest of the population—the working-class, poor, immigrant, and racial minority youth who in fact make up the majority of high school students. As the mission of the high school expanded to serve this population in the first half of the twentieth century, vocational programs were introduced to provide a more "relevant" curriculum for them (Kliebard 1999; see also chapter 1). The belief that schooling should prepare students for labor market roles—what is known as *vocationalism*—began to take root during this time (Kliebard 1999). Although the traditional academic or liberal arts curriculum is often framed as the opposite of vocationalism, some have argued that the liberal arts are a form of vocational education for the privileged—preparing them for admission to elite colleges and universities and, ultimately, for elite professional schools and managerial positions (Grubb and Lazerson 2004).

The division of the high school curriculum into academic and vocational tracks for college-bound and work-bound students, respectively, institutionalized the notion that these represented distinct types of knowledge. Indeed, the assumption of an academic-vocational divide has structured much of the secondary school curriculum over the past century of American schooling (Oakes and Saunders 2008a; Kliebard 1999). Mike Rose (2005b, 2008) has argued persuasively that this academic-vocational divide is a social construction, and that it maintains power asymmetries by privileging the knowledge and skills coded as academic over those coded as practical. The differentiation of knowledge into academic and vocational categories not only constructs difference, he claims, but also solidifies a hierarchy because the categories are not of equal status. Moreover, student placement into these differently valued categories has, over time, consistently broken down along lines of race and class—despite attempts to base placement decisions on "merit" alone (Oakes 1985; Rubin et al. 2008; Rose 2005a). Vocational programs have typically suffered from low status, which is impossible to separate from the low status of the students historically found in those programs (Rose 2008; Kliebard 1999). Critics of vocational education have long argued that it steers working-class and poor students into lower-status and lower-paid occupations, locking them into trajectories at a young age that are hard if not impossible to overcome (Oakes 1985; Rose 2005a, 2005b). As such, the academic-vocational divide may construct a hierarchy of knowledge that reflects and reinforces a hierarchy of *knowers*—reifying race- and class-based differences in educational and social status.

Since the 1980s, most American high schools have gradually eliminated formal, rigid divisions between academic and vocational programs.[3] As the high school curriculum became more homogenized around the traditional academic subjects, the status hierarchy grew more visible as terms such as *honors* and *accelerated* were added to distinguish higher tracks from lower. In chapter 1, I described this process of simultaneous standardization and stratification as the *hierarchization* of education. Debates continue to rage about the fairness of these tracks and the role that racism and classism play in assigning students to them. In theory, the standardized academic curriculum should offer students in lower tracks more opportunity for mobility than the previous, more rigid forms of separation into distinct academic and vocational programs. Exposure to similar academic content (even if covered in more or less depth according to track) should make it easier for students to "jump tracks" upward if their performance improves or it is determined that their initial placement was incorrect. But in practice, official and unofficial tracking mechanisms still function largely as pathways into distinct occupational and class futures, and they continue to primarily reinforce preexisting inequalities of race and class (Oakes 1985; Oakes and Saunders 2008; Rose 2005b; Rubin et al. 2008).

The idea of college for all as a frame and a policy goal gained prominence in the 1990s, when it was associated with the conservative-led movement for academic standards (Rothstein 2002). But its rhetoric also resonated with progressive, equity-seeking reforms such as detracking and increased college access for underserved students, and this blending of conservative and progressive ideals helped secure its hegemony as a dominant discourse (Glass and Nygreen 2011). In Labaree's (1997) terms, the discourse of college for all reflects and reinforces the goal of "social mobility": college is promoted on the basis that it enables individual students to achieve upward mobility and earn more money (Glass and Nygreen 2011; see the introduction for a summary of Labaree 1997). The discourse implicitly assumes that plenty of good, middle-income jobs are available to go around—if only students were educated enough to fill them (Rothstein 2002; Glass and Nygreen 2011). While there are many different angles from which to critique the discourse of college for all, the most popular critique of educators is that it is an impractical goal and does not advance the true needs of work-bound youth (e.g., Rosenbaum 2001; Cherry 2009; Symonds, Schwartz, and Ferguson 2011; Noddings 2011). Many argue that work-bound youth would be better served in vocational programs, providing not only technical training but also support with navigating the labor market, the same way college-bound youth are supported in navigating the higher-education system (Rosenbaum 2001; Symonds, Schwartz, and Ferguson 2011). This position, in Labaree's (1997) terms, reflects the "social efficiency" goal of education: preparing workers for jobs. In a social efficiency model of schooling, there are tight links between school curriculum and labor market needs, thereby making school (in theory) more relevant to youth at all points in the achievement hierarchy (Labaree 1997; Rosenbaum 2001).

The academic-vocational debate is particularly significant to continuation high schools, precisely because these schools serve students who are not traditionally seen as college-bound. As noted in chapter 1, defining the purpose of high school for "these kids" has been a long-standing dilemma, and debates about the relative merits of vocational versus academic and civic preparation in continuation high schools date back to their inception in the early 1900s (Imber 1985). Given the historic nature of the academic-vocational debate and its relevance to the last chance high school, it is not surprising that it should emerge within PARTY as we considered the meaning of social justice education at Jackson High. But significantly, PARTY members did not debate these issues until *after* we started teaching at Jackson. Before the class began, we shared a consensus on the primacy of the democratic equality goal (chapter 3)—the only one of Labaree's three goals that stresses the civic rather than economic purposes of education. It was only after PARTY entered the figured world of schooling that its role in labor market sorting and preparation became central and we had to take a position on it. It was (or felt to us) impossible in this figured world to advance the goal of democratic equality on its own; impossible to abstain completely from the academic-vocational debate; impossible to opt out altogether of the discourse on labor market preparation and sorting. As such, rather than a consensus on democratic equality, the relative importance of social mobility versus social efficiency emerged as a point of contention. That this was so even for a youth-led, once-a-week, informal social justice class suggests the degree to which the figured world of schooling is saturated with the assumptions of vocationalism.

The Standards Paradigm: College for All

Nowhere was the debate over standards and college for all more visible than in PARTY's weekly discussions of the journal assignment (chapter 4). Because this assignment, more than anything else in the social justice class, resembled other individual assignments that students did in school, it became a symbol for academic standards in my mind. The huge effort required to squeeze out even a handful of student journals each week was justified on precisely these grounds. In one meeting, I proposed requiring that journal entries be a full page in length. I argued that writing could foster meaningful reflection on the course material, but also appealed to the discourse of standards and college for all by saying, "If we dumb down the class, we are participating in the same racist system that doesn't prepare low-income kids, and black and brown kids, for college or, or anything else." Leila agreed on the point about standards, observing that Jackson students were routinely given "third-grade work," and that classes there were "so easy that my brain was melting." D and Suli protested that a page was too long for a journal assignment. Suli observed sarcastically, "Look at the students in that class and tell me that any of 'em is gonna write a page!" I suggested we push them to write a page but still give credit to any student whose answer was thoughtful. Suli shot back:

Suli: Hold on, though. Check this out, though. You say that you're trying to push them to write a page, but if they don't write a page, you're not gonna fail them anyway, right?

Kysa: Uh-huh.

Suli: Well, basically what you're saying is, "I want you to do this. This is the requirement. But if you don't meet the requirement, I'm just gonna pass you anyway." So aren't you part of that same system?

Kysa: Well, I want to push, I want to push them to do, to challenge them—

Suli: Hold on, though. You didn't answer my question. But you're part of the same system 'cause you're not failing them for not meeting the requirement, right? In college if you don't meet the requirement, you fail, right?

Kysa: Right, right.

Suli: So basically, you're saying that you're part of the same system.

Kysa: OK, good point. That's a good point.

[...]

Leila: I think just put like in parentheses, like half a page.

Suli: And we should do it differently if we gon' do that. If you don't want to be a part of that system, you should be like, "Man, you gotta write at *least* a half a page; otherwise, you gets no credit for this!" you feel? Otherwise, you tellin' them it's OK to do less than the requirement.

Kysa: Right.

Suli: I'm telling you. You don't get a half a page, it's no credit! For real, that's how you start doing it! Otherwise, you know, you're saying it ain't really work.

Suli had done a complete about-face. He had opened the conversation in a voice laced with sarcasm: "Look at the students in that class and tell me that any of 'em is gonna write a page!" Within minutes, he grew adamant about holding students to an explicit standard and failing those who did not meet the standard, for this is what would happen in college.

Suli (like Leila) frequently adopted the language of academic standards and college preparation when reflecting on his teaching practice. In one meeting, he talked about a student in his small group, Guillermo.

Suli: Guillermo, he was kinda just trying to sit in the back and not saying nothing. [...] I was like, "Man, you plan to go to college?" He was like, "Yeah." I was like, "Man, when you get to college, you feel, if you need to know something and you're scared to ask a question, I guarantee you there's other people in the room that want to ask the same question. But if you're scared to ask the group, you're never gonna learn nothing. 'Cause the professor don't care, he gonna move on. It's over with after they move on. 'Cause they don't be going back. I be noticing that. Most of the teachers there don't go back. If you didn't get it the first time, then you didn't get it." I was trying to tell him that, and he was, like, "OK I understand, it's cool, I'll do it." I was, like, "Yeah."

Suli beamed with pride as he told of this exchange with Guillermo. He had succeeded in getting Guillermo to participate in the discussion by giving a small pep talk about college, drawing from his own experience in community college. Suli's identity as a college student thus became significant, both in the PARTY classroom and in weekly meetings when reflecting on his teaching practice. But Suli also argued against giving written assignments and often engaged in active not-learning in the class, as seen in chapter 4. Suli's multiple identities and allegiances—as a college student wishing to uphold high standards and a cool guy wishing to subvert teachers' directives—were always in tension. Rather than synthesizing these two identities, Suli fluctuated between them and gave voice to both competing discourses within the space of weekly PARTY meetings.

As the above examples illustrate, appeals to academic standards were often justified in terms of college preparation. This was not accidental. The discourse of college for all is a ubiquitous public discourse, and was palpable at Jackson High. As in most American high schools, teachers at Jackson routinely emphasized the importance of college, and students regularly expressed plans to attend community college and transfer to a university. Whether they really hoped and planned to do so remains an open question, but certainly they knew this was the "right" answer to give when a teacher (or researcher) asked them about future goals. Despite ambivalence within the PARTY group, the social justice class also reproduced aspects of the college-for-all discourse—most notably when we invited a guest speaker, Jeffrey, to present in the class. Jeffrey was a Jackson graduate who had gone to community college and successfully transferred to the University of California. When D casually mentioned, in a PARTY meeting, that he and Jeffrey had grown up on the same block, I immediately began thinking aloud about the possibility of inviting Jeffrey to speak in the social justice class. Leila enthusiastically supported the idea. Suli asked what Jeffrey would talk about. I answered that he could share his story of transferring to a university from community college. Suli shrugged and said that was "cool." I pressed D about getting a phone number for Jeffrey. Rather than offering to give me the number, D said he wanted to call Jeffrey himself.

Three weeks later, Jeffrey came to speak in the social justice class, in a visit coordinated entirely by D. A tall, thin, and soft-spoken African American man in his mid- to late twenties, Jeffrey appeared humble as he stood before the class of twelve students, Ms. Barry, and the PARTY members. He began his presentation by sharing that he had been kicked out of Maytown High after receiving too many Fs and was involuntarily transferred to Jackson. After graduating from Jackson, he told us, he got a job stocking shelves at a warehouse. He worked side by side with other high school graduates, most of whom were older than he and many of whom were supporting their own children. He said he wanted to get his own apartment but could not afford to move out of his mother's home. Even without paying rent, Jeffrey said, his meager wages barely met his personal needs, and he wondered how his coworkers managed to raise children on the same wages. He recalled that many of them left the warehouse at the end of each long day only to head straight to a second job. After a year of this type of work, he realized it was not the future he wanted for himself. He acknowledged that the drug economy offered an alternative, but said he did not want to die as a young man or spend much of his adult life in prison. That was when, according to his story, he decided to enroll at the local community college.

The remainder of his speech focused on the grueling five years he spent in community college before transferring to the University of California. He said he was never a good student in high school and was not prepared for the academic rigor of college. He told the class that he failed all of his college courses in the first semester, and that he had to take the remedial English course four times before passing the test that made him eligible for transfer-credit courses. He told students not to get discouraged if they failed at community college. The important thing, he said, was to keep trying and to seek out tutors and mentors through various programs available on campus. Jeffrey insisted that hard work and motivation, not innate abilities or academic preparation, would determine if a student would ultimately succeed in community college. His story reinforced the prevailing narrative at Jackson High that anyone could transfer to a four-year university if they had enough perseverance, no matter what their high school preparation. But Jeffrey's story also offered a reality check. He talked about sleep deprivation, juggling school and work, feeling lost in classes that were over his head, and discouraged upon earning Fs despite sincere efforts to pass.

At the end of the class period, Ms. Barry initiated a round of applause and congratulated him on his academic success. On the spot, she invited him to be the keynote speaker at the upcoming graduation ceremony, adding almost as an afterthought that she was sure the principal, Mr. Galo, would agree. After class, she walked him over to Mr. Galo's office to propose the idea in person (Jeffrey would later decline the offer). Ms. Barry introduced Jeffrey to the principal as an alumnus who was now studying at UC. The office secretary, guidance counselor, and a teacher who happened to be in the office gathered around upon hearing the introduction, and continued to hover around Jeffrey in awe as if a celebrity were in their midst. Jeffrey appeared humble and a bit uncomfortable from all the attention.

As his visit to Jackson suggests, Jeffrey's existence appeared to bring school adults immeasurable pride and joy. Here was an exception: a Jackson student who had beaten the odds, "moving up" from the bottom of the educational achievement and social class hierarchies to a highly selective university and probably a solid middle-class job. It was with this ideal in mind that I pushed for academic "standards" in the social justice class, defined narrowly in terms of preparation for more schooling—in this case, college. In the paradigm of educational justice that I was operating within, traditional measures of academic achievement, especially college going, were evidence of agency and resistance, for they subverted the cycle of social reproduction. Throughout the semester, D leveled an implicit critique of my perspective, reminding us on one occasion that "college don't make you smart. And that's how I feel about a PhD too" (the latter part apparently an underhanded insult aimed at me). D explained further that "if you don't know how to survive with no money, then you're not really smart." Similar to the last chance students featured in Hatt's (2007) study of smartness, D framed street smarts as a superior form of intelligence that was associated with the exercise of agency, and school smarts as a form of conformity to dominant structures—the antithesis of agency.

D's Paradigm: Demystifying the Labor Market

As the teaching semester progressed, D appeared to grow increasingly disengaged from the social justice class. He often remained quiet during the class itself and during the portion of weekly meetings when we planned for and reflected on it. His gradual withdrawal from the work of teaching appeared to be an act of resistance to the direction the class had taken. There were some notable exceptions, however, when D grew animated and vociferously expressed an opinion. At these moments, it seemed, D was trying to assert a different paradigm of educational justice from the dominant paradigm of standards and college for all. D's paradigm of educational justice came into clearer focus as the teaching semester wore on. First, it rejected the use of individualized assessments as evidence of learning. And, second, it stressed learning goals of personal empowerment, survival, and demystification of the labor market.

In one of many discussions about the journal, for example, D had remained completely silent for nearly twenty minutes even as Suli, Leila, and I all spoke at length about our views. Noticing his withdrawal, I asked him directly:

Kysa: D, I want to know what you think about the journal. Honestly.

D: I don't care. [*four-second silence*] I don't care. That's it.

Kysa: Would you assign the journal if you were doing this class by yourself?

D: [*five-second silence*] I don't know. [*four-second silence*] Maybe.

Kysa: Really?

D: I doubt it, though. [*laughs slightly*] But that's just me, though. If it was my own class, though, I'd be chillin'. I'd get feedback *from* the class.

Kysa: What do you mean get feedback from the class?

D: But just 'cause they don't do the journal don't mean they ain't learning nothin'.

Kysa: Right. That's right.

D: And just 'cause they don't want to do it doesn't mean they ain't learning nothin'.

D's first response, "I don't care. I don't care. That's it," is characteristic of the indifference with which he approached much of the planning for the social justice class. But his indifference shifted to emotion when he asserted, "Just 'cause they don't do the journal don't mean they ain't learning." Here, rather than answering my question about how to get feedback from the class, D voiced his opposition to using the journal assignment as evidence of student learning. This was a theme that ran throughout the weekly meeting transcripts; consistently, D tried to separate discussions of student *learning* from discussions of student *evaluation*.

When debating my proposed one-page length requirement for the journal (discussed in the previous section), he insisted:

D: But what about if they is learning, you feel me, and they don't write a half a page? You give them an F?

Suli: All right, if you don't write a half a page—

D: But they *learning*! You feel? So they're like "Fuck it!" you feel? "I ain't gonna do *shit*!"

Leila: But they just don't get credit for the assignment, right? It doesn't mean they don't get credit for the class.

D: [*raising his voice*] That don't mean they ain't learning, though! Just 'cause they don't do the journal, it don't mean they ain't learning!

D was angry now. He insisted that completing the journal was not the same as actually learning. He expressed confidence that students *were* learning and there was no need to isolate, quantify, and measure that learning through individual displays of competence. It was not just written assignments he opposed but any individualized evaluation of students. For even when we discussed students' level of participation in class discussions and group activities as an alternative learning assessment, D rushed to the defense of the nonvocal students: "What makes you think just because they're quiet they ain't learning, though?"

D's paradigm was not simply a rejection of standards and college for all, however. He also attempted to advance an alternative vision of social justice as practical preparation for adult and labor market roles. About halfway into the teaching semester, D proposed a project in which students would research a career they wanted to pursue, including the wage they would earn and the type and amount of education or training they would need. We had been discussing strategies for engaging students in a longer-term project about a social issue, but D believed he had a better idea:

D: I'd rather get them to open their eyes to what I'm trying to do in five years. You know? Instead of just teaching them just straight political facts. 'Cause it's gonna help them better, you feel? Like, what type of job you want? What you want to do? Where you want to go? What do you need to do to get where you want to go? And if you don't know where you wanna go, you need to start thinking.

Suli: I mean, what makes you think they gonna do that? Take the time to research a job?

D: I mean, the ones that do it, you feel, are the ones that actually gonna have a future.

The other PARTY members and I questioned D's proposal, pointing out that ours was a *social justice* class, not a career exploration class. In my mind, these were different and incompatible kinds of knowledge, and I worried that D's project idea would undermine the intellectual and civic content of the class. D insisted that this practical knowledge was actually more helpful than the "straight political facts" we had been teaching about thus far.

In addition to demystifying the workings of the formal labor market, D expressed an occasional desire to help students navigate the informal and underground labor markets. In one meeting, he flipped through the pages of an information packet listing prison sentences for various drug-related crimes. Although we were not on the topic of lesson planning, D interrupted the conversation to insist that we teach the content to the class:

D: Hey, we should teach some of the facts in this packet, man, to the class. 'Cause they [students] need to know this.

Kysa: What facts?

D: They gotta lotta cool numbers, you feel? Especially about some of these, all these LSD-type drugs and how many years you get, you feel? You know, they need to know, they need to know all that. They need to know. I mean, about this. LSD—one gram equals five years, ten grams equal ten years.

Leila: That's some harsh shit.

D: And marijuana—a hundred plants equal five, a thousand plants get ten. And about crack—five grams get you five. You know, they need to know all that.

D's repeated insistence that students "need to know" this information revealed his assumption that some students participated in the underground drug economy. He wanted to help students think through the risks of this work and encourage them to be cautious, but not necessarily to abstain from extralegal work altogether.

In his interview at the end of the school year, D elaborated on this stance. His explanation is worth quoting at length for the insights it offers and the discourses it activates:

D: The only thing I can say [to students] is, if you're gonna be in the game [of drug sales], to be the man. You gotta be the *man*. All this nickel-and-dime stuff, it's not gonna add up. It's only a chosen few that can actually come up offa' nickel-and-dimin' it. So, you need to be the boss. Don't be the lowest person on the line, the one that's actually *on* the front line. You know, step up to the middle man or something; step up and be a boss!

D: Whatever you do, if it's legal or illegal, strive big. Set your goals up high. If you're gonna be in the legal or illegal game, don't set your mind on a thousand, or four or five hundred a night. Set your mind on *ten* thousand a night. If you're actually gonna take that fifty-fifty chance, make it worth it. So you won't be sitting up in jail like "Man, I got busted for a handful of rocks! I got to do two years for *nothing*!" Shit! If you're gonna get busted, get busted with a *kilo*. You feel me, a *pound* or something! So you can at least be sitting in jail like, "Man, at least I was trying to *do* something."

D: That's how I look at it. 'Cause some people may say, "Oh, that's so negative. How can you encourage them [to sell drugs]?" But seriously, though, you got to look at it another way. Why *not* tell them if they're gonna do something illegal [to] strive big? 'Cause you'll tell them to strive big and *not* do it [sell drugs], and go to school, get you a six-figure job. So why can't you tell them, if you *is* gonna do something illegal, be a six-figure nigga, you feel me? And be the man. That's what I'll tell 'em. Basically.

D: It's hard for people to just go to college when they ain't like high school in the first place. That's still not answering the question—the *first* question—like where's your money coming from? Shit, you're a grown-ass man, you can't depend on nobody else no more. Basically. So I don't know. That's what I tell them. [*pause*] That's what I *have* told them.

D's advice for students to "strive big" employs a dominant discourse of individual success and embraces many of the values prized in the broader American culture—work ethic, risk taking, entrepreneurialism, upward mobility, competitive individualism. He is in fact adopting and adapting this dominant public discourse to the lived social context of many Jackson students. He draws a parallel between his advice and the sanctioned advice of educators to work hard at school and go to college as the path to financial security (i.e., a "six-figure job"). But for students who "ain't like high school in the first place" and, moreover, lack the financial resources for college ("Where's your money coming from?"), D sees educators' sanctioned advice as an empty promise. Rather than asking students to accept their social location near the bottom of occupational hierarchies—whether as "nickel-and-dime" dealers in a hierarchical underground economy or as low-wage employees in a hierarchical legal economy—D mobilizes a familiar dominant discourse of individual success to motivate and inspire students to strive for something higher, more honorable, and more meaningful. Acknowledging that some may criticize him for condoning illicit activities, D insists he is merely acknowledging students' social reality. For some, drug sales may represent a rational calculation based on what opportunities exist for upward mobility and financial security. Far from being irrational, D's narrative about "striving big" reflects and extends a familiar dominant discourse of competitive individualism and upward mobility.

The mirror image to D's "strive big" narrative was the sanctioned advice of educators to "strive big" through education—specifically a *college* education. The emphasis on college as a primary alternative to drug sales exists in much public discourse about urban youth and was also part of the local discourse at Jackson High. The implicit framing of these two pathways as the exclusive options for last chance students obscures a third possible and likely pathway: direct entry into the blue-collar or retail-sector labor force. In broader public discourse, as in the local discourse at Jackson, this third pathway is largely absent. High school graduates who go directly into the labor force are rarely if ever held up as role models or examples, nor is their path imbued with the status of "striving big." Rather, it is implicitly framed as an inferior path for those not smart enough for college or brave enough for the streets. And yet, direct entry into the labor force is the path that a majority of high school graduates take.[4] The discursive silence about work in the local discourse of Jackson High and the broader public discourse may reflect the fact that the labor force possibilities for work-bound high school graduates are incredibly dismal. "Striving big"—choosing one of two extremely high-risk pathways—may in fact be the only way for most Jackson graduates, and others like them, to achieve financial security and experience a sense of professional dignity. To help contextualize these points, the next section traces the trajectories of four PARTY members in the labor force and community college after high school graduation, along with the statistical trajectories of similarly positioned youth. These stories paint a picture of the social context within which D's paradigm of educational justice can begin to "make sense."

Postgraduation Trajectories: Lolo, Louis, Suli, and D

Just two weeks after her high school graduation, Lolo began a summer "bridge" program at a local community college for first-generation college students, offering intensive academic and study-skills preparation. At the time, Lolo expressed the goal of transferring to a four-year university and majoring in sociology. At the end of the summer, she took a placement test and was assigned to remedial courses in math and English. Undeterred, she enrolled in these two courses along with Introduction to Sociology. During the fall semester, in addition to these three courses, Lolo worked full-time at a grocery store, where she earned just above the minimum wage. She also juggled numerous family obligations, the most time consuming of which was providing regular (uncompensated) child care for two nieces—an infant and a toddler. A few weeks before final exams, Lolo and her family became homeless, and she withdrew from all three classes. This was not the only time Lolo would become homeless during college. Nor was it the only semester in which Lolo would earn zero credits despite paying college tuition. It is important to emphasize that Lolo held a full-time job when she became homeless. Her wages were insufficient to cover rent, food, transportation, and tuition, and Lolo had no safety net from family or elsewhere to serve as a cushion.

For the rest of the two-year PARTY project and beyond, Lolo held a series of low-wage, service-sector retail jobs, and she reenrolled in community college every term even though her transcript accumulated more incompletes, withdrawals, and Fs than it did passing grades. Lolo's experiences in the workforce and community college were similar in significant ways to those of two other PARTY members, Suli and Louis. Over the two-year project, all three of these young high school graduates moved back and forth between periods of unemployment and periods of work in low-wage, service-sector jobs. Their jobs paid at or just above the minimum wage, offered no benefits such as health care and sick days, and typically allowed no control over their schedules. These PARTY members often left one job for another with the hope of finding more opportunities for mobility or a secure schedule, or at least a better work environment. This pattern of "horizontal mobility" (Royster 2003, 65) across a series of bottom-rung jobs closely resembles the postgraduation employment trajectories of many young, non-college-educated workers (Rosenbaum 2001; Royster 2003; Wilson 1997). The meager wages and unpredictable schedules at these jobs made it difficult if not impossible for the youth to support themselves while also paying community college tuition.

In addition to financial obstacles, their inadequate academic preparation meant a two-year college degree would take substantially longer and exact an enormous psychological cost. Lolo, Louis, and Suli were all were placed in remedial courses in college for which they paid tuition but did not receive transferable college credits. Although all three enrolled in community college with the goal of transferring to a four-year university, Lolo was the only one to eventually earn a postsecondary degree of any kind. She spent six years in community college before transferring to the California State University system, where, after another five years, she received a bachelor's degree in sociology and even spent a year abroad in Spain. She graduated at the age of thirty with over ten thousand dollars of student loan debt. Previous breaks in her schooling experience had left Lolo with gaps in her academic knowledge across a variety of subject areas, making college classes both difficult and overwhelming. Resonating with Jeffrey's story (told earlier in this chapter), Lolo repeated the remedial English course at community college six times before passing a writing test that made her eligible for the transfer-credit English requirements. Given the high proportion of community college students who are assigned to remedial courses,[5] we can infer that stories like Lolo's and Jeffrey's are not unique. Faced with such challenges, only the most exceptionally determined student would dream of persisting in community college long enough to transfer to a four-year university. And even those who do will find that a bachelor's degree is not the ticket to middle-income employment they might have hoped (Noddings 2011; Glass and Nygreen 2011).

For PARTY members who had graduated from high school, finding decent work was an ongoing challenge. Speaking about his high school diploma, Suli noted, "It really doesn't help you get a job. It hasn't helped *me* get a job. It really hasn't helped my friends either." His perception is consistent with much research showing that high school graduation may be necessary but not sufficient to gain access to stable, livable-wage employment (Goldin and Katz 2007, 148; MacLeod 2008, 124–28; Royster 2003; Rosenbaum 2001; Wilson 1997). Rather than the diploma, many studies suggest that access to social networks or social capital is the operative factor in obtaining quality work (Smith-Doerr and Powell 2005; Royster 2003). For example, in a study of the employment trajectories of fifty recent graduates from a vocational high school in Baltimore, Royster (2003) offers convincing evidence that access to social networks in blue-collar fields—not skills or qualifications as measured by school performance and achievements, even from a vocational high school where students specialized in a blue-collar trade—explained the type, length, and quality of their employment. But Royster also documents how the racialized nature of these networks was a significant barrier for the African American workers in her study, essentially locking them out of blue-collar professions even when they had excelled in vocational preparation programs at school.

The employment trajectories of PARTY members are consistent with those documented in Royster's study (ibid.). Over the course of the project, only D succeeded in obtaining something close to livable-wage work. In PARTY's second year, he got a position as a substitute member of the cleanup staff for the city's Parks and Recreation Department. D had learned about the opening through the personal connections of his grandmother, a clerical worker for the city. It was not on the basis of his high school performance but through social networks in the public sector—traditionally the most accessible employment sector for African American workers (Royster 2003, 190; Waldinger 1999)—that D learned about and was recommended for the position. Jobs in the public sector such as the one D's grandmother held, and D hoped to obtain, offered benefits, predictable schedules, and relative stability from seasonal and business cycle fluctuations. In this sense, they are significantly better jobs than the nonbenefited, unpredictable, low-wage service-sector work that other PARTY members pursued.

But PARTY members, including myself, did not know these details of the blue-collar and retail-sector labor market. As a teacher, I was well prepared to help the youth understand, decode, and navigate institutions of higher education. I could (and did) help them obtain financial aid, prepare essays for scholarship applications, put them in contact with professors and college students in particular (academic) fields of interest, and generally support them with academic coursework. But for all of us (with the possible exception of D), the workings of the blue-collar and retail-sector labor markets remained somewhat mysterious. I was not prepared to help PARTY members navigate this world, and Jackson High, like most high schools, did not offer counseling or support to work-bound students that might have prepared them to do so.[6] As a result, the youth struggled to find their way in a difficult labor market with no support system or guidance.

The situation for low-wage workers has never been easy, but it has arguably become worse in recent decades and continues to deteriorate. Since the 1970s, neither the minimum wage nor the average wages of non-college-educated workers have kept pace with inflation. The value of the minimum wage in 2003 was down 34 percent from its peak in 1968 (Wolff 2006, 23), and the purchasing power of the working class and the working poor has declined dramatically in these years (Mishel, Bernstein, and Shierholz 2009).[7] Falling wages at the bottom of the income distribution affect a vast number of Americans. In 2007, about a quarter of all workers (and more than a third of African American workers) earned "poverty level wages" (Economic Policy Institute 2011a, 2011b),[8] and 30 percent of the total population lived in families earning at or below 200 percent of the federal poverty level (Economic Policy Institute 2011c)—a fairly reasonable measure of the income needed for a decent living (Shipler 2005, 9–10). Corresponding with these trends has been a well-documented "shrinking" or "squeezing" of the middle class since the 1970s, and a growing polarization of jobs toward the top and bottom of the wage distribution (Autor, Katz, and Kearney 2006; Pastor 2008; Wolff 2006). These trends have made a bad economic situation worse for workers at the lower end of the occupational structure, where Jackson graduates are almost certain to find themselves.

In an interview at the end of the school year, D articulated the frustrations of Jackson youth who face a labor market offering little besides poverty-wage work, and the dangers it posed given the readily available alternative of drug sales.

D: They [Jackson students] see there's nothing in it from this nine-to-five. Nothing. You gotta wait two weeks for a check, no matter what you want to do until then. Work nine to five, for eight hours, come home tired, and then get your check in them two weeks—like four hundred dollars, five hundred dollars, six hundred dollars, seven hundred dollars. They [Jackson students] coulda made that in, like, three days! Or on a good night, one night. Or even on a better day, two hours, three hours. They're, like, "Oh, whatever." So they *see* that it's no, it's no way. [. . .] We see our friends struggling on a nine-to-five, barely makin' it.

[. . .] It's not just 'cause we see these rap videos, and people be singing. You think people actually gonna put theirself on the front lines, on the street, if the only reason is a rap video? No, it's not that. It's that we want to live comfortable.

Everything is going up, you feel me? [. . .] The cost of living is going up. Society is starting to cost more. And you gotta survive, you feel me? You gotta survive. And, people know you can't, you can't survive off five dollars an hour no more. You ain't gonna be able to get no decent meal that can fill you up. So, you got to start surviving off children too,[9] and how are you supposed to get it when their parents is goin' day to day, or week to week, paycheck to paycheck? You feel me? Ain't got enough money to get the necessities that they think they need. So, that's what I think.

D's assessment of the employment prospects for Jackson graduates is consistent with much research on the labor market for non-college-educated workers (Mishel, Bernstein, and Shierholz 2009; Wolff 2006).

His observations that "the cost of living is going up" and "you can't survive off five dollars an hour no more" reflect the economic truth that
wages have not kept up with prices, especially at the bottom of the wage
distribution. Countering dominant discourses that portray participation in the drug economy as malicious, irrational, or the result of negative media influences such as rap music, D depicts it as a rational choice
within the lived social context of students' lives. Rather than trying to locate deficiencies in the students who choose this route—such as broken
families, low self-esteem, reckless behavior, inability to reason through
consequences—D insists on a simpler explanation that almost anyone
can relate to: "we want to live comfortable."

A natural response to these PARTY members' stories is to call for
more and better college preparation at the K–12 level. If these youth had
been prepared for college success, they could have bypassed the low-
wage labor market and the temptations of the drug economy by head-
ing straight to four-year colleges—even if they did so by way of a successful two years in community college—and ultimately obtained good,
middle-income jobs. This is the stance that most educators and policymakers take when considering the dismal economic situation facing underserved students such as those at Jackson High. And given the existing
opportunity structure, it is eminently reasonable for individuals such as
Jeffrey and Lolo to pursue a college degree as a path to upward mobility, and for teachers and parents to encourage and support our own students in this direction. Most every caring teacher wants to create more
exceptions such as Jeffrey and Lolo, and it is logical for these exceptions
to be held up as role models for current Jackson students to emulate. The
labor force prospects for non-college-educated workers are so dismal
that well-meaning educators have few options except to try to turn more
work-bound students into college-bound ones; hence, the discourse of
college for all makes a lot of sense from the perspective of individual
teachers, students, and parents.

But what is reasonable for individuals may be unreasonable from a
public policy perspective (Labaree 1997; Rothstein 2002; Wolff 2006) as
well as a collective political empowerment perspective (Tannock 2006;
Glass and Nygreen 2011). The emphasis on creating exceptions raises
questions about the purposes of high school for everyone else—the inevitable *non*exceptions who make up the rule. Last chance high schools,
by definition, serve students who are socially located at the bottom of
the achievement distribution; therefore, students from these schools

who advance to a bachelor's degree—which represents the top 30 percent of educational achievement—are exceptional. The discourse of college for all offers no consolation prize to the many perfectly ordinary Jackson students who pass through its program every year. Instead, it focuses on increasing the number of exceptions such as Jeffrey and Lolo. At Jackson, this discourse was so hegemonic that staff lacked a model for articulating other compelling purposes of the high school for *all* students—exceptional and unexceptional alike. This lack of a compelling purpose for all Jackson students reflects the ongoing dilemma of hierarchy and the historic difficulty of defining the purpose of education for adolescents at the bottom of the educational hierarchy, as discussed in chapter 1. The inability of college for all to address the actual needs of Jackson students as a cohort reflects the limits posed by the paradox of getting ahead, a point I elaborate on in the next and final chapter.

Conclusion

The members of PARTY all agreed with the general goal of empowering Jackson students to become agents of social change. But we brought different paradigms of educational justice to the table that led us to emphasize different curricular goals in the social justice class. This chapter has examined our intragroup debates on these issues, and contextualized them within broader national debates about "college for all" and vocational education, as well as the labor market realities faced by PARTY members. The discourse of college for all was hegemonic at Jackson High, as it is today within the figured worlds of educational policy, practice, and research. The labor market for non-college-educated workers is so dismal that "striving big"—either by pursuing higher education or by joining the underground economy—appears to be necessary to achieve mobility, respect, and dignity in the world of work. Both options, unfortunately, represent extremely high-risk pathways for youth who are starting out at the bottom of multiple educational and social hierarchies.

The PARTY group's debate between competing paradigms of educational justice offers two key insights. First, it shows the extent to which the assumptions of vocationalism have saturated the figured world of schooling. The fact that PARTY members, myself included, were unable to work inside the school context *without* engaging a debate about labor market sorting reveals the hegemony of vocationalism in this space. Second, it shows the enduring relevance of educators' uncertainty about the purpose of high school for adolescents at the bottom of the educational hierarchy. Like reformers a century ago (discussed in chapter 1), we too wondered about the most socially just approach to take when educating last chance students in a system that channels youth into unequal labor market roles. Besides helping students "move up" within this hierarchy, how were we to conceptualize the purpose of social justice education for youth who were socially located at the bottom? Was there a way to avoid the trap of the social mobility paradigm without appearing to have "low expectations" of Jackson students or, worse, becoming resigned to the educational status quo?

Unable to answer these questions or resolve our intragroup conflicts, we ended up teaching a social justice class that reproduced, in large part, the dominant discourse of standards and college for all—albeit in watered-down and superficial form. This outcome is likely due in large part to my own disproportionate influence in the group, as well as our general tendency to reproduce rather than reimagine dominant practices and discourses of schooling in the social justice class (chapter 4). At the time, we were too steeped in the figured world of Jackson High and our solidifying teacher identities (chapter 4) to be able to "step back" and see the deeper, underlying issues at stake. To a great extent, I had naturalized these discourses and the false dichotomy that presents "college for all" as the only alternative to a racist and classist educational status quo. In the end, just like the continuation high school itself (discussed in chapter 1), we ended up giving students a vaguely "academic" type of class that reproduced mainstream definitions of "standards" and reinforced the dominant idea that the primary purpose of schooling is to prepare students for future levels of schooling. In short, we offered an unengaging, unchallenging, shallow version of traditional classrooms instead of a real alternative. What is most noteworthy is the extent to which these choices were made under the guise of upholding academic standards. The fear of lowering standards was precisely what held the most dull and alienating aspects of the grammar of schooling in place (Tyack and Cuban 1997; see also chapter 4).

This outcome hints at how the trend toward *hierarchization* in education makes it increasingly difficult to pursue alternative educational approaches: when one type of curriculum gets defined as high standards, any alternative to it gets defined as a lack of standards rather than an equally valuable if different set of knowledge and skills. In a hierarchizing educational system, it seems, there is less and less space for difference—in terms of types of knowledge, capacities, or educational purposes—that is not expressed in terms of hierarchy.[10] Instead of a diversity of talents, capacities, knowledges, and interests, we can see only gradations of inferiority and superiority. In practice, this value system may encourage educators, as it did PARTY members, to provide more of the same type of knowledge and instruction rather than pursuing genuine alternatives. This insight may help explain why my vision of social justice education so closely reflected traditional notions of an "academic" classroom, organized around the goal of college preparation and rooted in the assumption of an academic-vocational divide. But what vision of educational justice might have helped the PARTY group arrive at a different place? Given the sociopolitical and labor market context in which we find ourselves, how can and should educators prepare Jackson students and others like them to negotiate their social worlds? What visions of educational justice exist to guide our efforts? These are the questions I turn to in the next and final chapter.

CHAPTER SIX

Social Justice for "These Kids"

In the Jackson High multipurpose room, just under forty graduating seniors sat in metal folding chairs on an elevated platform serving as a makeshift stage. About sixty guests—parents, grandparents, siblings, and children—sat in rows facing the graduates, while members of the school staff stood around the periphery of the room. "Pomp and Circumstance" blasted from a boom box, creating a mood of positive anticipation and emotion. Camera flashes emanated from the audience, and the seniors seemed to struggle to maintain somber expressions amid the excitement of the moment. The principal, Mr. Galo, a slender white man in his early fifties, approached the podium to make his opening remarks. After welcoming the crowd, he turned to the graduating seniors—all but a handful of them African American, the rest Latino with the exception of one Filipino American—and told them they were "true warriors." He acknowledged that all had overcome significant obstacles to make it to this day, and congratulated them for their courage and strength. "Each and every one of you is special," he concluded. "I mean that from the bottom of my heart."

Three graduating seniors had been invited to deliver speeches at the ceremony. In the first, an African American student named Keisha opened by confessing she had failed nearly all of her classes in the first three years of high school. But, she said, everything had changed when her daughter was born in the summer after junior year. She realized then that she needed to graduate to be a positive role model for her daughter, asking rhetorically, "How could I expect *her* to graduate from high school if I didn't?" Keisha recalled that in September, the school counselor told her that graduation was impossible; she simply did not have enough credits. But, as Keisha told the crowd, "I wouldn't take no for an answer," and she insisted the counselor "map me a plan" to gradu- ate. She reenacted the back-and-forth between herself and the coun- selor with vivid intensity—the counselor repeating that she couldn't do it, Keisha insisting that she "map me a plan, 'cause I'm gonna gradu- ate this year!" In the end, she got her plan, which meant taking evening and weekend classes at the adult school and the community college six days a week, supplemented with a credit-earning internship at a local hospital, all in addition to a full load of courses at Jackson. Keisha pain- fully recounted the long hours and sacrifices it took to accumulate four years' worth of credits in one year's time—how she arrived home on slow city buses after 10:00 p.m. only to leave at 5:00 the next morning for her internship at the hospital, and sometimes went days without seeing her daughter—punctuating her list with the exclamation point: "*and* I'm a single mother!" The audience exploded with wild cheers and applause. Many rose to their feet and called out, "You go, Keisha!" "All right, girl!" "Good for you!" Tears began streaming down Keisha's face and she paused, taking in the warmth of the applause. When she regained her composure, her tone grew serious. She said the only thing that got her through each day was the desire "to prove all those people wrong," all those who had told her she couldn't do it: the counselor, her teachers, her family, and her friends.

Keisha's rendering of her story was heart wrenching, but the basic structure of her narrative was acutely familiar. The themes of accumu- lating credits in the senior year, working hard against seemingly impos- sible odds, and doing it all to "prove people wrong" echoed local nar- ratives about the high school diploma at Jackson and were a staple of graduation day speeches in all of the five years I attended them. These themes were repeated by two other student speakers that day, both of whom shared personal stories of believing they were losers, failures, and on a path toward becoming dropouts. Like Keisha, they described the pain of being expected to fail and attributed their will to stay in school to a deep desire to prove people wrong. The stories of these three young adults illustrate the difficulties "these kids" face just to maintain a sense of dignity as learners and respectable individuals. These youth were well aware of the processes through which their trajectories of failure were being predicted, solidified, and nurtured by the whole world around them, including school professionals.

The graduation day speeches articulated some of the meanings that were attached to the high school diploma at Jackson—as a sign of personal drive in the face of obstacles, a symbolic accomplishment to "prove people wrong," and a gateway to upward mobility. While the graduation ceremony provided occasion for voicing and celebrating these narratives, they were always part of the discursive landscape of Jackson High; teachers, students, and PARTY members employed them often. Suli, for example, recalled that his own motivation to graduate was "to show all you people you were wrong about me." Another student who had dropped out previously explained his choice to come back to Jackson as such: "I don't know. [*tentatively*] I didn't want to call myself a . . . [*pause*] failure or something. I'da let myself down." In this way, the high school diploma was positioned as a symbol of personal and academic success, partially insulating students from placement in the category of total failure. Dropping out of high school was tainted with stigma, a kind of proof that society and school people had been right in labeling one a failure all along.

It is not surprising that students who were on track to graduate from Jackson would embrace a narrative equating the diploma with personal success. The association of high school dropouts with ultimate (personal and academic) failure is a powerful trope in broader public discourse, and Jackson students are precisely those who have been and remain on the verge of dropping out. These students spend the bulk of their adolescent years teetering on the edge of a category that is broadly condemned and pitied. School adults and other professionals (social workers, psychologists, academics) label them "at risk" of dropping out, predict their failure, and then go about documenting and explaining it. Their figured worlds are populated with friends, allies, and role models who often have not graduated from high school and who offer a range of more rewarding and fulfilling ways to get through the day, including the fast money-making possibilities of the drug economy. Meanwhile, getting through the school day may be experienced as painful, dehumanizing, infantilizing, monotonous, irrelevant, and dull (Bettie 2003; Ferguson 2001; Kohl 1995; Nolan 2011). It is no wonder that students who find a way to persist in spite of this relentless countercurrent of pressure would find hope and meaning in a narrative that imbues the high school diploma with important symbolic power. And their persistence in the face of these odds should not be minimized. Jackson graduates really are "true warriors" as Principal Galo declared in his graduation day remarks.

But what to make of their futures beyond graduation? What probable futures await them? Statistics (reviewed in chapter 5) show that most young adults such as those at Jackson High—low-income, low-scoring, predominantly African American—will attempt to enter the labor force. Those who are lucky enough to find work at all will likely end up in low-wage, low-rights, service-sector jobs without benefits or opportunities for upward mobility. Those who attempt community college will likely struggle financially and academically, and discover that a two-year degree takes them substantially longer to achieve. Some of the most exceptionally determined and lucky among them may persist in college long enough to earn a postsecondary degree; many will not. Most will find it difficult or impossible to support themselves with the wages they are able to command, whether or not they have pursued postsecondary training. Access to health care and affordable housing will likely be a continuous struggle. Some will seek support from the limited public assistance that is still available in the United States. Some will turn to the extralegal economy. How, if at all, can and should education prepare them to face this probable future? How can and should *social justice* education contribute to improving the life chances and quality of life for "these kids" as a group?

Taking the interests of "these kids" to heart in a meaningful way requires us to confront the paradox of getting ahead. This paradox refers to the fact that schooling is structured to produce a hierarchy of achievement that sorts students into unequal labor market roles. Failure and success are mutually coconstructed and interdependent social categories, and when individual students get ahead in school, they always do so by getting ahead of others. No amount of "getting ahead" will eliminate the existence of students at the bottom of the educational hierarchy. They will always be with us no matter how well we close the achievement gap or raise overall levels of achievement. To transcend this paradox, we need a new discourse of educational justice and a new set of categories to reach beyond the limiting binaries of success and failure, winners and losers, top and bottom. In the remainder of this chapter, I first review the key arguments that I have advanced in this book. Then, I revisit the central dilemma of educational hierarchy and the limits posed by the paradox of getting ahead. Finally, I sketch out some principles for a new vision of educational justice that puts the interests of last chance students front and center. The vision I propose goes beyond closing the so-called achievement gap[1] and refocuses our attention on closing the *consequence gap*—in other words, reducing the consequences of educational failure and decoupling academic evaluations from judgments of character, deservedness, and worth.

These Kids: Identity, Agency, and Social Justice at a Last Chance High School

This book has examined the PARTY project as one modest attempt to enact social and educational change through PAR and social justice pedagogy in the context of a last chance high school. It explored some of the ways that youth PARTY members experienced, interpreted, and explained the social inequalities affecting their lives. It discussed how each of us, as individuals and as a group, attempted to exercise agency in the face of powerful social structures and discourses. And despite our acts of resistance, it showed numerous ways that the work of PARTY reproduced dominant educational discourses and practices. The story of PARTY is ultimately a story about social reproduction that draws our attention to the constraints on agency, particularly with regard to educational change. It also raises questions about the goals of social justice education—indeed, of secondary education generally—in the context of the last chance high school.

The choice to teach a social justice class at Jackson High reflected the youth PARTY members' desire to challenge and change the social inequalities affecting their lives and the lives of their fellow Jackson students. Through teaching this class, they sought to engage Jackson students in a process of collective inquiry and dialogue to deepen their critical consciousness and empower them as civic actors. As they planned for the class and prepared to teach it, the youth PARTY members defined its goals and methods in opposition to traditional classroom teaching and to the oppressive elements of mainstream schooling. Yet as they moved from the out-of-school context of weekly meetings to the in-school context of a classroom at Jackson High, their vision of educational change quickly transformed into a caricature of dominant educational practice and discourse. Rather than posing a challenge to mainstream schooling, the social justice class reproduced and parodied many of its most oppressive elements. This book has explored how and why these outcomes occurred and what educators might learn from them. Its two central arguments concerned, first, the power of discourse in shaping processes of identity formation and social reproduction, and second, the limits to educational justice posed by the paradox of getting ahead.

Discourse, Identity, and Agency

Drawing from critical and sociocultural theories of identity and agency, this book has examined the identity practices of PARTY members, including myself, as we wrestled with issues of educational and social inequality and attempted to take action for social change. In telling the story of PARTY, I have highlighted several acts of resistance and agency—as when D contested Yolanda's appropriation of the discourse of these kids and Lolo expressed reservations about Leila's deficit thinking (chapter 2); when D, Leila, and Suli chose to teach a social justice class for critical consciousness and social change (chapter 3); when Suli and Leila insisted they would not be "puppets" or "like the teacher of every day" (chapter 4); and when D advanced his own alternative paradigm of educational justice (chapter 5). In these moments, the youth refused to conform to dominant discourses and practices that they had experienced as dehumanizing and oppressive; instead, they took action to challenge, contest, or construct alternative discourses and practices. These small acts of resistance were consistent with their developing critical consciousness and the systemic analysis of inequality they articulated during the project (chapter 3). As seen in chapter 3, PARTY members grew increasingly skilled at identifying systemic causes of institutionalized oppression, and they often spoke about the need for transformative social change. The act of naming these issues can be classified as an act of resistance because naming is an essential step toward taking civic action.

I have also argued throughout this book that concepts of resistance and reproduction are not as clear-cut as they may initially seem. At some times, one might masquerade as the other; at other times, a single act might be classified as both resistive *and* reproductive. For example, when Leila and Yolanda chose to position themselves in opposition to the discourse of these kids during their interview with PARTY (chapter 2), they simultaneously resisted the power of this discourse to define them while reproducing its dominant deficit-oriented tropes. And when D and Suli chose to identify with "cool guys" in the social justice class at the expense of a commitment to more rigorous intellectual engagement (chapter 4), they rejected the oppressive institution of schooling while re-producing their positioning (and their students' positioning) as school failures. The same combination of resistance and reproduction could be found in the youth's approach to assigning final grades (chapter 4), a process that both trivialized and reified the imperative of individualized and hierarchical achievement as a necessary component of "doing school" (Pope 2003). Whether we choose to classify these acts as resistive or reproductive largely depends on our perspective and interpretation. But I also suggest that they might in fact be both: that resistance and reproduction can coexist within the very same actions and choices.

Social theorists have long debated precisely what kinds of actions constitute resistance. Must they be conscious, deliberate, and intentional? Explicitly geared toward social change? Public as opposed to covert? Collective as opposed to individual? At one end of the spectrum are those who interpret nearly any act of noncompliance as one of resistance. But many scholars have argued that this understanding is too broad: if almost everything is an act of resistance, the concept loses its analytical specificity and theoretical purpose (Giroux [1983] 2003; Solorzano and Delgado Bernal 2001). Complicating matters further is that resistance and reproduction are especially difficult constructs to disentangle in the context of schooling. Studying hard, pursuing higher education, trying to achieve academically—these are acts of compliance, but they are often framed as resistance when undertaken by low-income youth or youth of color because they challenge dominant patterns of social reproduction (Solorzano and Delgado Bernal 2001; Cammarota 2004; Fordham 1996; Brayboy 2005). For Jeffrey and Lolo (chapter 5), for example, making these choices seemed to represent a form of resistance. Lolo, in particular, clearly articulated a resistive stance (chapter 3). D made very different choices with regard to education. He was the only participant in PARTY who never even pretended to have an interest in pursuing higher education. And he, more so than other participants, unwaveringly embraced a "cool guy" identity in opposition to schoolteachers and school authorities (chapter 4). Alongside his rejection of schooling, though, was a steadfast support for liberatory education and an evident commitment to social justice. In my own rendering of D in this book, I have portrayed his stance as resistive. But his choices were also reproductive because they did little to challenge his own subordinate social positioning or that of other low-income students of color within the educational system.

Daniel Solorzano and Dolores Delgado Bernal (2001) outline a theoretical framework that allows us to understand how both Lolo and D exercised resistance to and within the institution of schooling while also differentiating between their choices and the implications of each. The authors identify four types of resistance: reactionary, self-defeating, conformist, and transformational. Each category corresponds to a quadrant on a grid, in which one axis represents the degree to which the actor is "motivated by social justice," and the other represents the degree to which the actor possesses a "critique of social oppression" (318). Applying their categories, a low-income student of color who studies hard to achieve upward mobility, as did Lolo and Jeffrey, would exemplify "conformist resistance" if they lacked a systemic critique of educational oppression and "transformational resistance" if they possessed such a critique.[2] In contrast, students such as D who rejected schooling and enacted oppositional behaviors in the classroom would exemplify "reactionary behavior" if they lacked a systemic critique of educational oppression and "self-defeating resistance" if they possessed such a critique. Self-defeating resistance, in Solorzano and Delgado Bernal's work, is motivated by a critique of oppression but ultimately "helps to recreate the oppressive conditions from which it originated" (310). The authors rightly point out that a great deal of writing about resistance in education has focused on—and often has glorified and romanticized—what they call self-defeating resistance while ignoring other types.

Solorzano and Delgado Bernal's framework is useful for distinguishing among different kinds of resistance with different motivations and implications, but its categories do not fully capture the complexity of resistance and agency seen within the PARTY project. In their framework, the four types of resistance appear to be arranged hierarchically, with transformational resistance positioned as the most desirable. Through the examples they offer to illustrate each type, they suggest that achieving academically in school is associated with being "motivated by social justice," while enacting oppositional behavior at school is interpreted as a lack of social justice motivation. This may imply too narrow a definition of what it means to be motivated by social justice. However, it is consistent with a resistance framework that sees greater inclusion of oppressed people in dominant educational and social institutions as its main goal. For youth participants in PARTY, inclusion may not have been their primary goal—at least not always, and not without qualifications. Moreover, they were likely motivated by a host of other goals, from the "bigger" goal of complete societal transformation (entailing the dismantling and replacement of dominant educational and social institutions rather than inclusion within them) to the "smaller" goal of self-preservation in the face of daily indignities. Many theorists have illuminated how small acts of resistance often serve the immediate psychological need of protecting the self against repeated "assaults on dignity" (Nolan 2011; see also Ferguson 2001; Scott 1990; Willis 1981). This is especially likely to be the case in the context of highly coercive and dehumanizing institutions, a description that applies to many high-poverty urban schools (Nolan 2011; Ferguson 2001). Such covert, "self-preserving and self-creating" acts of resistance (Nolan 2011) may or may not be entirely conscious, and they may or may not explicitly seek the goals of social justice, but I concur with theorists who treat these as legitimate forms of resistance rather than irrational, misguided, or self-defeating oppositional behaviors.

Current resistance theories attempt to disrupt the classic reproduction-resistance binary and advance a more fluid, less "teleological" understanding of resistance (Tuck and Yang 2011). In describing these emerging "non-teleological resistance theories" (ibid.), Tuck and Yang explain, they "do not fetishize progress, but understand that change happens in ways that make new, old-but-returned, and previously unseen possibilities available at each juncture" (522). Moreover, in nonteleological theories of resistance, "the endgame of such resistance is unfixed and always taking shape" (522). These theories are moving toward a more complex, fluid, and nonlinear understanding of resistance while hoping to avoid the trap of applying the term too broadly. Consistent with this emerging nonteleological theoretical perspective, I have argued that PARTY members' actions were often simultaneously both reproductive and resistive. Rather than framing these as mutually exclusive concepts, I examined how participants' choices, words, actions, and interactions could and often did embody both. This approach assumes there is no such thing as truly "authentic" resistance (Dimitriadis 2011); we are always implicated in and bound up with the social institutions, relations, and discourses of our social worlds. Every act of resistance might indeed reproduce particular kinds of dominant power relations and discourses while challenging or subverting others. A shortcoming of the PARTY project was, perhaps, our failure to recognize and name this complexity so that we could be more deliberate with our choices and conscious of their implications.

Although I have highlighted many small acts of resistance and sought to complexify our understanding of this concept, I have also shown a consistent tendency, throughout this book, toward socially reproductive results. This was most poignantly evident in the format and pedagogy of the social justice class at Jackson High. Chapters 4 and 5 argued that the class reproduced many aspects of the grammar of schooling (Tyack and Cuban 1997) while neglecting many of the ideals of liberatory education that had initially animated the youth. When we shifted from an out-of-school PAR project to the figured world of Jackson High, many dominant discourses of schooling were quickly adopted and naturalized, and the imperatives of schooling eventually trumped the ideals of education. Another example of unwitting reproduction in PARTY occurred when the youth participants were placed in the position of gatekeeper with real (if limited) distributional power—as seen during the interview process (chapter 2) and the assignment of final grades (chapter 4). In both cases, they employed dominant cultural scripts to make evaluative judgments about student ability based solely on the students' comportment, language use, and "attitude." As discussed in chapter 2, the experience of being gatekeepers was new and unfamiliar, necessitating improvisation and therefore heightening the possibilities for agency (Holland et al. 2001). In this situation, the youth engaged in practices of gatekeeping and exclusion that reinforced broader, societal-level exclusionary practices. D took visible steps in both situations to attempt to name and interrupt the reproductive and exclusionary practices that were playing out. These were significant acts of resistance, even though they did not succeed in preventing reproductive outcomes.

Many reformers today suggest that low-income students, students of color, and low-performing students in general need to be explicitly taught "professional" behaviors of schooling and the workplace (e.g., Payne 2005; Whitman 2008). However, the youth PARTY members' capacity to police and sanction behaviors coded as unprofessional suggests that, for them, explicit instruction in these areas was not needed. In their case, the relevant question was not whether they knew how to act in professional settings but what identities were "made possible and necessary" (McDermott 1997, 121) in any particular situation. The choices they made tended to be ones that preserved their dignity to the largest extent possible. When they attempted to construct a collective identity as "professionals" (chapter 2), or saw "good attitude" in students who reminded them of themselves and with whom they experienced empathy (chapter 4), they also reinforced their own goodness, deservedness, and dignity in the face of powerful school-based and societal discourses that framed them as criminal, undeserving, or victims. As well, their choices were shaped in each instance by the range of identities that were available to assume in a particular context or figured world (chapters 2 and 4), and by how other individuals in that context acted and interacted with *them*— what Gee (2000) calls the "recognition work" of identity (chapter 4).

The examples of identity and agency in PARTY that I explored throughout this book underscore the extent to which our identity choices, and our acts of agency and resistance, are situated within and shaped by the discursive terrain—the web of shared discourses, social categories, and social meanings we have to work with. My aim has been to help us think about the constraints on agency not only in terms of the material elements of structure but also its discursive, ideological, and cultural dimensions. By exposing and denaturalizing the role of discourse, I have tried to show ethnographically how and why it is central to the dialectic of structure and agency. Dominant discourses are often perpetuated through unconscious and taken-for-granted ways of speaking, acting, and interacting—part and parcel of our identities—and they constrain our capacity to exercise agency by shaping what we are capable of imagining.

Limits of the Paradox of Getting Ahead

In chapter 1, I situated the PARTY project and Jackson High within a historical analysis of continuation and other last chance high schools and their positioning vis-à-vis mainstream or "regular" high schools. Following Deirdre Kelly (1993a), I showed that continuation high schools periodically redefined their stated purpose and broadened their intended student constituency, but one thing that remained constant was the definition of their students in opposition to normative standards defining "regular" students, and the clear positioning of continuation students as deficient, defective, and inferior with regard to this norm. I identified a dominant discourse about last chance students as the *discourse of these kids*, characterizing this as a deficit-oriented discourse that defines who "these kids" are, why they are a problem, and what the purpose of schooling is for them. I argued that the last chance high school was constructed in tandem with the last chance student, both of them as distinct and inferior "kinds" understood in opposition to an untheorized mainstream.

This historical trajectory shaped the ground on which the PARTY project emerged. The youth participants in PARTY were well aware of their positioning at the bottom of the educational hierarchy, the implications of that positioning, and the social meanings attached to it. Their identities were constructed in dialogue with the discourse of these kids (chapter 2). And when we started teaching a social justice class at Jackson High, we found ourselves struggling with long-standing historic debates about the meaning of social justice and the purpose of education for "these kids" (chapters 1 and 5). In the context of the last chance high school, some enduring philosophical dilemmas of schooling became relevant: How and for what purpose should we educate youth who have already landed at the bottom of the achievement hierarchy and find themselves on a well-worn path into low-wage, low-status, low-rights jobs? Can education interrupt these paths? Certainly it can do so for a limited number of individuals, but what about the cohort of last chance students as a group? What does it mean to pursue social justice for "all" students inside a system such as this? Is it possible to reconceptualize schooling to eliminate such hierarchies altogether? What would we construct in its place?

PARTY members, including myself, lacked the appropriate conceptual frameworks that would have allowed us to articulate and engage these questions in a transformative way. The reality and inevitability of educational hierarchy appeared as a given, not something to be contested, and our work operated within the confines of that prevailing assumption. In what remains of this chapter, I attempt to take some small steps toward forging the type of alternative educational discourse that might have supported PARTY in arriving at a different outcome—or at least articulating a different set of possibilities. I seek to engage and reinvigorate the questions articulated above, by placing the interests of last chance students at the front and center of my discussion. I insist on considering the interests of last chance students as a group, rather than individuals, as a way to move beyond the paradox of getting ahead.

My first step is to revisit the discourse of "college for all" (chapter 5) and critically examine its logic, appeal, and limits. Not only is this discourse a powerful force in education today, but it is also strongly associated with notions of social justice and resonates with the "good sense" (Gramsci 1971; See also Lipman 2011) of many critical social justice educators. Therefore, as we construct a new vision of educational justice with the interests of last chance students at the center, it is important to interrogate the discourse of college for all and examine how it advances principles of critical, democratic, and social justice pedagogies as well as how it may undermine those very principles. Further, it is important to examine the promises and assumptions of this discourse in light of the paradox of getting ahead.

The Logic and Limits of College for All

College for all is a powerful ideal that resonates with all three of Labaree's (1997) educational goals (see the introduction for a summary). For proponents of "democratic equality," it promises equity and access for underserved student populations. For proponents of "social efficiency," it promises to meet employers' need for higher-skilled workers and to increase US competitiveness in the global economy. For proponents of "social mobility," it promises pathways for individual advancement and getting ahead. One of the most frequent arguments used to support college for all is to compare earnings of college graduates to those of non-college-educated workers. This argument directly appeals to the social mobility role of schooling by framing educational credentials as a private good that can be cashed in for higher earnings and individual advancement.

Since 1980, the income gap between college graduates and those with just a high school diploma has indeed grown wider (Goldin and Katz 2007). Many have interpreted this fact to be evidence of a growing demand for "higher-skilled" workers in the economy (ibid.). Based on this belief, educators and policymakers promote the idea of sending more students to college and assume that all or most of them will be rewarded with higher wages and better jobs at the other end. Few educators question the accuracy of this belief, but many social scientists contest it. Within this group, some argue the college wage premium is not the result of a labor market demand for high-skilled workers but rather of *decreasing* wages overall combined with soaring compensation at the very top of the income distribution (Krugman 2007; Mishel, Bernstein, and Shierholz 2009).[3] Concentration of income among the so-called hyperrich (Johnston 2005) may bring up the average earnings of college-educated workers but does not reflect a rise in wages among college graduates generally. The decline in unionization rates, the falling value of the federal minimum wage, and the deregulation of the financial sector may do more to explain the growing college wage premium than a changing labor market demand for better-educated workers (Philippon and Reshef 2009; DiNardo, Fortin, and Lemiuex 1996; Firpo, Fortin, and Lemieux 2009; Wolff 2006). Employment projections by the US Bureau of Labor Statistics (BLS) also cast doubts on the claim of an increasing demand for college-educated workers. As of this writing, the BLS projects that the overall share of jobs requiring a postsecondary degree in 2016 will be approximately 30 percent, and this is roughly the percentage of students who currently obtain one.[4]

Critics of college for all have emerged from both ends of the ideological spectrum. On the Right, some critics seem motivated by populist anti-intellectualism, as when Republican presidential candidate Rick Santorum called President Barack Obama a "snob" for encouraging all Americans to go to college (Caldwell 2012). Some may be motivated by implicit racism or classism when they suggest that traditionally workbound students (disproportionately poor and of color) are not capable of rigorous higher education. On the political Left, critics argue that college for all is a distraction from much-needed economic reforms. In this view, the interlocking problems of deindustrialization, growing income inequality, rising poverty rates, and a shrinking middle class—issues discussed in chapter 5 that present major barriers for Jackson students and graduates—must be understood as labor market issues and not primarily as educational ones (Grubb and Lazerson 2004; Rothstein 2002; Wolff 2006). As such, the proper response to these issues would be redistributive economic reforms such as raising the minimum wage and expanding the social safety net, not simply offering more or better education. For policymakers, educational reform may be a politically convenient response to economic inequality because it has the appearance of being redistributive without actually redistributing many resources. From this perspective, the discourse of college for all might be seen as a naïve hope or a deliberate deception—but surely a misplaced emphasis that may reinforce economic inequality rather than ameliorate it.

The history of American education is replete with attempts to promote education reform as a solution to economic problems and inequalities (Grubb and Lazerson 2004; Labaree 2010; Tyack and Cuban 1997; Perkinson 1995). The view of education as a panacea places unrealistic demands on educators, ultimately casting them as scapegoats when those demands are not met, and diverts political attention from reforms that might actually address the root causes of economic inequality (Tyack and Cuban 1997; Labaree 2010). As Anyon (2005) summarizes, "As a nation, we have been counting on education to solve the problems of un- employment, joblessness, and poverty for many years. But education did not cause these problems, and education cannot solve them. An eco- nomic system that chases profits and casts people aside (especially peo- ple of color) is culpable" (3). The rhetoric of college for all reflects and reinforces the view of education as a panacea. According to its logic, it is schools and students that need changing—not the economic system. If schools would just prepare all students for college, and if students would just apply themselves to academic achievement, the problems of growing income inequality and under- and unemployment would be greatly miti- gated if not solved outright. This message encourages policymakers and the public to scapegoat teachers and students for growing economic in- equality rather than shifting their gaze to the political-economic system itself and to economic reforms that might actually raise the standard of living for all workers—the college-educated and non-college-educated alike.

Nevertheless, educators who support the broader aims of educational equity might reasonably ask what harm there is in the discourse of col- lege for all. There are many good reasons to support policies that expand college access to more students. These include the intellectual, cultural, and political benefits of higher education, and the benefits of democra- tizing access to higher education for underserved students. If the dis- course of college for all brings us closer to these ends, what is the value in advancing a critique? Educators with commitments to social justice should always support better, more intellectually rigorous, and more eq- uitable schools for underserved students, and this must include vigorous support for greater access to higher education. But it is unwise to rely on misleading economic rationales to support these aims. My reading of the available research suggests it is extremely unlikely that growing income inequality, poverty-wage jobs, and high unemployment for last chance students can be solved by sending all of them to college. College for all may enable some individual students to achieve upward mobility, but it does not provide the possibility of mobility for the cohort of "these kids" as a group. In fact, as more and more students pursue college de- grees, the value of the degree is declining and the credentials race is in- tensifying, with no appreciable change in overall levels of mobility (La- baree 1997; Wolff 2006). Moreover, the rhetoric of college for all may be politically demobilizing because it encourages students—especially low-income, urban, and of-color youth who want to change the social conditions of their lives and communities—to channel their time and energy into the individualistic pursuit of educational credentials rather than collective organizing for social change and economic justice (Tannock 2006). This message resonates with the achievement ideology but may undermine the collective, democratic goals of critical and social justice pedagogy.

The debate on college for all is contentious precisely because of the role that schools play in sorting students into different labor market positions and therefore social class positions. The deeply unequal quality of the US class structure makes educational outcomes particularly consequential. Many aspects of students' lives and well-being are potentially affected by them: their future paychecks and standard of living; their ability to access adequate health care and housing; their sense of dignity and humanity in the workplace; their capacity and sense of entitlement to exercise political voice. The consequential nature of educational outcomes gives privileged groups a great deal of incentive to maintain the educational status quo, or at least to maintain their own positions of relative advantage within it. It also puts pressure on the system to offer numerous second chances and reentry points (Kantor and Tyack 1982; Brint and Karabel 1991), of which the last chance high school is one. The existence of numerous such reentry points sustains the idea that educational failure is never permanent, that mobility always remains an option. This belief in the possibility of second chances is essential to the American achievement ideology. In the end, however, we are still left with winners and losers, and hence a cohort of "these kids," and this is by design. That is why I propose a shift in focus from the achievement gap to the consequence gap. Such a shift would help us imagine educational interventions that improve the life chances and quality of life for last chance students as a group. Further, it would support the use of more critical, democratic, and social justice pedagogies in schools.

Closing the Consequence Gap

Educators and policymakers from across the political spectrum are eager to close the achievement gap. But almost nothing is said about the consequence gap—that is, the disproportionate economic consequences of educational underachievement, especially for youth who begin their lives in positions of economic and racial marginalization. For these students, the consequences of school failure in today's postindustrial economy are severe. It is popular to blame the education system for the economic struggles that Jackson students and others like them face, and to imagine that closing the achievement gap would improve these conditions and reduce inequalities. But economic inequality is not primarily caused by the achievement gap; it is caused by the academic *consequence* gap. In fact, the consequence gap has continued to grow wider even as the achievement gap has declined slightly and overall levels of achievement have risen (Rothstein 2002; Wolff 2006). If failure for some is indeed "produced" by the education system, then its consequences should be softened. Social justice for "these kids" cannot only be about equalizing achievement, although enhancing the intellectual capacities and curiosities of all students is no doubt an important component. It must also be about reducing the consequences of achievement differences—consequences measured in terms of access to livable-wage work, political voice, and dignified selves.

Reducing the consequence gap would mean substantially reducing income inequality and the social distance between the top and bottom ends of the income distribution. To achieve this, educational policy and curricular reform must be joined with and supported by economic and social policy reforms that reduce economic inequality and strengthen the social safety net. An important step toward this goal, as Anyon (2005) persuasively argues, is to redefine what counts as educational policy so it includes these other social arenas—for example, raising the minimum wage, providing affordable health care and housing, and improving working conditions for low-wage workers. Not only would such policies directly reduce the consequence gap, but some research suggests they can also help reduce the achievement gap (this research is summarized in Anyon 2005 and Rothstein 2002). This is because children whose basic economic needs are met—and who do not experience the household stress caused by a parent's loss of a job, eviction from an apartment, inability to access health care when sick—are likely to be more focused and perform better in school. Therefore, educators who care about the achievement gap have an interest in social reforms that reduce the consequence gap.

Reducing the consequence gap would also support efforts to implement more democratic, critical, and social justice pedagogies in schools. This is because by lowering the economic stakes attached to achievement disparities, it would likely alleviate some of the pressure toward ever-greater hierarchization, commodification, and credentialism in schools. The race for educational credentials and for access to ever-scarcer positions of privilege would likely become less frantic, less fierce, and less all-consuming to the system. The exchange value of credentials would be less significant, so students and teachers might more readily pursue education for its use value. Rather than increased educational hierarchization, we might construct an educational system that provides every student with multiple opportunities to excel and develop his or her talents across a wide variety of arenas. We might nurture and reward students' diverse ways of knowing without arranging these hierarchically. We might pursue more altruistic learning goals such as fostering a love of learning for its own sake, unleashing the innate creativity and curiosity of every student, and strengthening every student's capacity for social critique and political engagement. We would likely find it easier to talk about the idea of education for the public good, since the pressures to frame it as a private good for individual gain would be substantially reduced. These ideas do not have to mean a complete elimination of all "incentives" for studying hard. They just mean the consequences of being average, or even below average, would no longer equate to total economic marginalization and uncertainty. This could free up space in schools to get back to the work of educating for democracy.

Reducing the consequence gap also means challenging the hegemony of meritocracy as the end point of educational justice. The ideal of meritocracy is central to almost every definition of educational justice but does not bring us closer to social justice for "these kids."[5] The goal of meritocracy is not an equitable society but a "level playing field" on which to compete for society's scarce, and unevenly divided, rewards. Social inequality is justified and even beneficial in this model as long as income and status disparities reflect "true" differences in merit, *and* everyone is given equal opportunities to develop and display their merit in exchange for societal rewards (M. Young 1994). When these conditions are met, income inequality is actually seen as beneficial because it provides incentives for hard work (ibid.; Becker and Murphy 2007). Some political conservatives suggest that our current education system is basically meritocratic already, but the prevailing view among liberals and most education reformers is that we still have a long way to go toward this goal. In short, while the more conservative position uses meritocracy as an *ideology* to justify privilege, the more liberal position advances meritocracy as an *ideal* we have not yet reached. Pursuing meritocracy as an ideal is inherently complicated because definitions of merit and ideas about how to measure it are substantially contested. The complex whole of human capability and creativity cannot adequately be quantified, and attempts to do so inherently reflect particular interests, values, and perspectives. Moreover, those who have obtained societal privileges will always be better positioned to secure advantages for their children and to have those advantages recognized as "merit" (Bourdieu and Passeron 1990; Lareau 2003). Therefore, a perfect meritocracy is not likely to be an attainable goal. Yet a great deal of education reform is aimed at pursuing it anyway, and this is often seen as essential to the project of creating a more just society.

Given the popular belief in meritocracy as an ideal, it is worth considering whether it offers an adequate vision of social justice for "these kids." In an ideal meritocracy, we might imagine that all educational decisions and assessments would reflect a pure measure of merit (defined as some combination of a student's inherent ability and effort), with no exceptions. There would be no controversy about the definition of merit, the evidence for demonstrating it, or the fairness and accuracy of procedures for measuring it. Every individual would end up precisely where he or she "deserved" to be on the basis of merit alone. The playing field would be level, and the system would be fully transparent, objective, and uncontested. If such a true meritocracy existed, would it then be acceptable for a high school graduate with a full-time job at a grocery store to become homeless simply because the minimum wage was insufficient for securing shelter (as happened to Lolo, chapter 5)? Would it then be acceptable for millions of workers in low-wage, low-status, low-rights jobs to go without basic health care or to experience stigma and shame for having "failed" in the race to get ahead? After all, in this ideal meritocracy, would they not "deserve" these economic hardships and assaults on their dignity?

If this degree of social inequality does not appear just in a hypothetical but impossible ideal meritocracy, then it must be even less so in the context of the imperfect, partial meritocracy we are bound to have in practice. An education system that creates losers and relegates them to poverty-wage jobs, extreme financial insecurity, and stigmatization cannot embody social justice—even if its winners and losers are determined on the basis of merit. As both Varenne and McDermott (1999) and Labaree (1999) have pointed out, such an ideal meritocracy may be a fairer world than the one we currently have, but that does not mean it is the world we should strive for. Existing levels of social inequality are unjust not only because they are not based on merit but because they dehumanize, stigmatize, and exploit large proportions of the population by structural necessity. A consequence of meritocratic ideology is that people with insufficient amounts of socially recognized merit get positioned as undeserving citizens and lesser people (Katz 1990). This is antithetical to social justice, and it is morally wrong. It is not merely a more meritocratic system we need; it is a more compelling vision of social justice that insists on the essential dignity and deservedness of all people and the inherent value of a well-rounded, broad, and critical education for democracy.

To begin taking us in this direction, I believe we must find ways to decouple educational assessments from judgments of personal worth, character, and deservedness. We must forcefully assert and actually believe that all human beings are morally deserving, politically entitled, and intellectually capable. We must vigorously defend and seek to restore the civic purposes of education and the value of education for democracy. We need an education system that recognizes and values the cognitive demands of so-called practical labor, as well as the kinesthetic and embodied demands of so-called academic labor (Rose 2005b). This must go beyond the trite lip service of slogans about the value of all honest work. It must be reflected in the societal rewards that are in fact accrued to all honest work. But how do we get from here to there? What concrete things can educators do to begin closing the consequence gap now?

First, we need to be clear that no education reform to advance the interests of "these kids" should be targeted only at last chance or low-scoring students alone. These students exist because the larger system does not serve all students well (Kelly 1993a). Therefore, advancing their needs requires change *throughout* the broader education system. This is an important point that cannot be overstated. Too often, reforms to help "these kids" take place at the margins of the education system—in alternative and continuation programs, remedial and special education classes, or outside of school altogether—precisely where "these kids" are likely to be found (see the introduction). Such reforms leave the basic structure and practices of the education system intact. They do nothing to address the production of hierarchy that creates "these kids" in the first place. Social justice for last chance students requires radical transformation *throughout* the education system, not just at its margins and lower rungs.

It also requires substantial social change outside education, most notably by reducing income inequality and strengthening the social safety net, to close the consequence gap.

Within education, we should start by increasing and equalizing school funding, reducing the emphasis on standardized tests, eliminating the corporate influence in education, and returning public schools to public control (e.g., see Lipman 2011). We should also think about new frameworks for organizing curriculum and pedagogy that take labor market realities seriously, challenge the academic-vocational divide (chapter 5), and integrate social justice across the curriculum rather than confining it to so-called academic subject areas. One possible approach for translating these values into practice is a civically focused multiple pathways framework (e.g., Oakes and Saunders 2008b; Rose 2008; Rogers, Kahne, and Middaugh 2008). *Multiple pathways* is a general term that typically applies to programs integrating academic with career and technical content through thematic, contextualized, project-based learning (Oakes and Saunders 2008b). Some advocates of multiple pathways emphasize the framework's economic purpose of labor market preparation and neglect the democratic function of schools. But the civically focused multiple pathways approaches described by Oakes and Saunders (2008b), Rose (2008), and Rogers, Kahne, and Middaugh (2008) explicitly aim to revitalize the civic mission of schools by challenging the academic-vocational divide and weaving social analysis and critique throughout the curriculum in diverse, heterogeneous classrooms.

These authors suggest different details, but their work converges in advocating a curriculum and pedagogy that would help students navigate the postindustrial labor market and higher education system while also critiquing and challenging instances of economic exploitation and inequality in both. This combination of navigating *and* critiquing the labor market resonates with theorists of critical pedagogy who call on teachers to help students master and critique the dominant school curriculum (e.g., Tejeda, Espinosa, and Gutierrez 2003; Kincheloe 1995; Delpit 1988). It aims to empower all students, including work-bound students, as critical agents of social change by linking social justice issues to the world of work and to other contexts such as home, neighborhood, and community. The workplace, even the low-wage workplace, is framed as an arena of political engagement in which students—as democratic citizens and as workers—have the right and responsibility to exercise political voice. This approach helps all students learn to see themselves as

SOCIAL JUSTICE FOR "THESE KIDS"   177

potential advocates for social justice across the many contexts of their lives and the range of pathways in which they might end up. Social justice work needs to happen everywhere, not only within professionalized "social justice" careers such as law, politics, teaching, and professional activism.

Of course, a civically focused multiple pathways program is no panacea. It is merely one way to rethink the organization of curriculum and pedagogy to help educators foster difference without hierarchy, and without neglecting low-income students' legitimate interest in obtaining economic security and dignified work. To really make progress in closing the achievement and consequence gaps, any education reform must also be accompanied by social reforms that actually create opportunities for livable-wage work, reduce overall income inequality, and strengthen the social safety net. A good place to start is by supporting efforts to strengthen labor unions, raise wages at the lower end of the income distribution, and provide housing and health care for all. As Anyon (2005) persuasively argues, these social reforms should "count" as educational policy, and educators should advocate for them as such.

Concluding Thoughts

The vision of educational justice I advance in this chapter is based on my central concern with the paradox of getting ahead and the limits it places on achieving social justice for "these kids." These limits are exposed and magnified in the context of the last chance high school, but they are indicative of broader contradictions inherent to American schooling. In particular, they reflect the contradictory imperatives of schools to sort children into unequal labor market roles while also providing multiple opportunities for upward mobility. As long as schooling produces a hierarchy of achievement, "these kids" will be with us. What does it mean to pursue social justice for "all" within a system like this? In this book, I have attempted to take this question seriously and suggest possible ways of rethinking education that might help us begin to transcend this paradox of getting ahead. I have argued that we need a radical rethinking and transformation of the education system and our educational value system. We must reclaim as a core value the belief that every person, no matter what he or she did in school, is entitled to dignified work, a livable wage, and a political voice. We must do more than state this ideal;

we must work tirelessly to operationalize it through social, political, economic, and pedagogical change.

Clearly, this is a very tall order. I have argued throughout the pages of this book that discourses—the systems of meaning that structure our consciousness and identities—are powerful, durable, and resilient. Dominant discourses are often perpetuated through unconscious and taken-for-granted ways of speaking, acting, and interacting, and they often constrain our capacity to exercise agency or even to imagine what kinds of action might constitute agency. Without underestimating the challenges inherent in such a goal, I have tried to demonstrate the need for a new discourse of educational justice throughout this book, and to point toward the direction that such discursive change should take. Social justice for "these kids" requires a new way to talk about education and its purpose, a new set of categories and assumptions to frame our discussion. Constructing this language must be part of our work as social justice educators. We cannot do it alone; closing the consequence gap requires a broad social movement and a profound transformation of values. But we must be willing to imagine the world and the educational system we want to build. This is a first necessary step toward exercising agency.

Appendix:
Last Chance Literature Review
Coding Methods

This appendix describes the procedures used in my review of policy, practitioner, and research texts about last chance high schools and their students.1 The purpose of this review was to examine the national-level discourse defining who last chance students are, what they are like, and what the purpose of schooling is for them. The insights gleaned from this review are the basis of my arguments about the nature and contours of the discourse of these kids (chapter 1).

Text Selection

From three database searches in ERIC (the Education Resources Information Center) and Google Scholar, I selected all published works dated 1990 or later that I determined to be "about" last chance high schools and/or their students. After all applicable texts were combined and redundancies eliminated, the sample consisted of 221 published works.

1. A search in Google Scholar for "continuation high school" (conducted March 2, 2009) yielded 492 hits, of which 88 were determined to be applicable.
2. A search in ERIC for "continuation high school," "continuation school," and "continuation education" (conducted February 10, 2009) yielded 48 hits, of which 23 were determined to be applicable.

3. A search in ERIC for "alternative high school" or "alternative education" or "alternative school" AND "fail*" or "risk" or "dropout" (conducted April 15, 2009) yielded 163 hits, of which 142 were determined to be applicable. (The asterisk after the word *fail* instructs the search engine to include all terms beginning with those letters, including *failure* and *failing*.)

To determine if a text was applicable, I applied two criteria:

1. It was published in the United States, based on research conducted in the United States, in 1990 or later. I defined as "published" all doctoral dissertations (EdD and PhD), conference papers, and professional association newsletters, but excluded master's theses.
2. It was "about" last chance high schools or their students. I determined a text to be about last chance high schools or their students if it met *any one* of the following three qualifications:

   a. A last chance high school, group of last chance high schools, or the continuation high school system was a primary unit of analysis in the study or text. (Last chance high schools included all continuation high schools in California and any alternative high schools specifically targeting low-scoring or at-risk students.)
   b. Last chance high school students as a group constituted a significant unit of analysis in the text, either on their own or in comparison to another group of students. (This included students in any continuation high school in California or any alternative high school specifically targeting low-scoring or at-risk students.)
   c. The sample of research subjects in the study was comprised wholly or partially of continuation/alternative high school students, and identified as such in the text.

The most common reasons for excluding a text from the sample were the following:

1. Last chance high schools or their students were mentioned in the text but were neither a central unit of analysis nor an explicit part of the sample of the research subjects.
2. An alternative high school was featured that did not specifically target low-scoring or at-risk students.
3. The text was not published (this included all master's theses).

4. The text was published or based on research done outside the United States.
5. The text was published before 1990.

Coding and Analysis Procedures

After determining the sample from the three database searches, I coded each text to identify its central topic, audience, and disciplinary orientation. I employed an open coding approach in the first round, choosing codes for each text based on the abstract and, when necessary, a cursory reading of the text. From this first round of open coding, I identified three topics that repeated most frequently across the sample: substance abuse, criminality/violence, and explaining school failure. I conducted a second round of coding with these three topics as codes to apply systematically. I applied the following criteria to determine if a text could be categorized in each one:

*   *Substance abuse*: A text was considered to be about substance abuse if its focus was wholly or partially about substance abuse, including risk factors, treatment models, prevention models, intervention programs, and so forth. Substance abuse texts include those focused on the use or abuse of alcohol, tobacco, caffeine, marijuana, and other illicit drugs. This category includes articles focused solely on substance abuse as well as those looking at substance abuse in conjunction with other issues (such as violence, academic achievement, and self-esteem).
*   *Violence/criminality*: A text was considered to be about violence/criminality if its focus was wholly or partially about violence, gun possession, gun violence, gang membership, or criminal behavior. This category includes articles in which the primary research subjects are identified as juvenile offenders or students on parole. The texts may be focused solely on violence/criminality, or they may examine violence/criminality in conjunction with other issues (such as substance abuse, academic achievement, and self-esteem).
*   *Explaining failure*: A text was considered to be about explaining failure if its focus was wholly or partially about explaining *why* students in the study performed poorly in school (including dropping out, receiving failing grades, transferring to a continuation high school, etc.). This category also included articles/studies focused on explaining strategies/reforms to help such students perform better in school (whether by graduating, not transferring to a continuation high school, raising test scores, etc.).

The second round of coding also involved categorizing research texts by academic discipline. I skipped this step in ERIC because all of the texts in the database come from education, but in Google Scholar I found a significant number of texts from fields such as public health, psychology, and criminology. Therefore, in the second round of coding, I added the primary academic discipline for each text. To determine the discipline for a journal article, I looked up the journal to determine how it defined itself. When in doubt, I looked up the author to find her or his departmental affiliation.

I knew from the first two rounds of coding that a large proportion of texts in the sample focused on problem- or deviant-coded behaviors of students. Therefore, in the third round, I added an additional set of codes to gather more systematic information about what types of behaviors dominated the literature. I coded each text according to:

1. *Audience*: Texts were coded as research, policy, or practitioner texts based on their primary audience.

    - Research: academic articles published in peer-reviewed scholarly journals, written by and for academic researchers. This includes all doctoral dissertations.
    - Policy: policy documents and texts written by and/or for educational policymakers, including district-level and school administrators. This category includes actual policy documents in the sample, as well as policy analyses and executive summaries of policy analyses, when their intended audience is primarily policymakers (rather than policy researchers).
    - Practice: texts written by and/or for practicing teachers, other educators, and education support professionals. This category includes texts presenting curriculum ideas or teaching strategies, reflecting on teaching practice, and so forth.

2. *Problem-focused*: Texts were coded according to whether they focused on a deviant-coded behavior of students (e.g., teen pregnancy, delinquency, violence, or dropping out).

3. *Problem definition*: If coded as a problem-focused text, the problem(s) at the center of the analysis was/were identified. An attempt was made to systematize the categories as much as possible. (For example, the text was coded as "dropout" if it focused on dropouts, pushouts, retention, or attrition.) If the text was not considered to be problem focused, then this code was left blank.

TABLE A.I. **Most common textual descriptions of last chance students in abstracts**

Concept/term	Number	Percentage of sample*
Risk (at-risk, high-risk)	108	49
Delinquent	10	5
Dropout / potential dropout	22	10
Low-achieving / failing	17	8
Disruptive / problem behavior	21	10

*Sample = 221 articles.

4. *Textual descriptions of students*: For each text, I recorded the primary terms used to describe last chance students in the abstract or opening paragraph of the text. (See table A.1 for a summary.)

At this stage, I conducted a basic analysis of the findings in order to determine the dominant audiences, topics, and disciplinary orientations in the published literature on last chance high schools and their students. I ran numerical tallies to sort the results by topic, disciplinary orientation, audience, purpose, and "problem" under study. I also looked for correlations and relationships among different categories—for example, whether texts from different academic disciplines focused on different topics and problems. I also examined whether texts for different audiences (researchers, policymakers, practitioners) employed different frames or focused on different topics. In the final coding stage, I combined all the available abstracts into a single document and read them as a whole, identifying statements about who last chance students are, what they are like, and what the purpose of the last chance high school is or should be. I paid attention to what key terms were used to describe last chance students and to repeated phrases, terminology, and frames.

Findings

More than three-quarters of the texts in the sample—77 percent ($N = 168$)—focused on a problem or deviant-coded behavior of students such as criminal activity, substance abuse, failing, or dropping out of school. (See tables A.2 and A.3.) These were more or less evenly distributed across policy, practitioner, and research texts. As is to be expected, articles about substance abuse were more common in the research literature from public health; those about violence and criminality were more

TABLE A.2. **Problem-focused texts in sample**

	Number	Proportion (%) of text in sample ($N = 221$)
Problem-focused	148	67
Not problem-focused	73	33

TABLE A.3. **Breakdown of problem-coded texts**

Problem- or deviant-coded behavior	Number of texts about this problem	Proportion (%) of problem-coded texts ($N = 168$)*	Proportion (%) of all texts in sample ($N = 221$)
Substance abuse	73	43	33
Dropout, pushout, attrition, or retention	37	22	17
Academic failure, low achievement	24	14	11
Criminality, violence, or delinquent behavior	24	14	11
Depression, stress, low self-esteem	8	5	4
Sexual behavior, teen pregnancy	7	4	3
Truancy, attendance problems, tardiness	5	3	2
Poor physical health, nutrition, exercise	3	2	1
Lack of motivation	2	1	<1
Other**	5	3	2

*Does not add to 100% because some texts focused on more than one problem.
**These were: "problem-saturated families," "social dysfunction," "risk behavior," "poor attitude," and "motor vehicle safety."

TABLE A.4. **Deficit and antideficit perspectives in problem-focused texts**

Analytical perspective	Number of texts	Percentage of problem-coded texts ($N = 168$)	Percentage of sample ($N = 221$)
Deficit	112	67	51
Mixed	12	7	6
Antideficit	21	12.5	9.5
Not applicable / could not determine	23	14	10

common in the research literature from criminology; and those about school failure were more common in the research literature from education. I coded each of these problem-focused texts for its primary unit of analysis, or where it located the cause/solution of the problematic behavior under study. I specifically sought to determine the degree to which social context, social structure, and/or social inequality were considered in the discussion of the students' problematic behavior. I coded 67 percent ($N = 112$) of these problem-focused texts as reflecting a primarily *deficit* perspective because they focused solely on problems with the student, his or her family, peer group, culture/ethnic group, or community as the primary unit of analysis or cause of the deviant-coded behavior. An additional 7 percent of the texts ($N = 12$) were coded as *mixed* because they focused on problems with the student or his or her immediate surroundings as well as a larger social-institutional cause, and 12.5 percent ($N = 21$) were coded as *antideficit* because they focused primarily on social-institutional levels of analysis such as the school, curriculum, district policy, or educational inequality (table A.4).

Of the 21 problem-focused texts that I coded as *antideficit*, only 2 had analyses focused on structural or institutional factors beyond the level of the school. The first of these was Deirdre Kelly's *Last Chance High* (1993a), coded as problem focused because it examines the issue of high school dropouts, and antideficit because its analysis of why students drop out considers historical factors, racial inequality, gender inequality, formal and hidden curricula (ideology), school and district-level tracking policies, state-level educational policies, and peer group influence. The second antideficit text to include larger-level structural analysis beyond the school was Debbie Smith and Kathryn Whitmore's *Literacy and Advocacy in Adolescent Family, Gang, School, and Juvenile Court Communities* (2006). This book was coded as problem focused because it examines youth gang activity, and antideficit because its analysis of youth gangs considers the influences of social, economic, political, and ideological factors such as social injustice, institutionalized racism, and educational inequality. In other words, just 2 out of the 168 texts that focused on last chance students' problem- or deviant-coded behavior paid serious consideration to social-structural inequalities beyond the level of the school, such as historical forces; district-level tracking policies; state-level education policies; ideological forces; or racial/gender/economic inequalities in education, housing, and labor markets. These findings are the basis of my claim, in chapter 1, that decontextualized and deficit-oriented analyses are prevalent within the literature on last chance schools and their students.

Notes

Introduction

1. An enormous range of educational researchers have weighed in on the structure-agency debate, far too many to list in an exhaustive way. Some of the works that influenced my thinking for this book are Bettie 2003; Demerath 2009; Ferguson 2001; Fine 1991; Foley 1990; Gibson 1988; Lareau 2003; MacLeod 2008; Ogbu 1978; Varenne and McDermott 1999; Willis 1981; and Weis 1990.

2. My understanding of social justice education is influenced by the vast and varied literature on this topic. This literature encompasses a range of different pedagogical and political traditions that vary according to whether they focus on the education of children or adults, in formal or nonformal settings, in the United States or the global South. They also differ according to whether they are written for a scholarly, activist, or practitioner audience and the extent to which they come out of an anticapitalist, feminist, antiracist, or antioppression tradition. However, all authors writing about social justice education tend to align around a few key concepts: the notion of critical consciousness; the assumption that education is inherently political; the value placed on popular and marginalized knowledge; the commitment to processes of problem posing and critical dialogue; and the ultimate goal of collective action for social change. See Nygreen 2010 for a more lengthy discussion of these principles and their diverse political-pedagogical traditions, and introduction, n. 3, for a list of influential authors.

3. Influential authors who have defined the field of critical or social justice pedagogy within education include Giroux ([1983] 2003); McLaren (1995); Duncan-Andrade and Morrell (2008); Darder (2002); hooks (1994); and Freire (2000). Scholar-educators who have adapted these principles to K–12 classroom settings include Sleeter (2005); Nieto and Bode (2012); Bigelow (1990); Christensen (2009); Ayers (2004); and Gutstein (2005).

4. I credit Cathy Luna for suggesting this terminology and for helping me

identify the dialogue between the "me of then" and the "me of now" as a running theme of the book.

Chapter 1

1. Unless otherwise noted, all of the statistics presented in this section are taken from the 2000 US census. Some figures for Maytown are rounded to protect confidentiality of the school and research subjects.

2. In 1999, median family income was $70,400—40 percent higher than the national median of $50,046 and 33 percent higher than the state median of $53,025.

3. Jackson High was also 10.0 percent Latino (compared with 11.0 percent at Maytown High) and 3.4 percent Asian / Pacific Islander (compared with 11.0 percent at Maytown High) in 1997–98. Data accessed from the California Department of Education's DataQuest website: http://dq.cde.ca.gov/Dataquest.

4. Although the name change occurred midway through my research, I continue to refer to the school as Jackson High in this book. This is for reasons of simplicity and consistency, and because the new name never caught on with students or PARTY members during the research period for this book.

5. The social justice class that PARTY members taught met for eighty-minute blocks, because the school schedule was changed yet again in the following year.

6. Jackson's student population by gender remained very close to 50–50 percent male/female throughout the 1990s and early 2000s.

7. Official demographic figures for the school are not available for the year in question because enrollment data for MAP/Jackson were combined with those of Maytown High for two years. These approximate figures are my own estimation, based on participant observation and work at the school during those years.

8. The US Department of Commerce and Bureau of the Census (1941) report that 4,145,669 students were enrolled in public secondary schools in 1930. If 340,000 students were enrolled in continuation or part-time programs (as documented in Kelly 1993a, 40; and Mayman 1933, 195), they would represent 8.2 percent of all public secondary school enrollment.

9. For example, the 1950 edition of the handbook called on continuation school staff to "carry on a continuous program of public relations" (ibid., 21) to counter negative images of their schools, and advised them to stress that "the program is established to help [students] continue their education and improve their status and that it is an honor to be enrolled. Such a positive approach will do much to counteract the impression that in being transferred to continuation school students are being 'banished,' 'disciplined,' or 'committed' because of their failure in school" (ibid., 23). A district superintendent wrote, "Any school

administrator who writes or talks about his own continuation school does so apologetically. If he is conscientiously concerned about the welfare of youth, he will admit readily that this department of his school is weak and ineffective and that the young people who are compelled to be in continuation school are really the forgotten youth of his community so far as their education is concerned" (Hicks 1945, 75).

10. The word *alternative* first appeared in the 1973 edition of the *Handbook on Continuation Education in California*. The foreword to the handbook states that continuation education offers "an alternative method of schooling that has a flexible, personalized program of instruction" (Eales 1973). It claims that potential high school dropouts would "profit from the availability of an alternative—a different secondary education that can lead to a high-school diploma, that serves their special needs and problems, that offers smaller classes with individualized instruction, and that enhances their feelings of satisfaction in completing subject matter requirements" (foreword). In the 1968 edition of the handbook, an entire paragraph was devoted to a discussion of one continuation school that had implemented alternative pedagogy.

11. "Continuation Education," on the California Department of Education website, accessed June 14, 2011, http://www.cde.ca.gov/sp/eo/ce/.

12. For example, several scholars have noted that leaders in the movement for high-stakes testing and accountability use the language of the civil rights movement to portray these reforms as a move toward educational equity and access for underrepresented students (e.g., Labaree 2010; Lipman 2003, 2011; Watkins 2011).

13. See the appendix for a description of the methods used for this review. My review included an analysis of 221 texts published between 1990 and 2009 about continuation and/or alternative high schools designed to serve students who had failed or been kicked out of regular high schools.

14. See Nygreen (2006) for a more thorough discussion of the problems with a decontextualized analysis of school failure.

Chapter 2

1. The interviews and debriefing session occurred over two consecutive two-hour meetings in the fall of PARTY's first year. Following Bloome's (1993) discussion of the microethnographic approach, this chapter contains: "(a) a detailed, thick description of how people act and react to each other, and the ways they use language (including written language) to act and react, and (b) an emic interpretation of what is happening in the event, moment by moment as the event evolves, and as what is happening in the event changes and is contested" (103).

2. Chapter 4 contains further discussion of these points.

3. Much of the literature on low-performing students in high-poverty communities suggests these students are unaware of the "hidden rules" (Payne 2005) of the middle class and therefore need explicit instruction in how to follow them. The preservice teachers I work with in urban schools often report that students need to be taught "manners" so that they know how to behave in job interviews. The PARTY interview sequence suggests that, at least in one case, the students knew very well how to behave in a job interview. For them, the issue at stake may not be the lack of knowledge about the "hidden rules" but rather the lack of opportunities for decent jobs. See chapter 5 for further discussion of these points.

4. My use of the term *everyday resistance* echoes Mica Pollock's use of "everyday anti-racism" (2008) and "everyday justice" (2010) to refer to the small, daily actions that ordinary people take all the time to resist patterns of oppression, racism, or injustice.

5. The term *discursive-ideological* is used in the work of Claire Kim (2000) to differentiate this realm from the "social-structural" realm of institutionalized racism. I make a similar distinction here between the "discursive" and "structural" realms, but I am blending these ideas to define what I call the "discursive dimension of structure." The analysis in this paragraph is strongly influenced by, and resonates with, the work of Kim (2000) and Holland et al. (2001), who have advanced similar arguments about the role of discourse and the nature of agency.

Chapter 3

1. Although Leila's encounters with police were restricted to political organizing events and not her everyday life, she affirmed the other PARTY members' stories of daily harassment and appeared convinced of their veracity. See Nygreen 2008 (92–93) for an illustration of the contrast between Leila's criminal justice experiences and those of D and Suli.

2. My goal in inviting guest speakers was to expose PARTY members to a range of research and researchers, and in particular, to scholars of color from working-class backgrounds who could speak about the role of research in social change as well as their own personal journeys through schooling, college, and beyond. I hoped that PARTY members might come to see themselves as critical researchers for social change, in part by seeing this identity as both viable and transgressive. I invited speakers who I believed could relate to PARTY members and contribute insight to our project.

Chapter 4

1. I am adapting Gee's (2000) definition of identity as "acting and interacting as a particular 'kind of person'" to apply to teacher identity.

2. Errors of spelling and usage are reproduced exactly as in the originals.

3. I acknowledge Denise Ives and Flavio Azavedo for helping me develop the self-critique in this paragraph, and Denise in particular for suggesting the treadmill example.

4. *On one* is a slang term used locally to mean acting crazy or foolish, as if induced by alcohol or drugs, though not necessarily implying inebriation. The term is defined by http://www.urbandictionary.com as follows: "Just generally trippin,' tweakin,' weird, actin' a fool, blackin' out, goin' off. Not necessarily due to drugs, though that's the obvious reference."

5. *Hella* is a slang term used locally to mean "really," "very," or "a lot of." It likely derived from the phrase "hell of a lot."

6. The distinction between a reasonable response to unreasonable circumstances and a willful act of noncompliance is adapted here from Ferguson (2001), who also made this distinction. Ferguson's analysis reveals the significance of race in shaping how teachers interpret students' noncompliant acts.

Chapter 5

1. I acknowledge Ronald Glass for helping me make this shift.

2. The history of the academic-vocational divide has been written about extensively. All the scholarly works I consulted agree on the general historical progression of this debate, which I summarize in this section. Unless otherwise stated, the historical facts and arguments in the first three paragraphs of this section are supported by the following works: Grubb 1995; Grubb and Lazerson 2004; Kliebard 1999; Imber 1985; and Tyack and Kantor 1982.

3. Of course, vocational programs never completely disappeared. Many remained and are now commonly referred to as career and technical education (CTE) programs. There have been periodic attempts to reemphasize the high school's vocational mission and revitalize CTE programs throughout the years. For example, in the 1990s there was a movement to reform high schools into career academies. The School-to-Work Opportunities Act of 1994 attempted to revitalize vocational education and better align the high school curriculum with workplace preparation (Grubb 1995).

4. According to the National Center for Education Statistics (NCES 2005), more than half of all high school graduates in the class of 2004 (55.7 percent) entered the civilian labor force immediately after graduation (this includes those who were working as well as those who were officially registered as unemployed).

Among graduates who did *not* enroll in any college, more than three-quarters (77.5 percent) entered immediately into the labor force. Among graduates who enrolled as part-time college students, 82.4 percent were in the labor force. And of graduates who enrolled at two-year colleges, 61.1 percent were in the labor force. I was not able to obtain data on the actual pathways of Jackson graduates.

5. According to the National Center for Education Statistics (Wirt et al. 2004), 61 percent of 1992 twelfth graders who enrolled in a public two-year postsecondary institution had taken at least one remedial college course by 2000. The proportion was notably higher for low-income students in this cohort (those in the bottom 20 percent of the income distribution), at 63.2 percent, and for those in the lowest quintile of high school standardized test scores (which would apply to all or nearly all Jackson students), at 79.3 percent. See Wirt et al. 2004, 140, table 18-1, for a summary of these statistics. The most recent published NCES figures on postsecondary remedial course taking are not disaggregated by student income level or high school test scores. However, they show that 20.2 percent of all first-year undergraduates in 2007–8 enrolled in at least one remedial course in their first year of college (Aud et al. 2011). This proportion was higher for African American students (24.7 percent), Latinos (23.3 percent), those living with parents or relatives while attending college (25.4 percent), and those attending public two-year institutions (23.9 percent). See Aud et al. 2011, 225, table A-22-1, for a summary of these statistics.

6. Many scholars have pointed out that there is a systematic lack of support and career counseling for work-bound students in American high schools, and that this is a stark contrast from the high levels of support and guidance provided to college-bound students (e.g., Grubb and Lazerson 2004; Royster 2003, 41; Rosenbaum 2001). Royster (2003) writes, "The contrast in how schools assist college-bound and work-bound students is stark. The early schooling, intermediate training, and occupational trajectories of college-bound students tend to flow in a carefully coordinated sequence, whereas noncollege-bound students typically find themselves searching for some pathway to skilled and semi-skilled jobs with little assistance from schools" (41).

7. The value of the minimum wage is significant because it sets the benchmark for all wages at the lower end of the income distribution, even those above the legal minimum. A rise in the minimum wage tends to push all wages up at the bottom of the income distribution, since other low-paid positions must raise wages just enough to compete for quality workers. Likewise, a stagnant or falling minimum wage (in real value) will pull down wages across the lower end of the income distribution. For instance, economists DiNardo, Fortin, and Lemieux (1996) found that about 25 percent of the overall rise in inequality over the 1980s could be traced to minimum-wage policies.

8. The Economic Policy Institute (2011a, 2011b) defines poverty-level wage as "the wage that a full-time, full-year worker would have to earn to live above

the federally defined poverty threshold for a family of four. In 2009, this wage is $10.55 an hour." In 2007, 26.4 percent of all workers earned poverty-level wages (2011b), and 34.0 percent of black workers earned poverty-level wages (2011a).

9. In other words, families must rely on the income generated from children's economic activities.

10. I credit Deirdre Kelly (1993a, 215–25) for connecting the continuation high school's dilemma of hierarchy to the more general question of whether or not it is possible to have difference without hierarchy. Her arguments, and use of the terminology of difference versus hierarchy, were influential in shaping the ideas in this paragraph.

Chapter 6

1. The term *achievement gap* has been thoroughly challenged by critical educational scholars, most notably by Gloria Ladson-Billings, who sought to reframe this concept as an "education debt" in her 2006 Presidential Address to the American Educational Research Association (AERA). I support the attempts to reframe this concept as an education debt (Ladson-Billings 2006) or opportunity gap (Oakes et al. 2004), but in this chapter I avoid a thorough discussion of these terms because my central goal is to advance the alternative concept of a "consequence gap." A full engagement with the debate over the term *achievement gap* and alternative terms is beyond the purview of this chapter.

2. This example of a striving, upwardly mobile student of color is described in their work as a case of "internal" transformational resistance. The authors state that such resistance may appear conformist "on the surface" but is motivated by social justice (Solorzano and Delgado Bernal 2001, 325). Internal transformational resistance is differentiated from external transformational resistance, which is conspicuous, overt, and often organized.

3. Mishel, Bernstein, and Shierholz (2009), 174, table 3.20, "Hourly wages by decile within education groups: 1973–2007," shows that most of the gain in college-educated workers' wages between 1995 and 2007 was concentrated among workers in the 90th percentile of wages rather than being spread across all college-educated workers. Between 2000 and 2007, the wages of college graduates at the 10th and 50th percentiles either fell or stayed relatively flat. Only the wages of college graduates in the 90th percentile rose more than 1.5 percent during this period, with men in the 90th percentile seeing a much higher gain than women in the 90th percentile (8.6 percent versus 3.9 percent, respectively).

4. The BLS projects that the overall share of jobs requiring a bachelor's degree or higher will be 21.7 percent in 2016, with another 9 percent requiring an associate's degree or certificate from a vocational program. The remaining 70 percent of job openings will require just on-the-job training. In short, only

about 30 percent of new jobs created will require a postsecondary degree of any kind, which is roughly the percentage of students who currently obtain one (NCES 2011). Of course, there is some debate over the accuracy of BLS projections, and supply-side factors such as a large increase in college-educated workers could have an impact on these projections (see Tyler, Murane, and Levy 1995 for a review; Gottschalk and Hansen 2003). Nevertheless, there is reason to suspect that the widely assumed need for more college graduates in the labor market may be overstated (Handel 2005; Lafer 2002; Grubb and Lazerson 2004; Rothstein 2002; Rosenbaum, 2001; Stern and Stearns 2008; Wolff 2006).

5. I am indebted to an in-class lecture by Stuart Tannock at the University of California–Berkeley in 2004 (date unknown) for the points about meritocracy articulated in this paragraph.

Appendix

1. This review was completed with a team of research assistants at the University of California–Santa Cruz. Yazmin Duarte served from September 2008 to June 2009. Yolanda Diaz-Houston and Mariella Saba served from March to June 2009. Linnea Becket served from June to August 2009.

References

Alexander, Michelle. 2010. *The New Jim Crow: Mass Incarceration in the Age of Colorblindness*. 1st ed. New York: New Press.

Anyon, Jean. 2005. *Radical Possibilities: Public Policy, Urban Education, and a New Social Movement*. New York: Routledge.

Apple, Michael W. 1979. *Ideology and Curriculum*. New York: Routledge and Kegan Paul.

Aud, Susan, William Hussar, Grace Kena, Kevin Bianco, Lauren Frohlich, Jana Kemp, and Kim Tahan. 2011. *The Condition of Education 2011* (NCES 2011-033). US Department of Education, National Center for Education Statistics. Washington, DC: US Government Printing Office. Accessed August 31, 2012. http://nces.ed.gov/pubsearch/pubsinfo.asp?pubid=2011033.

Autor, David H., Lawrence F. Katz, and Melissa S. Kearney. 2006. "The Polarization of the U.S. Labor Market." *American Economic Review* 96 (2): 189–94. doi:10.1257/000282806777212620.

Ayers, William. 2004. *Teaching toward Freedom: Moral Commitment and Ethical Action in the Classroom*. New York: Beacon Press.

Bashi, Joseph. 1990. "School Culture and the Second Chance." In *Second Chance in Education: An Interdisciplinary and International Perspective*, edited by Dan E. Inbar, 129–39. New York: Falmer Press.

Battey, Dan, and Megan L. Franke. 2008. "Transforming Identities: Understanding Teachers across Professional Development and Classroom Practice." *Teacher Education Quarterly* 35 (3): 127–49.

Beales, LeVerne. 1941. "Statistical Abstract of the United States 1940. U.S. Department of Commerce & Bureau of the Census." Washington, DC. http://www2.census.gov/prod2/statcomp/documents/1940-01.pdf.

Becker, Gary S., and Kevin M. Murphy. 2007. "The Upside of Income Inequality." *American*. http://www.american.com/archive/2007/may-june-magazine-contents/the-upside-of-income-inequality/.

Berg, Marlene J., and Jean Schensul. 2004. Introduction. "Approaches to Conducting Action Research with Youth." Special issue, *Practicing Anthropology* 26 (2).

Bettie, Julie. 2003. *Women without Class: Girls, Race, and Identity*. Berkeley: University of California Press.

Bigelow, W. 1990. "Inside the Classroom: Social Vision and Critical Pedagogy." *Teachers College Record* 91: 437–48.

Black, Timothy. 2009. *When a Heart Turns Rock Solid: The Lives of Three Puerto Rican Brothers on and off the Streets*. New York: Pantheon.

Blommaert, Jan. 2005. *Discourse: A Critical Introduction*. Cambridge: Cambridge University Press.

Bloome, David. 1993. "Necessary Indeterminacy and the Microethnographic Study of Reading as a Social Process." *Journal of Research in Reading* 16 (2): 98–111.

Boaler, Jo, and James G. Greeno. 2000. "Identity, Agency, and Knowing in Mathematics Worlds." In *Multiple Perspectives on Mathematics Teaching and Learning*, edited by Jo Boaler, 171–200. Westport, CT: Ablex.

Bonilla-Silva, Eduardo. 2006. *Racism without Racists: Color-Blind Racism and the Persistence of Racial Inequality in the United States*. New York: Rowman & Littlefield.

Bourdieu, Pierre. 1993. *The Field of Cultural Production*, edited by Randal Johnson. New York: Columbia University Press.

———. 1994. "Structures, Habitus, Power: Basis for a Theory of Symbolic Power." In *Culture/Power/History: A Reader in Contemporary Social Theory*, edited by Nicholas B. Dirks, Geoff Eley, and Sherry B. Ortner, 155–99. Princeton, NJ: Princeton University Press.

Bourdieu, Pierre, and Jean-Claude Passeron. 1990. *Reproduction in Education, Society and Culture*. 2nd ed. Thousand Oaks, CA: Sage.

Bowles, Samuel, and Herbert Gintis. 1976. *Schooling in Capitalist America: Educational Reform and the Contradictions of Economic Life*. New York: Routledge and Kegan Paul.

Brayboy, Bryan McKinley Jones. 2005. "Transformational Resistance and Social Justice: American Indians in Ivy League Universities." *Anthropology and Education Quarterly* 36 (3): 193–211.

Brint, Steven, and Jerome Karabel. 1991. *The Diverted Dream: Community Colleges and the Promise of Educational Opportunity in America, 1900–1985*. New York: Oxford University Press.

Brydon-Miller, Mary, Budd Hall, Ted Jackson, and Peter Park. 1993. *Voices of Change: Participatory Research in the United States and Canada*. Westport, CT: Praeger.

Cain, Carole. 1991. "Personal Stories: Identity Acquisition and Self-Understanding in Alcoholics Anonymous." *Ethos* 19 (2) (June 1): 210–53.

Caldwell, Tanya. 2012. "Santorum Calls Obama a 'Snob' for Promoting Higher Education." *The Choice* (blog), *New York Times*, February 27. Accessed August 29, 2012. http://thechoice.blogs.nytimes.com/2012/02/27/rick-santorum-calls-obama-a-snob-for-encouraging-higher-education/.

Callahan, David. 2004. *The Cheating Culture: Why More Americans Are Doing Wrong to Get Ahead*. Boston: Houghton Mifflin Harcourt.

Cammarota, Julio. 2004. "The Gendered and Racialized Pathways of Latina and Latino Youth: Different Struggles, Different Resistances in the Urban Context." *Anthropology and Education Quarterly* 35 (1): 53–74.

Cammarota, Julio, and Michelle Fine, eds. 2008. *Revolutionizing Education: Youth Participatory Action Research in Motion*. 1st ed. New York: Routledge.

Camp, Catherine. 1980. "School Dropouts: A Discussion Paper." Sacramento: California State Legislature, Assembly Office of Research.

Carnoy, Martin, and Henry M. Levin. 1985. *Schooling and Work in the Democratic State*. 1st ed. Palo Alto, CA: Stanford University Press.

Cherry, Robert. 2009. "The Folly of Academic College for All." *Teachers College Record* (August 24). ID no. 15755. Accessed: August 29, 2012. http://www.tcrecord.org.

Christensen, Linda. 2009. *Teaching for Joy and Justice: Re-imagining the Language Arts Classroom*. 1st ed. Milwaukee: Rethinking Schools.

Cochran-Smith, Marilyn, and Kenneth M. Zeichner, eds. 2005. *Studying Teacher Education: The Report of the AERA Panel on Research and Teacher Education*. Mahwah, NJ: Lawrence Erlbaum Associates.

Conrath Jerry. 2001. "Changing the Odds for Young People: Next Steps for Alternative Education." *Phi Delta Kappan* 82 (8) (April): 585–87.

Darder, Antonia. 2002. *Reinventing Paulo Freire: A Pedagogy of Love*. Boulder, CO: Westview Press.

Davidson, Ann Locke. 1996. *Making and Molding Identity in Schools: Student Narratives on Race, Gender, and Academic Engagement*. SUNY Series, Power, Social Identity, and Education. Albany: State University of New York Press.

Delpit, Lisa. 1988. "The Silenced Dialogue: Power and Pedagogy in Educating Other People's Children." *Harvard Educational Review* 18 (3): 280–98.

———. 2002. Introduction to *The Skin That We Speak: Thoughts on Language and Culture in the Classroom*, edited by Lisa D. Delpit and Joanne Kilgour Dowdy. New York: New Press.

Delpit, Lisa, and Joanne Kilgour Dowdy, eds. 2002. *The Skin That We Speak: Thoughts on Language and Culture in the Classroom*. New York: New Press.

Demerath, Peter. 2009. *Producing Success: The Culture of Personal Advancement in an American High School*. Chicago: University of Chicago Press.

Dimitriadis, Greg. 2011. "Studying Resistance: Some Cautionary Notes." *Inter-

national Journal of Qualitative Studies in Education 24 (5): 649–54. doi:10.10 80/09518398.2011.600260.

DiNardo, John, Nicole Fortin, and Thomas Lemieux. 1996. "Labor Market Institutions and the Distribution of Wages, 1973–1992: A Semiparametric Approach." *Econometrica* 64 (5) (September): 1001–44.

Duncan-Andrade, Jeffrey M. R., and Ernest Morrell. 2008. *The Art of Critical Pedagogy: Possibilities for Moving from Theory to Practice in Urban Schools.* New York: Peter Lang.

Dyrness, Andrea. 2011. *Mothers United: An Immigrant Struggle for Socially Just Education.* Minneapolis: University of Minnesota Press.

Eales, John R. 1973. *Handbook on Continuation Education in California.* Sacramento: California State Printing Office, California State Department of Education.

Eckert, Penelope. 1989. *Jocks and Burnouts: Social Categories and Identity in the High School.* New York: Teachers College Press.

Economic Policy Institute. 2011a. "Minorities Are More Likely to Be Low-Wage Earners." Accessed August 29, 2012. http://stateofworkingamerica.org/ charts/share-of-workers-earning-poverty-level-wages-by-race-1973-2009/.

———. 2011b. "Percentage Earning Poverty-Level Wage Is High." Accessed August 29, 2012. http://stateofworkingamerica.org/charts/share-of-workers-earning-poverty-level-wages-by-gender-1973-2009/.

———. 2011c. "Poverty Rises in Recessions and Falls in Recoveries." Accessed August 29, 2012. http://stateofworkingamerica.org/charts/poverty-and-twice-poverty-rates-1959-2010/.

EdSource. 2008. *California's Continuation High Schools.* Mountain View, CA: EdSource.

Elder, Glen H. 1966. "The Schooling of Outsiders." *Sociology of Education* 39 (4) (October 1): 324–43. doi:10.2307/2111917.

Ellis, Carolyn, and Arthur P. Bochner. 2000. "Autoethnography, Personal Narrative, Reflexivity: Researcher as Subject." In *Handbook of Qualitative Research*, edited by Norman K. Denzin, 733–68. 2nd ed. Thousand Oaks, CA: Sage Publications.

Epstein, Terrie. 2001. "Adolescents' Perspective on Racial Diversity in U.S. History: Case Studies from an Urban Classroom." *American Educational Research Journal* 37: 185–214.

Estrella, Marisol, and John Gaventa. 1998. "Who Counts Reality? Participatory Monitoring and Evaluation: A Literature Review." Brighton, UK: Institute of Development Studies.

Fairclough, Norman. 2003. *Analysing Discourse: Textual Analysis for Social Research.* Vol. 57. Taylor and Francis eBook Collection. New York: Routledge.

Ferguson, Ann Arnett. 2001. *Bad Boys: Public Schools in the Making of Black Masculinity.* Ann Arbor: University of Michigan Press.

Fine, Michelle. 1991. *Framing Dropouts: Notes on the Politics of an Urban Public High School*. New York: State University of New York Press.

Firpo, Sergio, Nicole M. Fortin, and Thomas Lemieux. 2009. "Unconditional Quantile Regressions." *Econometrica* 77 (3) (May 1): 953–73.

Flanagan, Constance, and Leslie Gallay. 1995. "Reframing the Meaning of 'Political' in Research with Adolescents." *Perspectives on Political Science* 24 (1): 34–41.

Foley, Douglas E. 1990. *Learning Capitalist Culture: Deep in the Heart of Tejas*. Philadelphia: University of Pennsylvania Press.

Fordham, Signithia. 1996. *Blacked Out: Dilemmas of Race, Identity, and Success at Capital High*. Chicago: University of Chicago Press.

Foucault, Michel. 1980. "Truth and Power." In *Power/Knowledge: Selected Interviews and Other Writings, 1972–1977*, edited by Colin Gordon. 1st American ed. New York: Vintage.

———. 1995. *Discipline and Punish: The Birth of the Prison*. New York: Vintage Books.

Freedman, Sarah, and Deborah Appleman. 2008. "'What Else Would I Be Doing?' Teacher Identity and Teacher Retention in Urban Schools." *Teacher Education Quarterly* 35 (3): 109–26.

Freire, Paulo. 2000. *Pedagogy of the Oppressed*, translated by Myra Bergman Ramos. 30th anniv. ed. New York: Continuum.

Gatto, John Taylor. 1992. "The Seven-Lesson Schoolteacher." In *Dumbing Us Down: The Hidden Curriculum of Compulsory Schooling*, 1–22. Philadelphia: New Society Publishers.

Gee, James Paul. 2000. "Identity as an Analytic Lens for Research in Education." *Review of Research in Education* 25 (January 1): 99–125. doi:10.2307/1167322.

———. 2005. *An Introduction to Discourse Analysis: Theory and Method*. 2nd ed. New York: Routledge.

Gibson, Margaret A. 1988. *Accommodation without Assimilation: Sikh Immigrants in an American High School*. Ithaca, NY: Cornell University Press.

Gilmore, Perry. 1985. "Gimme Room: School Resistance, Attitude, and Access to Literacy." *Journal of Education* 167: 111–28.

Gilmore, Ruth Wilson. 2007. *Golden Gulag: Prisons, Surplus, Crisis, and Opposition in Globalizing California*. Berkeley: University of California Press.

Ginwright, Shawn, and Taj James. 2003. "From Assets to Agents of Change: Social Justice, Organizing, and Youth Development." *New Directions for Youth Development* 96 (Winter): 27–46.

Giroux, Henry A. (1983) 2001. *Theory and Resistance in Education: Towards a Pedagogy for the Opposition*. Rev. and exp. ed. Westport, CT: Praeger. First published by Bergin and Garvey, 1983.

Glass, Ronald D., and Kysa Nygreen. 2011. "Class, Race, and the Discourse of

'College for All.' A Response to 'Schooling for Democracy.'" *Democracy and Education* 19 (1). Article 7. http://democracyeducationjournal.org/home/vol19/iss1/7.

Goldberger, Anthony M. 1931. *Variability in Continuation School Populations: A Study of the Significance of Differences in the Proportions of Child Workers*. New York: Bureau of Publications, Teachers College, Columbia University.

Goldin, Claudia, and Lawrence F. Katz. 2007. "Long-Run Changes in the Wage Structure: Narrowing, Widening, Polarizing." *Brookings Papers on Economic Activity* 38 (2): 135–68.

Gonzalez, Norma, Luis C. Moll, and Cathy Amanti, eds. 2005. *Funds of Knowledge: Theorizing Practices in Households and Classrooms*. 1st ed. Mahwah, NJ: Lawrence Erlbaum Associates.

Gottschalk, Peter, and Michael Hansen. 2003. "Is the Proportion of College Workers in Noncollege Jobs Increasing?" *Journal of Labor Economics* 21 (2): 409–48.

Gramsci, Antonio. 1971. *Selections from the Prison Notebooks*. New York: International Publishers.

Grubb, W. Norton. 1995. "Introduction: Resolving the Paradox of the High School." In *Education through Occupations in American High Schools: Approaches to Integrating Academic and Vocational Education*, edited by W. Norton Grubb. New York: Teachers College Press.

Grubb, W. Norton, and Marvin Lazerson. 2004. *The Education Gospel: The Economic Power of Schooling*. Cambridge, MA: Harvard University Press.

Gutstein, Eric. 2005. *Reading and Writing the World with Mathematics: Toward a Pedagogy for Social Justice*. New York: Routledge.

Handel, Michael J. 2005. *Worker Skills and Job Requirements: Is There a Mismatch?* Washington, DC: Economic Policy Institute.

Hatt, Beth. 2007. "Street Smarts vs. Book Smarts: The Figured World of Smartness in the Lives of Marginalized, Urban Youth." *Urban Review* 39 (2) (June): 145–66.

Henry, Dooley William. 1916. *The Education of the Ne'er-do-well*. Boston: Riverside Press.

Hicks, Robert A. 1945. "Continuation Pupils Are Our Forgotten Youth." *California Journal of Secondary Education* 20 (2) (February): 75–78.

Hirschfield, Paul, Jr. 2008. "Preparing for Prison? The Criminalization of School Discipline in the USA." *Theoretical Criminology* 12 (1): 79–101.

Holland, Dorothy C., and Margaret A. Eisenhart. 1992. *Educated in Romance: Women, Achievement, and College Culture*. Chicago: University of Chicago Press.

Holland, Dorothy C., William Lachicotte Jr., Debra Skinner, and Carole Cain.

2001. *Identity and Agency in Cultural Worlds.* Cambridge, MA: President and Fellows of Harvard College.

Hollins, Etta, and Maria Torres Guzman. 2005. "Research on Preparing Teachers for Diverse Populations." In *Studying Teacher Education: The Report of the AERA Panel on Research and Teacher Education,* edited by Marilyn Cochran-Smith and Kenneth M. Zeichner, 477–548. Mahwah, NJ: Lawrence Erlbaum Associates.

hooks, bell. 1994. *Teaching to Transgress: Education as the Practice of Freedom.* New York: Routledge.

Imber, Michael. 1985. "The Continuation School 1910–1940: An Historical Case Study of an Early Work Study Programme in the United States with Implications for Current Practice." *Journal of Educational Administration and History* 17 (1): 49–61.

Inbar, Dan, and Rita Sever. 1989. "The Importance of Making Promises: An Analysis of Second-Chance Policies." *Comparative Education Review* 33 (2) (May 1): 232–42.

Inbar, Dan E. 1990. "The Legitimation of a Second Chance." In *Second Chance in Education: An Interdisciplinary and International Perspective,* edited by Dan E. Inbar, 1–18. New York: Falmer Press.

Johnston, David Cay. 2005. "Richest Are Leaving Even the Rich Far Behind." In *Class Matters,* edited by The New York Times. New York: New York Times Books / Henry Holt Company.

Jones, Leo. 1950. *Handbook on Continuation Education in California.* Sacramento: Bulletin of the California State Department of Education.

Jurow, A. Susan. 2005. "Shifting Engagements in Figured Worlds: Middle School Mathematics Students' Participation in an Architectural Design Project." *Journal of the Learning Sciences* 14 (1) (January 1): 35–67.

Kantor, Harvey, and David B. Tyack. 1982. "Introduction: Historical Perspectives on Vocationalism in American Education." In *Work, Youth, and Schooling: Historical Perspectives on Vocationalism in American Education,* edited by Harvey Kantor and David B. Tyack. 1st ed. Palo Alto, CA: Stanford University Press.

Katz, Michael B. 1990. *The Undeserving Poor: From the War on Poverty to the War on Welfare.* New York: Pantheon.

Katznelson, Ira, and Margaret Weir. 1988. *Schooling for All: Class, Race, and the Decline of the Democratic Ideal.* Berkeley: University of California Press.

Keller, Franklin Jefferson. 1924. *Day Schools for Young Workers: The Organization and Management of Part-Time and Continuation Schools.* New York: Century Company.

Kelly, Deirdre M. 1993a. *Last Chance High: How Girls and Boys Drop In and Out of Alternative Schools.* New Haven, CT: Yale University Press.

———. 1993b. "Secondary Power Source: High School Students as Participatory Researchers." *American Sociologist* 24 (1) (April 1): 8–26.

Khan, Lindy. 2008. "Literature Review: Characteristics of Successful Alternative School Settings." *Journal of Juvenile Court, Community, and Alternative School Administrators of California* 21: 56–65.

Kim, Claire Jean. 2000. *Bitter Fruit: The Politics of Black-Korean Conflict in New York City*. New Haven, CT: Yale University Press.

Kincheloe, Joe L. 1995. *Critical Pedagogy Primer*. New York: Peter Lang Publishing.

Kirshner, Ben. 2010. "Productive Tensions in Youth Participatory Action Research." *Yearbook of the National Society for the Study of Education* 109 (1): 238–51.

Kleiner, Brian, Rebecca Porch, and Elizabeth Farris. 2002. "Public Alternative Schools and Programs for Students at Risk of Education Failure: 2000–01." *Education Statistics Quarterly* 4 (3). http://nces.ed.gov/programs/quarterly/vol _4/4_3/3_3.asp.

Kliebard, Herbert M. 1999. *Schooled to Work: Vocationalism and the American Curriculum, 1876–1946*. New York: Teachers College Press.

Knoeppel, Janet. 2007. "A Better Alternative: A Philosophy of Educating the Whole Child and a Willingness to Experiment with Differing Instructional Strategies Is What Makes Continuation Schools Work." *Leadership* 36 (4): 36–38.

Kohl, Herbert R. 1995. *"I Won't Learn from You": And Other Thoughts on Creative Maladjustment*. 2nd ed. New York: New Press.

Krugman, Paul. 2007. *The Conscience of a Liberal*. 1st ed. New York: Norton.

Kwon, Soo Ah. 2006. "Youth of Color Organizing for Juvenile Justice." In *Beyond Resistance! Youth Activism and Community Change: New Democratic Possibilities for Practice and Policy for America's Youth*, edited by Shawn Ginwright, Pedro Noguera, and Julio Cammarota, 197–214. New York: Routledge.

Labaree, David F. 1997. "Public Goods, Private Goods: The American Struggle over Educational Goals." *American Educational Research Journal* 34 (1) (April 1): 39–81. doi:10.2307/1163342.

———. 1999. *How to Succeed in School without Really Learning: The Credentials Race in American Education*. New Haven, CT: Yale University Press.

———. 2010. *Somebody Has to Fail: The Zero-Sum Game of Public Schooling*. Cambridge, MA: Harvard Education Press.

Ladson-Billings, Gloria. 2004. "Culture Versus Citizenship: The Challenge of Racialized Citizenship in the United States." In *Diversity and Citizenship Education*, edited by James Banks, 99–126. San Francisco: Jossey Bass.

———. 2006. "From the Achievement Gap to the Education Debt: Understanding Achievement in U.S. Schools." *Educational Researcher* 35 (7): 3–12.

Lafer, Gordon. 2002. *The Job Training Charade*. Ithaca, NY: Cornell University Press.

Langhout, Regina. 2006. "Where Am I? Locating Myself and Its Implications for Collaborative Research." *American Journal of Community Psychology* 37: 267–74.

Lareau, Annette. 2003. *Unequal Childhoods: Class, Race, and Family Life*. 1st ed. Berkeley: University of California Press.

Laudan, Aron Y. 2006. *An Overview of Alternative Education*. Washington, DC: Urban Institute.

Lave, Jean, and Etienne Wenger. 2008. *Situated Learning: Legitimate Peripheral Participation*. New York: Cambridge University Press.

LeCompte, Margaret. 1995. "Some Notes on Power, Agenda and Voice: A Researcher's Personal Evolution toward Critical Collaborative Research." In *Critical Theory and Educational Research*, edited by Peter McLaren and James M. Giarelli, 91–112. Albany: State University of New York Press.

Lesko, Nancy. 2001. *Act Your Age: A Cultural Construction of Adolescence*. New York: Routledge.

Lipman, Pauline. 1997. "Restructuring in Context: A Case Study of Teacher Participation and the Dynamics of Ideology, Race, and Power." *American Educational Research Journal* 34 (1) (April 1): 3–37. doi:10.2307/1163341.

———. 2003. *High Stakes Education: Inequality, Globalization, and Urban School Reform*. 1st ed. New York: Routledge.

———. 2011. *The New Political Economy of Urban Education: Neoliberalism, Race, and the Right to the City*. 1st ed. New York: Routledge.

Lopez, Nancy. 2002. *Hopeful Girls, Troubled Boys: Race and Gender Disparity in Urban Education*. 1st ed. New York: Routledge.

MacLeod, Jay. 2008. *Ain't No Makin' It: Aspirations and Attainment in a Low-Income Neighborhood*. 3rd ed. Boulder, CO: Westview Press.

Maguire, Patricia. 1987. *Doing Participatory Research: A Feminist Approach*. University of Massachusetts Center for International Education / School of Education.

Maguire, Patricia. 1993. "Challenges, Contradictions, and Celebrations: Attempting Participatory Research as a Doctoral Student." In *Voices of Change: Participatory Research in the United States and Canada*, edited by Peter Park, Mary Brydon-Miller, Budd Hall, and Ted Jackson, 157–75. Westport, CT: Bergin and Garvey.

Mahiri, Jabari. 2000. "Pop Culture Pedagogy and the End(s) of School." *Journal of Adolescent & Adult Literacy* 44 (4) (December 1): 382–85.

Mansbridge, Jane. 2001. "Complicating Oppositional Consciousness." In *Oppositional Consciousness: The Subjective Roots of Social Protest*, edited by Jane J. Mansbridge and Aldon Morris, 238–64. 1st ed. Chicago: University of Chicago Press.

Markey, Kathryn. 1940. "This Continuation High School Has Room for All." *California Journal of Secondary Education* 15 (3): 160–63.

Martin, Trow. 1961. "The Second Transformation of American Secondary Education." *International Journal of Comparative Sociology* 2: 144–66.

Mauer, Marc and Meda Chesney-Lind. 2002a. Introduction to *Invisible Punishment: The Collateral Consequences of Mass Imprisonment*, edited by Marc Mauer and Meda Chesney-Lind, 1–12. New York: New Press.

——, eds. 2002b. *Invisible Punishment: The Collateral Consequences of Mass Imprisonment*. New York: New Press.

Mayman, J. Edward. 1933. "The Evolution of the Continuation School in New York City." *School Review* 41 (3) (March 1): 193–205.

McDermott, Raymond. 1987. "The Explanation of Minority School Failure, Again." *Anthropology & Education Quarterly* 18 (4): 361–64.

——. 1997. "Achieving School Failure: 1972–1997." In *Education and Cultural Process: Anthropological Approaches*, edited by George D. Spindler, 110–35. Long Grove, IL: Waveland Press.

McGee, Jay. 2001. "Reflections of an Alternative School Administrator." *Phi Delta Kappan* 82 (8) (April 1): 588–91.

McIntyre, Alice. 2000. *Inner City Kids: Adolescents Confront Life and Violence in an Urban Community*. New York: NYU Press.

McLaren, Peter. 1995. *Critical Pedagogy and Predatory Culture: Oppositional Politics in a Postmodern Era*. New York: Routledge.

Mishel, Lawrence, Jared Bernstein, and Heidi Shierholz. 2009. *The State of Working America, 2008/2009*. New York: ILR Press.

Monroe, Carla R. 2006. "African American Boys and the Discipline Gap: Balancing Educators' Uneven Hand." *Educational Horizons* 85 (1): 102.

Mottaz, Carole. 2002. *Breaking the Cycle of Failure: How to Build and Maintain Quality Alternative Schools*. Lanham, MD: R&L Education.

NCES (National Center for Education Statistics). 2005. "Table 380: College Enrollment and Labor Force Status of 2002, 2003, and 2004 High School Completers, by Sex and Race/Ethnicity: 2002, 2003, and 2004." *Digest of Education Statistics: 2005*. Washington, DC: US Government Printing Office. Accessed September 3, 2012. http://nces.ed.gov/programs/digest/d04/tables/dt04_380.asp.

——. 2011. "Table 8: Percentage of Persons Age 25 and Over and of Persons 25 to 29 Years Old with High School Completion or Higher and a Bachelor's or Higher Degree, by Race/Ethnicity and Sex: Selected Years, 1910 through 2011." *Digest of Education Statistics: 2011*. Washington, DC: US Government Printing Office. Accessed August 31, 2012. http://nces.ed.gov/programs/digest/d11/tables/dt11_008.asp.

Nieto, Sonia, and Patty Bode. 2012. *Affirming Diversity: The Sociopolitical Context of Multicultural Education*. 6th ed. Boston: Pearson Education.

Noddings, Nel. 2011. "Schooling for Democracy." *Democracy and Education* 19 (1). Article 1. http://democracyeducationjournal.org/home/vol19/iss1/1.

Noguera, Pedro. 2003. "The Trouble with Black Boys: The Role and Influence of Environmental and Cultural Factors on the Academic Performance of African American Males." *Urban Education* 38 (4): 431–59.

Nolan, Kathleen M. 2011. "Oppositional Behavior in Urban Schooling: Toward a Theory of Resistance for New Times." *International Journal of Qualitative Studies in Education* 24 (5): 559–72. doi:10.1080/09518398.2011.600263.

Nygreen, Kysa. 2006. "Reproducing or Challenging Power in the Questions We Ask and the Methods We Use." *Urban Review* 38 (1): 1–26.

———. 2008. "Urban Youth and the Construction of Racialized and Classed Political Identities." In *Educating Democratic Citizens in Troubled Times: Qualitative Studies of Current Efforts*, edited by Janet S. Bixby and Judith L. Pace. Albany: State University of New York Press.

———. 2009. "Critical Dilemmas in PAR: Toward a New Theory of Engaged Research for Social Change." *Social Justice* 36 (4) (January 1): 14–35.

———. 2010. "The Central Paradox of Critical Pedagogy: Learning from Practice at a Last-Chance High School." In *Culturally Relevant Pedagogy: Clashes and Confrontations*, edited by Lisa Scherff and Karen Spector. Lanham, MD: R&L Education.

Oakes, Jeannie. 1985. *Keeping Track: How Schools Structure Inequality*. New Haven, CT: Yale University Press.

Oakes, Jeannie, and Marisa Saunders, eds. 2008a. *Beyond Tracking: Multiple Pathways to College, Career, and Civic Participation*. Cambridge, MA: Harvard Education Press.

———. 2008b. "Multiple Pathways: Promising to Prepare All High School Students for College, Career, and Civic Participation." In *Beyond Tracking: Multiple Pathways to College, Career, and Civic Participation*, edited by Jeannie Oakes and Marisa Saunders, 1–16. Cambridge, MA: Harvard Education Press.

Oakes, Jeannie, John Rogers, David Silver, and Joanna Goode. 2004. "Separate and Unequal 50 Years after *Brown*: California's Racial 'Opportunity Gap.'" UCLA Institute for Democracy, Education, and Access (IDEA). http://idea.gseis.ucla.edu/publications/files/brownsu2.pdf.

Ogbu, John U. 1978. *Minority Education and Caste: The American System in Cross-Cultural Perspective*. 1st ed. San Diego: Academic Press.

Olsen, Brad. 2008. "How Reasons for Entry into the Profession Illuminate Teacher Identity Development." *Teacher Education Quarterly* 35 (3): 23.

Parenti, Christian. 2000. *Lockdown America: Police and Prisons in the Age of Crisis*. New York: Verso.

Pastor, Manuel. 2008. "United or Divided: Can Multiple Pathways Bring Together Multiple Communities?" In *Beyond Tracking: Multiple Pathways to*

College, Career, and Civic Participation, edited by Jeannie Oakes and Marisa Saunders, 91–112. Cambridge, MA: Harvard Education Press.

Payne, Ruby K. 2005. *Framework for Understanding Poverty*. 3rd ed. Highlands, TX: aha! Process.

Pease-Alvarez, Lucinda, and Alisun Thompson. 2011. "Teachers Organizing to Resist in a Context of Compliance." In *Critique Qualitative Research in Second Language Studies: Agency and Advocacy*, edited by Kathryn A. Davis, 277–98. Charlotte, NC: Information Age Publishing.

Perkinson, Henry J. 1995. *The Imperfect Panacea: American Faith in Education*. 4th ed. New York: McGraw-Hill Humanities / Social Sciences / Languages.

Philippon, Thomas, and Ariell Reshef. 2009. "Wages and Human Capital in the U.S. Financial Industry: 1909–2006." http://pages.stern.nyu.edu/%7Etphilipp/papers/pr_rev15.pdf.

Phillips, Margaret. (1922) 2009. *The Young Industrial Worker: A Study of His Educational Needs*. Ithaca, NY: Cornell University Library.

Pine, Gerald J. 2008. *Teacher Action Research: Building Knowledge Democracies*. Thousand Oaks, CA: Sage Publications.

Pollock, Mica. 2005. *Colormute: Race Talk Dilemmas in an American School*. Princeton, NJ: Princeton University Press.

———. 2008. *Everyday Antiracism: Getting Real about Race in School*. New York: New Press.

———. 2010. *Because of Race: How Americans Debate Harm and Opportunity in Our Schools*. Princeton, NJ: Princeton University Press.

Pope, Denise Clark. 2003. *Doing School: How We Are Creating a Generation of Stressed-Out, Materialistic, and Miseducated Students*. New Haven, CT: Yale University Press.

Price, Ted. 2008. "Alternative Education: How the Community Benefits When All Students Succeed." *Journal of Juvenile Court, Community, and Alternative School Administrators of California* 21: 42–48.

Ravitch, Diane. 2011. *The Death and Life of the Great American School System*. New York: Basic Books.

Raywid, Mary Anne. 1994. "Alternative Schools: The State of the Art." *Educational Leadership* 52 (1): 26–31.

Rogers, John, Joseph Kahne, and Ellen Middaugh. 2008. "Multiple Pathways and the Future of Democracy." In *Beyond Tracking: Multiple Pathways to College, Career, and Civic Participation*, edited by Jeannie Oakes and Joseph Saunders, 153–70. Cambridge, MA: Harvard Education Press.

Rose, Mike. 2005a. *Lives on the Boundary: A Moving Account of the Struggles and Achievements of America's Educationally Underprepared*. New York: Penguin (Non-Classics).

———. 2005b. *The Mind at Work: Valuing the Intelligence of the American Worker*. New York: Penguin (Non-Classics).

———. 2008. "Blending 'Hand Work' and 'Brain Work': Can Multiple Pathways Deepen Learning?" In *Beyond Tracking: Multiple Pathways to College, Career, and Civic Participation*, edited by Jeannie Oakes and Marisa Saunders, 21–36. Cambridge, MA: Harvard Education Press.

Rosenbaum, James E. 2001. *Beyond College for All: Career Paths for the Forgotten Half.* New York: Russell Sage Foundation.

Rothstein, Richard. 2002. *Out of Balance: Our Understanding of How Schools Affect Society and How Society Affects Schools.* Chicago: Spencer Foundation.

Royster, Deirdre A. 2003. *Race and the Invisible Hand: How White Networks Exclude Black Men from Blue-Collar Jobs.* 1st ed. Berkeley: University of California Press.

Rubin, Beth C. 2007a. "Learner Identity amid Figured Worlds: Constructing (In)competence at an Urban High School." *Urban Review* 39 (2): 217–49.

———. 2007b. "There's Still Not Justice: Youth Civic Identity Development amid Distinct School and Community Contexts." *Teachers College Record* 109 (2): 449–81.

Rubin, Beth C., and Brian F. Hayes. 2010. "'No Backpacks' versus 'Drugs and Murder': The Promise and Complexity of Youth Civic Action Research." *Harvard Educational Review* 80 (3): 352–79.

Rubin, Beth C., Jean Yonemura Wing, Pedro A. Noguera, Emma Fuentes, Daniel Liou, Alicia P. Rodriguez, and Lance T. McCready. 2008. "Structuring Inequality at Berkeley High." In *Unfinished Business: Closing the Racial Achievement Gap in Our Schools*, edited by Pedro Noguera and Jean Yonemura Wing, 29–86. San Francisco: Jossey-Bass.

Ruiz de Velasco, Jorge. 2008. "Alternative Education in Continuation High Schools: Meeting the Needs of Over-aged Under-credited Youth." Stanford, CA: John W. Gardner Center, Stanford University. WestEd.

Ruiz de Velasco, Jorge, Gregory Austin, Don Dixon, Joseph Johnson, Milbrey McLaughlin, and Lynne Perez. 2008. "Alternative Education Options: A Descriptive Study of California Continuation High Schools." Stanford, CA: John W. Gardner Center, Stanford University.

Sadker, Myra, and David Sadker. 1995. *Failing at Fairness: How Our Schools Cheat Girls.* 4th ed. New York: Scribner.

Saffold, Felicia, and Hope Longwell-Grice. 2008. "White Women Preparing to Teach in Urban Schools: Looking for Similarity and Finding Difference." *Urban Review* 40: 186–209.

Sánchez-Jankowski, Martin. 2002. "Minority Youth and Civic Engagement: The Impact of Group Relations." *Applied Developmental Studies* 6 (4): 237–45.

Scott, James. 1990. *Domination and the Arts of Resistance: Hidden Transcripts.* New Haven, CT: Yale University Press.

Shaffer, Evan E. 1955. *A Study of Continuation Education in California.* Sacramento: California State Printing Office, California State Department of Education.

Shipler, David K. 2005. *The Working Poor: Invisible in America.* New York: Vintage.

Sleeter, Christine E. 2005. *Un-standardizing Curriculum: Multicultural Teaching in the Standards-Based Classroom.* Multicultural Education series. New York: Teachers College Press.

Smith, Debbie, and Kathryn Whitmore. 2006. *Literacy and Advocacy in Adolescent Family, Gang, School, and Juvenile Court Communities.* Mahwah, NJ: Lawrence Erlbaum Associates.

Smith-Doerr, Laurel, and Walter W. Powell. 2005. "Networks and Economic Life." In *The Handbook of Economic Sociology,* edited by Neil J. Smelser and Richard Swedberg, 379–402. 2nd ed. Princeton, NJ: Princeton University Press.

Solorzano, Daniel, and Dolores Delgado Bernal. 2001. "Examining Transformative Resistance through a Critical Race and Latcrit Theory Framework: Chicana and Chicano Students in an Urban Context." *Urban Education* 36 (3): 308–42.

Spindler, George D. 1982. "Roger Harker and Schonhausen: From Familiar to Strange and Back Again." In *Doing the Ethnography of Schooling: Educational Anthropology in Action,* edited by George D. Spindler. New York: Holt Rinehart & Winston.

Stern, David, and Roman Stearns. 2008. "Evidence and Challenges: Will Multiple Pathways Improve Students' Outcomes?" In *Beyond Tracking: Multiple Pathways to College, Career, and Civic Participation,* edited by Jeannie Oakes and Marisa Saunders, 37–54. Cambridge, MA: Harvard Education Press.

Stevens, Lisa Patel, Lisa Hunter, Donna Pendergast, Victoria Carrington, Nan Bahr, Cushla Kapitzke, and Jane Mitchell. 2007. "ReConceptualizing the Possible Narratives of Adolescence." *Australian Educational Researcher* 34 (2): 107–27.

Swidler, Ann. 1980. *Organization without Authority: Dilemmas of Social Control in Free Schools.* Cambridge, MA: Harvard University Press.

Symonds, William C., Robert Schwartz, and Ronald F. Ferguson. 2011. "Pathways to Prosperity: Meeting the Challenge of Preparing Young Americans for the 21st Century." Cambridge, MA: Pathways to Prosperity Project, Harvard University Graduate School of Education.

———. 2006. "The Trouble with Getting Ahead: Youth Employment, Labor Organizing, and the Higher Education Question." *WorkingUSA: Journal of Labor and Society* 9: 185–98.

Tatum, Beverly Daniel. 2003. *"Why Are All the Black Kids Sitting Together in the Cafeteria?" A Psychologist Explains the Development of Racial Identity.* 5th anniv. ed., rev. New York: Basic Books.

Tejeda, Carlos, Manuel Espinosa, and Kris Gutierrez. 2003. "Toward a Decolonizing Pedagogy: Social Justice Reconsidered." In *Pedagogies of Difference: Rethinking Education for Social Change,* edited by Peter Pericles Trifonas, 2–38. New York: RoutledgeFalmer.

Tuck, Eve, and K. Wayne Yang. 2011. "Youth Resistance Revisited: New Theories of Youth Negotiations of Educational Injustices." *International Journal of Qualitative Studies in Education* 24 (5): 521–30. doi:10.1080/09518398.2011 .600274.

Tyack, David, and Larry Cuban. 1997. *Tinkering toward Utopia: A Century of Public School Reform.* Cambridge, MA: Harvard University Press.

Tyler, John, Richard J. Murane, and Frank Levy. 1995. "Are More College Graduates Really Taking 'High School' Jobs?" *Monthly Labor Review* 118 (2) (December): 18–27.

Valencia, Richard. 1997. "Conceptualizing the Notion of Deficit Thinking." In *The Evolution of Deficit Thinking: Educational Thought and Practice,* edited by R. Valencia, 1–12. New York: Routledge.

Varenne, Hervé, Shelley Goldman, and Raymond P. McDermott. 1997. "Racing in Place: Middle Class Work in Success/Failure." In *Education and Cultural Process: Anthropological Approaches,* edited by George Dearborn Spindler, 136–57. 3rd ed. Long Grove, IL: Waveland Press.

Varenne, Hervé, and Ray McDermott. 1999. *Successful Failure: The School America Builds.* New York: Westview Press.

Vojak, Colleen. 2006. "What Market Culture Teaches Students about Ethical Behavior." *Ethics and Education* 1 (2) (October): 177–95.

Voss, John W. 1968. *Handbook on Continuation Education in California.* Prepared for the Bureau of Elementary and Secondary Education. Sacramento: California State Department of Education.

Waldinger, Roger. 1999. *Still the Promised City? African-Americans and New Immigrants in Postindustrial New York.* Cambridge, MA: Harvard University Press.

Watkins, William H. 2011. "The New Social Order: An Educator Looks at Economics, Politics, and Race." In *The Assault on Public Education: Confronting the Politics of Corporate School Reform,* edited by William H. Watkins, 7–32. New York: Teachers College Press.

Weis, Lois. 1990. *Working Class without Work: High School Students in a Deindustrializing Economy.* New York: Routledge.

Whitman, David. 2008. *Sweating the Small Stuff: Inner-City Schools and the New Paternalism.* 1st ed. Washington, DC: Thomas B. Fordham Institute.

Williamson, Devon. 2008. *Legislative History of Alternative Education: The*

Policy Context of Continuation High Schools. Stanford, CA: John W. Gardner Center, Stanford University.

Willis, Paul. 1981. *Learning to Labor: How Working Class Kids Get Working Class Jobs.* Morningside, NY: Columbia University Press. First published 1977.

Wilson, William Julius. 1997. *When Work Disappears: The World of the New Urban Poor.* 1st ed. New York: Vintage.

Wirt, John, Susan Choy, Patrick Rooney, Stephen Provasnik, Anindita Sen, and Richard Tobin. 2004. *The Condition of Education 2004* (NCES 2004-077). Washington, DC: US Government Printing Office. Accessed August 31, 2012. http://nces.ed.gov/pubsearch/pubsinfo.asp?pubid=2004077.

Wolff, Edward N. 2006. *Does Education Really Help? Skill, Work, and Inequality.* A Century Foundation Book. New York: Oxford University Press.

Woodson, Carter G. 2006. *The Mis-education of the Negro.* Trenton, NJ: Africa World Press.

Wortham, Stanton. 2006. *Learning Identity: The Joint Emergence of Social Identification and Academic Learning.* New York: Cambridge University Press.

Wright, J. C. 1929. "The Continuation School Program in the United States." *New York State Education* 7 (4): 291–92.

Young, Michael. 1994. *The Rise of the Meritocracy.* Piscataway, NJ: Transaction Publishers.

Young, Timothy W. 1990. *Public Alternative Education: Options and Choice for Today's Schools.* New York: Teachers College Press.

Index